DEIN COACH ZUM ERFOLG!

Dein ActiveBook auf My**STARK**:

Du kannst auf alle digitalen Inhalte (Prüfung 2022, Hördateien, interaktive Aufgaben, Videos, „MindCards") online zugreifen. Registriere dich dazu unter **www.stark-verlag.de/mystark** mit deinem **persönlichen Zugangscode:**

C03551-001873

Die Inhalte dieser Auflage stehen bis Schuljahresende zur Verfügung.

MySTARK

Das Active**Book** *bietet dir:*

- MP3-Dateien der Hörtexte
- Lernvideos zum Umgang mit Textaufgaben
- Interaktive Aufgaben zu sprachlichen Grundlagen
- Web-App mit hilfreichen Wendungen

DEIN COACH ZUM ERFOLG!

So kannst du interaktiv lernen:

Interaktive Aufgaben

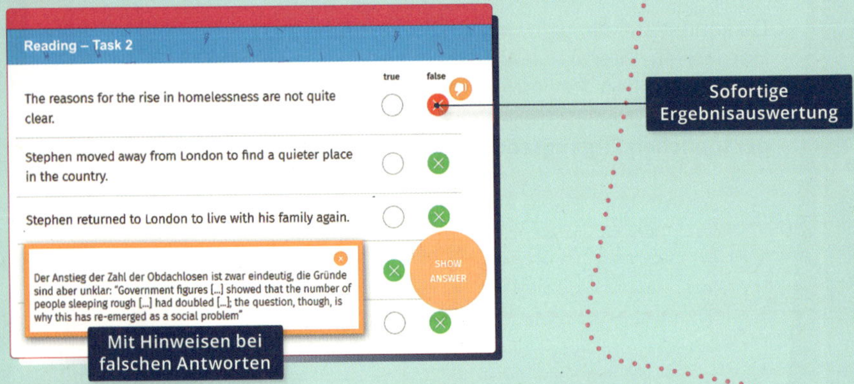

Lernvideos

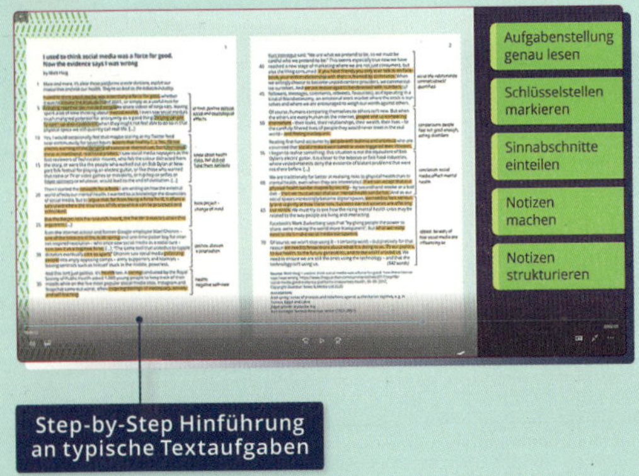

Web-App „MindCards"

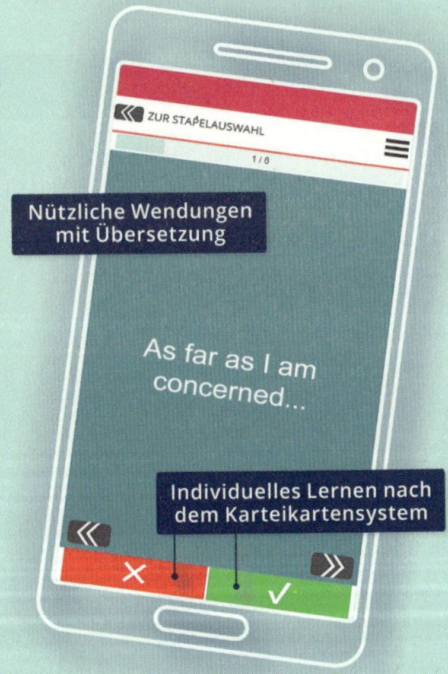

Systemvoraussetzungen:
- Mindestens 1024×768 Pixel Bildschirmauflösung
- Chrome, Firefox oder ähnlicher Webbrowser
- Adobe Reader oder kompatibler anderer PDF-Reader
- Internetzugang

Speaking

Writing

2023

Abitur

Original-Prüfungsaufgaben
mit Lösungen

Niedersachsen

Englisch eA

STARK

17. ergänzte Auflage
www.stark-verlag.de

Inhaltsverzeichnis

Sobald die Original-Prüfungsaufgaben 2022 freigegeben sind, können sie als PDF auf der Plattform MyStark heruntergeladen werden (Zugangscode vgl. Farbseiten vorne im Buch).

MP3-Dateien

Sprecher*innen (MP3-Dateien)

Eva Adelseck, Daniel Beaver, Clare Gnasmüller, Daniel Holzberg, Daria Kozlova, Barbara Krzoska, Jennifer Mikulla, Veronica Stivala

FAQs: Redaktion

Hinweise, Tipps und Übungsaufgaben zu den Prüfungsbereichen:

Hörverstehen: Redaktion (Aufbau des Prüfungsteils, Vorgehen)
Dorothée Just (Set 1, Task 1; Set 2, Task 3)
Paul Jenkinson (Set 1, Tasks 2/3; Set 2, Tasks 1/2)
Constantin Rieske (Set 3)

Sprachmittlung: Redaktion (Aufbau des Prüfungsteils, Vorgehen; Übungsaufgabe 2)
Mareike Hasselmann (Übungsaufgabe 1)
Christian Fischer (Übungsaufgabe 3)
Paul Jenkinson (Übungsaufgabe 4)

Textaufgabe: Redaktion (Aufbau des Prüfungsteils, Vorgehen)
Rainer Jacob (Übersicht Stilmittel, hilfreiche Wendungen zu Cartoons/Statistiken)
Birgit Holtwick (Übungsaufgaben 1 und 4)
Birte Bökel/Henning Christiansen (Übungsaufgabe 2)
Karin Feldner (Übungsaufgabe 3)

Lösungen zu den Original-Prüfungsaufgaben

Abitur 2017: Redaktion (Hörverstehen)
Robert Klimmt (Sprachmittlung)
Christian Fischer (Textaufgaben)

Abitur 2018: Redaktion (Hörverstehen)
Robert Klimmt (Sprachmittlung)
Christian Fischer (Textaufgaben)

Abitur 2019: Redaktion (Hörverstehen)
Johannes Schmidt-Wellenburg/Gertrude Weber (Sprachmittlung)

Abitur 2021: Redaktion (Hörverstehen)
Rainer Jacob (Sprachmittlung)
Christian Fischer (Textaufgaben)

Vorwort

Liebe Schülerinnen, liebe Schüler,

dieses Buch (und seine digitalen Zusätze, siehe Folgeseiten) soll Sie auf dem Weg zu einer erfolgreichen Abiturprüfung im Fach Englisch begleiten. Es ist folgendermaßen aufgebaut:

- Die **FAQs** enthalten alles Wichtige rund um die Abiturprüfung in aller Kürze. Hier können Sie sich einen ersten Überblick verschaffen, was Sie in der Prüfung erwartet.
- Im zweiten Teil des Buches finden Sie **Hinweise**, **Tipps** und **Übungsaufgaben zu den Prüfungsbereichen Hörverstehen**, **Sprachmittlung** und **Textaufgabe**. Zu Beginn jedes Kapitels erfahren Sie, welche **Aufgabenformate** auf Sie zukommen können und wie Sie in der Prüfung am besten **vorgehen**. Außerdem finden Sie hier nützliche **Übersichten** zu Operatoren, Textsorten, hilfreichen Wendungen und vielem mehr. Nach dieser theoretischen Hinführung können Sie Ihre Kenntnisse in den **Übungsaufgaben** praktisch anwenden. Bei der jeweils ersten Übungsaufgabe bzw. dem ersten Übungsset werden Sie Schritt für Schritt angeleitet (bei der Textaufgabe in Form von Lernvideos). Die weiteren Übungsaufgaben enthalten keine solche zusätzliche Hilfestellung. Wenn Sie möchten, können Sie sich auch ein vollständiges Abiturprüfungsset (bestehend aus je einer Übungsaufgabe Hörverstehen, Sprachmittlung und Textaufgabe) zusammenstellen und damit den „Ernstfall“ simulieren.
- Am Ende des Buches finden Sie **Original-Prüfungsaufgaben** der letzten Jahre, die Ihnen einen Eindruck vermitteln, wie die zentral gestellte Abiturprüfung aussieht. Beachten Sie, dass sich einzelne Aufgabenstellungen im Bereich „Textaufgabe“ auf die damals gültigen Pflichtlektüren beziehen. Die Aufgaben eignen sich dennoch weiterhin gut zum Üben.
- Zu allen Übungsaufgaben und Original-Prüfungen gibt es ausführliche **Lösungsvorschläge**. In den Tippkästen finden Sie nützliche Hinweise zum Bearbeiten der Aufgaben bzw. wesentliche Aspekte, die in Ihrer Lösung enthalten sein sollten. Hier können Sie also bei Bedarf nachschlagen, wenn Sie Hilfestellung benötigen. Anschließend können Sie Ihre Lösung mit unserer (Beispiel-)Lösung vergleichen.

Wir wünschen Ihnen schon jetzt viel Erfolg in der Prüfung!

Hinweise zu den digitalen Zusätzen

Auf alle digitalen Zusätze können Sie online über die Plattform **MyStark** zugreifen. Ihren persönlichen Zugangscode finden Sie auf den Farbseiten vorne im Buch.

PDF der Original-Prüfungsaufgaben 2022

Um Ihnen die Prüfung 2022 schnellstmöglich zur Verfügung stellen zu können, bringen wir sie in digitaler Form heraus. Sobald die Original-Prüfungsaufgaben 2022 freigegeben sind, können Sie sie als PDF auf der Plattform MyStark herunterladen.

Lernvideos

Textaufgaben sind Teil vieler Prüfungen und Klausuren – und machen oft einen Großteil der Prüfungsleistung aus. Mithilfe der **Lernvideos zum richtigen Umgang mit Textaufgaben** können Sie sich optimal auf die Anforderungen in diesem Bereich vorbereiten. Am Beispiel von zwei Texten mit je drei Aufgabenstellungen wird gezeigt, wie man an eine Textaufgabe herangeht und sie erfolgreich löst.

Die Lernvideos beinhalten:

- **Schritt-für-Schritt-Anleitungen** zum richtigen Vorgehen in der Prüfung
- einen **Sachtext** und **literarischen Text** als Grundlage
- nützliche Hinweise zu **häufigen Operatoren** und **Zieltextsorten**

MP3-Dateien

Über die Plattform **MyStark** können Sie sich außerdem die Hörverstehenstexte der Übungsaufgaben und Original-Prüfungen anhören und zum Offline-Gebrauch herunterladen.

Interaktive Aufgaben – „ActiveBook“

Im **ActiveBook „Basic Language Skills“** erhalten Sie Zugriff auf zahlreiche **interaktive Aufgaben** zu Grundlagen wie **Hörverstehen**, **Leseverstehen** und **Sprachverwendung im Kontext**. Dies sind ganz wichtige „Basics“, die Sie für eine gute Sprachbeherrschung brauchen.

Das ActiveBook „Basic Language Skills“ bietet Ihnen:

- „**Listening**“ – authentische Audiodateien mit vielfältigen Aufgaben, die Ihr Hörverstehen testen
- „**Reading**“ – abwechslungsreiche Lesetexte und dazugehörige Aufgaben
- „**English in Use**“ mit gemischten Aufgaben rund um den Gebrauch der englischen Sprache

ActiveBook
Interaktives
Training

Alle Aufgaben sind interaktiv, d. h., Sie können sie direkt am PC oder Tablet bearbeiten und erhalten sofort eine Rückmeldung zu Ihren Antworten.

Web-App „MindCards“

Mit der Web-App „**MindCards**“ können Sie am Smartphone Vokabeln lernen. Auf diesen interaktiven Karteikarten finden Sie hilfreiche Wendungen, die Sie beim Schreiben von Texten oder im mündlichen Sprachgebrauch einsetzen können.
Scannen Sie einfach die QR-Codes oder verwenden Sie folgende Links, um zu den „MindCards“ zu gelangen:
https://www.stark-verlag.de/mindcards/writing-2
https://www.stark-verlag.de/mindcards/speaking-2

Writing

Speaking

FAQs – Häufige Fragen

FAQs – Häufige Fragen zur Abiturprüfung

Wie ist die Prüfung aufgebaut und wie viel Zeit habe ich?

Die schriftliche Abiturprüfung besteht aus den Teilen **Hörverstehen**, **Sprachmittlung** und **Textaufgabe**. Als erstes findet der *listening comprehension test* statt, im Anschluss daran erhalten Sie die Sprachmittlungsaufgabe. Beim dritten und letzten Prüfungsteil, der Textaufgabe, können Sie zwischen zwei Vorschlägen auswählen.

Prüfungsteil	Zeit
Hörverstehen	30 Minuten
Sprachmittlung	60 Minuten
Textaufgabe (2 Vorschläge zur Auswahl)	240 Minuten (einschließlich Auswahlzeit)

Welche Hilfsmittel darf ich verwenden?

In allen Prüfungsteilen stehen Ihnen sowohl ein **einsprachiges** als auch ein **zweisprachiges Wörterbuch** zur Verfügung. Anstelle der gedruckten Wörterbücher kann auch ein elektronisches Wörterbuch verwendet werden, sofern es bereits in der Qualifikationsphase eingeführt wurde und für jeden Prüfling ein Exemplar bereitsteht.

Welche Textsorten und Aufgabentypen können vorkommen?

Genaue Informationen zu den Textsorten und Aufgabenformaten, die Sie in den einzelnen Prüfungsteilen erwarten können, erhalten Sie im Kapitel „**Hinweise, Tipps und Übungsaufgaben zu den Prüfungsteilen**". Dort finden Sie auch Schritt-für-Schritt Anleitungen zum richtigen Vorgehen in der Prüfung sowie Übungsaufgaben, mit denen Sie die „Theorie" gleich praktisch anwenden können.

Gibt es inhaltliche/thematische Schwerpunkte?

Die Abiturvorbereitung im Englischunterricht stützt sich auf das **Kerncurriculum**, das wesentliche Unterrichtsinhalte und -methoden festlegt. Folgende Themenfelder werden danach in der Oberstufe behandelt und sind Grundlage für das Abitur:

- *Beliefs, values and norms in society – tradition and change:*
  Britishness; the American experience; Postcolonial/Neo-colonial experiences; migration effects on the world of work
- *Individual and society:*
  identity; ethnic, cultural and linguistic diversity; gender and sexual diversity
- *Globalisation:*
  effects on the world of work; impact on personal lives; global responsibility concerning e. g. politics, the environment, economy; English as a global language
- *Science and technology:*
  chances and risks; visions of the future; the media, e. g. the influence of the media on public opinion and personal life; the digital revolution
- *Shakespeare: the world that made him; modern adaptations*

Ergänzend veröffentlicht das Kultusministerium eine Liste mit **verbindlichen Materialien**, die im Unterricht behandelt werden müssen. Diese sind speziell für den Prüfungsteil „Textaufgabe“ relevant: Zwar entstammt der Prüfungstext im Abitur nicht einer der Pflichtlektüren – es kann aber sein, dass von Ihnen verlangt wird, den Prüfungstext in Bezug zu den verbindlichen Materialien zu setzen. Für das Abitur 2023 wurden folgende Texte und Filme als verbindliche Materialien festgelegt:

Verbindliche Materialien	verbindliche Unterrichtsaspekte
Roman: Mary Shelley, *Frankenstein* (1831)	ethics of science; the role of nature; questions of (human) identity
Short story (Allgemeinbildende Schulen): Jhumpa Lahiri, “The Third and Final Continent” (1999); Andrea Levy, “Loose Change” (2005); Shereen Pandit, “She Shall Not Be Moved” (2005); Qaisra Shahraz, “The Escape” (2009)	postcolonial experience; displacement: questions of belonging and identity
Short story (Berufliche Gymnasien): Saeed Taji Farouky, “The Rain Missed My Face and Fell Straight to My Shoes” (2005); Jhumpa Lahiri, “The Third and Final Continent” (1999); Andrea Levy, “Loose Change” (2005); Qaisra Shahraz, “The Escape” (2009)	postcolonial experience; displacement: questions of belonging and identity
Film: *Gran Torino* (2008)	ethnic and cultural diversity: cultural clashes; the role of gang culture and violence
Drama: Auszüge aus William Shakespeare, *Hamlet*	fate vs. free will; the role(s) of women; questions of morality

Wie werden die einzelnen Prüfungsteile bewertet?

Sie bekommen für jeden der drei Prüfungsteile eine Note. Aus diesen drei Teilnoten wird am Ende durch prozentuale Gewichtung Ihre Gesamtnote für die schriftliche Prüfung ermittelt (siehe Tabelle unten).
Die Bewertung des **Hörverstehens** erfolgt über sog. Bewertungseinheiten (BE). In den Prüfungsteilen **Sprachmittlung** und **Textaufgabe** werden Sprache und Inhalt zunächst getrennt voneinander bewertet.

Folgende Kriterien sind für die Bewertung der **sprachlichen Leistung** relevant:
- kommunikative Textgestaltung:
  Textaufbau, Textsortenspezifik, Situationsangemessenheit und Adressatenbezug
- Ausdrucksvermögen/Verwendung sprachlicher Mittel:
  eigenständige Bearbeitung, angemessener und reichhaltiger Wortschatz, Verwendung idiomatischer Konstruktionen, abwechslungsreicher und angemessen komplexer Satzbau, korrekte Zitiertechnik
- Sprachrichtigkeit:
  korrekte Rechtschreibung/Grammatik/Satzbau/Wortschatz; Verständlichkeit

Bei der Bewertung der **inhaltlichen Leistung** werden folgende Kriterien angelegt:
- Aufgabenerfüllung:
  Umsetzung der Aufgabenstellung, Textsortenspezifik, Situations-/Adressatenbezug
- Erläutern kulturspezifischer Aspekte (bei der Sprachmittlung)
- Text- und Problemverständnis:
  Durchdringung der Textvorlage, Problemverständnis/ggf. Einordnen in größere Zusammenhänge
- Darstellung und Gliederung:
  Umsetzung des Operators; selbstständige und differenzierte Entfaltung des Themas; Verständlichkeit, Klarheit und Schlüssigkeit der Darstellung

Prüfungsteil	Ermittlung der Teilnote	Anteil der Teilnote an Gesamtnote
Hörverstehen	Bewertung über Bewertungseinheiten (BEs): Pro richtige Antwort 1 BE; für eine ausreichende Leistung (5 Notenpunkte) ist das Erreichen von 45 % der BE notwendig	20 %
Sprachmittlung	60 % auf Sprache, 40 % auf Inhalt	25 %
Textaufgabe	60 % auf Sprache (wird ganzheitlich für alle Teilaufgaben ermittelt) 40 % auf Inhalt (wird zunächst einzeln für jede Teilaufgabe ermittelt und danach entsprechend der prozentualen Vorgabe in der Prüfung gewichtet)	55 %

Zur Veranschaulichung hier ein **Beispiel, wie Ihre Note errechnet wird:**
Nehmen wir einmal an, Sie haben bei der Textaufgabe für Ihre Arbeit im Bereich „Sprache“ 11 Punkte bekommen. Im Bereich „Inhalt“ ergibt sich für Sie bei drei Aufgaben und prozentualer Gewichtung ein Mittelwert von 9,3 Punkten. Für das Endergebnis multiplizieren Sie Ihre sprachliche Note mit 0,6 und die inhaltliche Note mit 0,4 und addieren dann beide Ergebnisse. Es ergibt sich 10,32 – dieser Prüfungsteil wird also mit „noch gut (10 Punkte)“ bewertet.
Nehmen wir zudem an, Sie haben im Hörverstehen eine Teilnote von 9 Punkten erzielt und in der Sprachmittlung eine Teilnote von 8 Punkten. Multiplizieren Sie nun die 10 Punkte aus der Textaufgabe mit 0,55, die 9 Punkte aus dem Hörverstehen mit 0,2 und die 8 Punkte aus der Sprachmittlung mit 0,25 und addieren Sie anschließend die drei Werte. Es ergibt sich ein Wert von 9,3. Ihre Gesamtnote für die schriftliche Prüfung ist also „befriedigend (9 Punkte)“.

Wie bereite ich mich am besten auf die Prüfung vor?

Inhaltliche Vorbereitung

Sie werden in der Abiturprüfung Texte und Aufgaben vorgelegt bekommen, die für Sie neu sind, die Sie also noch nicht zuvor im Unterricht behandelt haben. Für Ihre Vorbereitung bedeutet das Folgendes:

- Arbeiten Sie vor allem an Ihrer **Methodik**. Trainieren Sie also, wie man an die verschiedenen Aufgabenstellungen herangeht – das ist insbesondere für die Sprachmittlung und Textaufgabe von entscheidender Bedeutung. Die nachfolgenden Kapitel enthalten detaillierte Informationen, was Sie in den einzelnen Prüfungsteilen beachten müssen und wie Sie in der Prüfungssituation am besten vorgehen. Diese Abschnitte sollten Sie unbedingt genau durchlesen. Mit den Übungsaufgaben haben Sie anschließend die Möglichkeit, Ihr methodisches Wissen in der Praxis zu testen.
- Für die Textaufgabe ist zudem wichtig, dass Sie mit den **Pflichtlektüren bzw. -filmen** vertraut sind. Neben der Vorbereitung im Unterricht hilft Ihnen hier das „**AbiturSkript Englisch Niedersachsen 2023**“ (Bestell-Nr. 3546S3). Sie finden darin knapp zusammengefasst alles Wichtige zu Handlung, Figuren und relevanten Themen sowie nützliche Schaubilder, mit denen Sie sich das Gelernte besser einprägen können.

Sprachliche Vorbereitung

Mindestens ebenso wichtig wie die inhaltliche Vorbereitung ist die sprachliche Vorbereitung auf die Prüfung. Im *listening comprehension test* müssen Sie mit dem normalen Sprechtempo von *native speakers* zurechtkommen. In den Prüfungsteilen Sprachmittlung und Textaufgabe fließt Ihre sprachliche Leistung mit 60% in die Teilnote ein und wird damit sogar stärker gewichtet als Ihre inhaltliche Leistung. Eine flüssige Ausdrucksweise, ein vielseitiger Wortschatz sowie grammatikalische und orthografische Richtigkeit sind hier von besonderer Bedeutung. Länger- und mittelfristig können Sie u. a. folgende Strategien zur Vorbereitung anwenden:

- Schauen Sie englischsprachige Filme oder Serien, hören Sie englische Hörbücher oder Podcasts und lesen Sie Artikel oder Bücher auf Englisch.
- Auch mit dem ActiveBook zu diesem Band können Sie sprachliche Grundlagen wie Hörverstehen, Wortschatz und Strukturen trainieren (Zugang vgl. Farbseiten vorne im Buch).
- Sehen Sie sich Ihre korrigierten Englisch-Klausuren an und notieren Sie, was Ihre häufigsten Fehler sind. Üben Sie diese Bereiche dann ganz gezielt. Zur Wiederholung von Grammatik und Wortschatz eignen sich beispielsweise die Abitur-Trainings-Bände „Englisch Grammatikübungen“ (82452V) und „Englisch Themenwortschatz“ (82451D).
- Speziell als Vorbereitung auf die Sprachmittlungsaufgabe sollten Sie außerdem üben, deutsche Zeitungsartikel für (imaginäre) englische Bekannte zusammenzufassen – das entspricht dem üblichen Szenario, das Ihnen auch in der Prüfung begegnet.

ÜBUNGSAUFGABEN

Hörverstehen

Aufbau des Prüfungsteils „Hörverstehen“

Der *listening comprehension test* im Abitur besteht meist aus **zwei bis vier einzelnen Hörtexten**, die jeweils **zweimal hintereinander abgespielt** werden. Häufig handelt es sich dabei um Radiobeiträge, Interviews, Nachrichtenmeldungen oder mehrere kurze Monologe. Die Themen der Texte können sehr vielfältig sein (von Politik über Kultur bis hin zu Umweltschutz) und müssen nicht in Bezug zu den Pflichtlektüren oder den Themen der anderen Prüfungsteile stehen. Die einzelnen Hörtexte sind in der Regel maximal fünf Minuten lang. Die gesamte Bearbeitungszeit beträgt **30 Minuten**. In diesem Prüfungsteil können **geschlossene** bzw. **halboffene Aufgabenformate** vorkommen, z. B. *multiple choice,* Zuordnung *(multiple matching)* und *table completion.* Dabei steht das reine Hörverstehen im Vordergrund. Deshalb werden Sie – wenn überhaupt – nur kurze Phrasen oder Sätze schreiben müssen. Sprachliche Fehler werden nur dann gewertet, wenn sie das Verständnis beeinträchtigen.

Aufgabenformat	Merkmale	Beispiel
multiple choice	• i.d.R. ist ein Satzanfang vorgegeben und Sie müssen aus mehreren möglichen Satzenden das richtige auswählen und abhaken • die Aufgaben können sich auf Detailinformationen oder den Text als Ganzes beziehen	*[…] tick (✓) the correct answer (a, b, c or d). There is only one correct answer.*
multiple matching	• Sie sollen mehreren kurzen Texten/Monologen von verschiedenen Sprechern die passende Überschrift oder Aussage zuordnen • häufig sind mehr Möglichkeiten vorgegeben als zugeordnet werden müssen	*[…] match the statements A to G with the speakers 1 to 6. There is one more statement than you need.*
table completion/ filling in information	• Sie müssen fehlende Informationen ergänzen (meist in einer Tabelle) • in der Regel sind keine vollständigen Sätze nötig • Sie können den Wortlaut des Texts übernehmen oder in eigenen Worten formulieren	*[…] fill in the missing information. You do not need to write complete sentences.*

Vorgehen in der Prüfung

Schritt 1 Vor dem ersten Hören: Aufgaben lesen

Meist haben Sie vor dem ersten Hören etwas Zeit, um sich mit den Aufgaben vertraut zu machen und sich auf das Thema des jeweiligen Texts einzustellen. Lesen Sie die Aufgabenstellung genau und unterstreichen Sie **Schlüsselbegriffe** oder Eigennamen mit Bleistift.

Schritt 2 Erstes Hören: möglichst viele Aufgaben lösen

Jetzt wird Ihnen der Text ein erstes Mal vorgespielt.

- Achten Sie beim Hören besonders auf die **Schlüsselbegriffe** aus der Aufgabe und damit verwandte Formulierungen (z. B. **Synonyme**, **Wörter derselben Wortfamilie** oder **aus demselben Wortfeld**). So erkennen Sie schnell die für die Lösung relevanten Stellen. Wird in der Aufgabenstellung beispielsweise das Wort „legislation“ verwendet, ist im Hörtext möglicherweise von „laws“ oder dem „legislative process“ die Rede. Machen Sie bei *multiple choice*- und *matching*-Aufgaben aber nicht den Fehler, „automatisch“ auf eine bestimmte Lösung zu schließen, nur weil ein bestimmter Begriff auch im Hörtext vorkommt. Manchmal enthalten die Aufgabenstellungen auch **Distraktoren**, also Antwortmöglichkeiten, die Sie auf eine falsche Fährte locken sollen. Beziehen Sie daher immer den **Kontext** mit ein, in dem ein Begriff im Hörtext genannt wird. Achten Sie außerdem auf die genaue **Formulierung in der Aufgabenstellung** (z. B. ob Verneinungen oder Relativierungen enthalten sind).
- Versuchen Sie während des ersten Hörens, sofort alle **Lösungen festzuhalten**, von deren Richtigkeit Sie überzeugt sind.
- Wenn Sie sich unsicher sind, dann halten Sie sich nicht lange mit einer Teilaufgabe auf. In der Regel sind die Aufgaben in der Reihenfolge angeordnet, in der auch die Lösungen im Text vorkommen. Sollten Sie sich also zu lange mit einer noch offenen Lücke beschäftigen, dann laufen Sie Gefahr, auch die nächste Lösung zu verpassen. **Markieren Sie** stattdessen **Aufgaben, bei denen Sie noch nicht ganz von Ihrer Antwort überzeugt sind**, mit Bleistift, damit Sie dort beim zweiten Durchgang ganz genau hinhören.
- Ist der erste Durchlauf beendet, gibt es eine kurze **Pause**, während der Sie Ihre Aufzeichnungen weiter **ergänzen** können.

Schritt 3 Zweites Hören: Lösungen kontrollieren und vervollständigen

Nun wird der Text ein zweites Mal vorgespielt.

- Sie haben jetzt die Gelegenheit, Ihre Lösungen aus dem ersten Durchgang noch einmal zu **kontrollieren**.
- Wenn Sie beim ersten Hören Informationen für eine Aufgabe verpasst haben, achten Sie jetzt besonders auf diese Stellen und **tragen Sie die Lösung(en) nach**.
- Auch nach dem zweiten Durchgang folgt meist eine kurze **Pause**. Nutzen Sie die Zeit, um Ihre **Lösungen** weiter zu **vervollständigen**. Sollten Sie die Antwort zu einer Aufgabe einmal gar nicht wissen, ist es besser, zu raten (etwa bei *multiple choice*- und *matching*-Aufgaben) als eine Aufgabe gar nicht zu bearbeiten. So besteht zumindest noch eine kleine Chance, einen Punkt zu bekommen.

Neben den Übungsaufgaben und Original-Prüfungen in diesem Buch können Sie Ihr Hörverstehen auch hervorragend mit den **interaktiven Aufgaben im ActiveBook** trainieren. Das ActiveBook und alle Hördateien zu diesem Band stehen Ihnen auf der Plattform MyStark zur Verfügung (Zugangscode vgl. Farbseiten vorne im Buch).

Hörverstehen: Übungsset 1

Mit Schritt-für-Schritt-Anleitung

You will hear each recording twice. After each listening you will have time to complete your answers.

Task 1: Protecting the Climate

You will hear six people talking about climate change. Match each speaker (1 to 6) with one of the statements (A to G). There is one more statement than you need.

- **Before listening:** use the time before the recording starts to read through the statements below and underline the key words.
- **First listening:** if you are certain which statement goes with which speaker, write the letter in the table below. If you are not sure yet, write down the possible solution(s) in pencil first.
- **Second listening:** check your solutions and pay particular attention to those speakers where you haven't been sure yet which statement to choose. Don't just rely on the key words but also listen out for synonyms or paraphrases, and always take into consideration the context in which the terms are mentioned. In some cases, you can also find the correct solution by excluding statements that obviously don't fit a certain speaker *(Ausschlussverfahren)*.

The speaker …

A believes that higher costs would make people change their habits concerning behaviour that is damaging to the environment.

B says politics will adopt measures to deal with the problem of climate change.

C is pointing the finger at individuals who refuse to bear responsibility for their actions.

D blames older generations and their blindness with regard to the future.

E wants politicians to take action but does not think the measures they take are sufficient.

F believes that everybody can do something to live a sustainable life.

G questions the impact an individual has and is against restricting people's freedom.

speaker	1	2	3	4	5	6
statement						

Task 2: Purple Door Coffee Shop: Changing lives one cup at a time

You will hear a recording about how a project is helping young homeless people in Denver. While listening, tick (✓) the correct answer (a, b or c). There is only one correct answer.

- **Before listening:** use the time before the recording starts to underline the key words and attune yourself to the topic.
- **First listening:** keep in mind that the tasks usually follow the order of the text. This helps you assess when the relevant passage might appear. If you miss an important passage or aren't sure which answer to choose, make a note next to the task with pencil.
- **Second listening:** check your answers and pay particular attention to the passages that you missed before.

1 The aim of the scheme is …

a ☐ to give homeless young people a job.
b ☐ to raise money to provide shelter for homeless young people.
c ☐ to give homeless young people a chance to change their lives.

2 The young people are found through …

a ☐ advertisements.
b ☐ suggestions by partner organisations.
c ☐ voluntary internships.

3 A big problem of young homeless people is that they …

a ☐ lack many basic life skills.
b ☐ often fight each other.
c ☐ do not eat healthily.

4 The coffee shop owners …

a ☐ provide an education for the young people.
b ☐ meet once a week to talk about their employees.
c ☐ help their employees to manage their lives.

5 What Kevin likes about working at the "Coffee Shop" is …

a ☐ gaining new ideas through the programme.
b ☐ the approach the owners adopt towards their employees.
c ☐ that employees can talk openly to the owners.

6 The owners feel that the best thing is seeing the people in the scheme …

a ☐ grow up.

b ☐ gain self-confidence.

c ☐ enjoy themselves.

Task 3: Teen Business Owner Creates Recipe for Success

You will hear a recording about a teenager who has started her own business. While listening, fill in the missing information. You need not write complete sentences. Unless otherwise specified, one aspect is enough. There is one example **(0)**.

- **Before listening:** begin by underlining key words and proper names in the task.
- **First listening:** the information that you need in order to fill the table will appear in the same order as in text. You only have to note down one aspect per line, except in tasks 3 to 5, where you are meant fill in two pieces of information. It is probably easiest to use the words from the text, but you may also use your own words.
- **Second listening:** check your answers and concentrate on passages you missed the first time round.

0 How Bree feels when baking:	innovative/creative/in another world
1 How her great-grandmother influenced Bree:	
2 What Bree's mother advised her daughter to do:	
3 What role Bree's mother has in the business today:	• •
4 What Leo Harrington thinks of Bree's work:	• •
5 What Bree has learnt through working in her bakery:	• •
6 What ingredient makes Bree's sweets special:	

Lösung

Transkript 1 Protecting the Climate

Speaker 1: For my generation – I'm 17 – climate change is a big issue. My friends and I have been to several demonstrations against man-made global warming. Politicians and lawmakers finally need a wake-up call to do more to protect the climate now. I mean, the older generations have lived at our expense! What about the future of the younger generations? We want to live on a planet that's still worth living in! I do hope we can make a difference and manage to change course.

Speaker 2: It worries me to see that the climate is changing at such a fast pace! In my opinion, individuals can do a great deal to contribute to protecting the climate and emitting less CO2, for example. I live in the city with my family – I'm a mother of two – so it's easy to do without a car – even with two little children. We use public transport, and when we go on holiday we take the train. You'd be surprised how far you can get by railway in Europe – and it can be much more comfortable than flying! We've also met a lot of lovely people on our train journeys – we're still in touch with some of them!

Speaker 3: I'm from the countryside and public transport there is dreadful. So I definitely need my car to get around. I don't know whether you can make a difference as an individual – it's the politicians who have to act. I asked the MP for my constituency to speak up for a regular bus connection to the nearest city, but nothing has been done. There's always a lack of funds. If the government increased its expenditure on rural infrastructure, the number of people who left their car in the garage would rise. That's for sure!

Speaker 4: In my opinion, both individuals and politicians need to act to slow or stop global warming. I only vote for parties that take global warming seriously and support legislation that gives incentives for environmentally friendly behaviour. And why isn't there a tax on jet fuel? If flying got more expensive, maybe fewer people would fly? I, for one, try to fly as little as possible – and what I also do is eat less meat. You know that the methane gas cattle emit contributes a great deal to global warming?

Speaker 5: I don't agree. What difference does it make if some people, say, avoid flying? Other people will take their places. And why should we cut back on our lifestyle? Don't I have the right to fly to Bali in winter when the weather is dreadful here? I can afford it and I just do it. Wouldn't it be unfair to less affluent people if the price of flying increased? They also have the right to fly to Majorca for their summer holidays, for example. And, by the way, if I feel like it, I also treat myself to a juicy steak. I can't make a difference anyway.

Speaker 6: I'm an MP from the south of England. I really understand that an increasing number of citizens are getting more and more impatient with politics as far as global warming is concerned. But I can assure people who are worried that the topic is high on my party's agenda. I know the legislative process can be lengthy and that compromises have to be made, but we're working hard on a ground-breaking legislative package. Both lawmakers and citizens should do their very best to tackle the pressing issue of global warming, however.

TIPP

These text passages will help you find the correct answer:

1 "I mean, the older generations have lived at our expense! What about the future of the younger generations?" (ll. 4/5)
In this case, the same keyword ("older generations") is used both in the task (statement D) and in the listening text.

2 "In my opinion, individuals can do a great deal to contribute to protecting the climate and emitting less CO_2, for example." (ll. 7–9)
Here, you might be tempted to choose statement C or G, as they both contain the keyword "individual(s)". However, neither of the two is correct. Statement C does not fit the text, because speaker 2 does not blame anyone. Statement G is wrong, because speaker 2 actually believes in the power of individuals to make a difference. Thus, statement F has to be correct: "Everybody" can be seen as a synonym of "individuals".

3 "it's the politicians who have to act. I asked the MP for my constituency […], but nothing has been done. There's always a lack of funds." (ll. 17–19)
Speaker 3 mentions the terms "politicians", "MP" and "government", which indicates that either statement B or E could be correct. Now you have to take the context into consideration: Speaker 3 sounds disappointed with what politicians have done so far rather than optimistic about what they will do – thus, E is the right solution.

4 "And why isn't there a tax on jet fuel? If flying got more expensive, maybe fewer people would fly?" (ll. 25/26)
Here, statement A is correct. The phrase "more expensive" in the text corresponds to "higher costs"; "fewer people would fly" corresponds to "change their habit".

5 "What difference does it make if some people, say, avoid flying? Other people will take their places. And why should we cut back on our lifestyle?" (ll. 29–31)
The correct solution for speaker 5 has to be statement G. "[R]estricting people's freedom" corresponds to "cut back on our lifestyle" and the question "What difference does it make" corresponds to "questions the impact an individual has".

6 "But I can assure people who are worried that the topic is high on my party's agenda. […] we're working hard on a ground-breaking legislative package." (ll. 38–41)
The word "party" indicates that the speaker is talking about "politics" and the expression "legislative package" corresponds to "measures" – thus, both B and E could be correct. Due to the speaker's positive view of politics (and because E has already been used for speaker 3), only statement B can be correct.

The speaker …

A believes that higher costs would make people change their habits concerning behaviour that is damaging to the environment.

B says politics will adopt measures to deal with the problem of climate change.

C is pointing the finger at individuals who refuse to bear responsibility for their actions.

D blames older generations and their blindness with regard to the future.

E wants politicians to take action but does not think the measures they take are sufficient.

F believes that everybody can do something to live a sustainable life.

G questions the impact an individual has and is against restricting people's freedom.

speaker	1	2	3	4	5	6
statement	D	F	E	A	G	B

Transkript 2 Purple Door Coffee Shop: Changing lives one cup at a time

Paula Vargas: Kevin Person had been homeless for a quarter of his life. Today, he works at this espresso bar and is transitioning into a home.

Kevin Person: The struggle to get a job even when you have a house nowadays, but when you don't have a house, trying to get a job is so much harder.

Paula Vargas: The mission of the Purple Door Coffee Shop goes beyond serving coffee. The owners want to turn lives around and for two years the non-profit has hired three to four young adults per year. They work with shelters like Urban Peak, where Kevin was staying, for recommendations on who to hire. Kim Easton, who runs Urban Peak, says the partnership is vital to this community.

Kim Easton: When someone has lived in chronic stress and trauma for as long as these young people have, everyday fighting for survival, they haven't had the opportunity nor the example of how to learn conflict management, how to manage money, how to cook a meal, how to pay their rent on time – nor do they understand even why that's important.

Paula Vargas: Purple Door co-founder, Madison Chandler, and her partner meet with each worker once a week. They discuss 52 topics ranging from mental health, finance, hygiene and customer service, and provide a life coaching tour, they will help their employees put their past behind them. But there are success stories.

Madison Chandler: Our very first guy that ever graduated from the programme; he's been working at an Auto Parts Warehouse since he left, which has been over a year now.

Paula Vargas: Kevin appreciates the chance to learn new skills. He says the programme is giving him things he never had.

Kevin Person: They seem to have the philosophy that they don't want to change us, they want to help us change ourselves and to have, like, a purpose and a goal that's, like, tangible.

Madison Chandler: The more rewarding things are watching somebody start to believe in themselves and to believe that they can achieve a life for themselves that they have dreamed of, or to believe that they are worth it.

Paula Vargas: As for Kevin, who turns 25 this month, living off the streets in a home and having a job will be the best gift he gives himself. For VOA news, Paula Vargas in Denver.

From: Paula Vargas, "Purple Door Coffee Shop: Changing Lives One Cup at a Time".
In: Voice of America News, *29 May 2015.*

TIPP

These text passages will help you find the correct answer:

1. "The mission of the Purple Door Coffee Shop goes beyond serving coffee. The owners want to turn lives around" (ll. 5/6)
2. "They work with shelters like Urban Peak, where Kevin was staying, for recommendations on who to hire." (ll. 7/8)
3. "they haven't had the opportunity nor the example of how to learn conflict management, how to manage money, how to cook a meal, how to pay their rent on time – nor do they understand even why that's important." (ll. 11–14)
4. "Purple Door co-founder, Madison Chandler, and her partner meet with each worker once a week. They discuss 52 topics ranging from mental health, finance, hygiene and customer service, and provide a life coaching tour; they will help their employees put their past behind them." (ll. 15–18)
5. "They seem to have the philosophy that they don't want to change us, they want to help us change ourselves and to have, like, a purpose and a goal that's, like, tangible." (ll. 24–26)
6. "The more rewarding things are watching somebody start to believe in themselves and to believe that they can achieve a life for themselves that they have dreamed of, or to believe that they are worth it." (ll. 27–29)

1 The aim of the scheme is …

c [✓] to give homeless young people a chance to change their lives.

2 The young people are found through …

b [✓] suggestions by partner organisations.

3 A big problem of young homeless people is that they …

a [✓] lack many basic life skills.

4 The coffee shop owners …

c ☑ help their employees to manage their lives.

5 What Kevin likes about working at the "Coffee Shop" is …

b ☑ the approach the owners adopt towards their employees.

6 The owners feel that the best thing is seeing the people in the scheme …

b ☑ gain self-confidence.

Transkript 3 Teen Business Owner Creates Recipe for Success

Faith Lapidus: For Bree Britt nothing is more enjoyable, soothing and fulfilling than working in the kitchen.

Bree Britt: I can be in the worst of moods and … once I get started baking it's just … something turns on where I'm just … in my whole … another world.

Faith Lapidus: Here she says she can be innovative and creative.

Bree Britt: I'd like to compare myself to an artist, sort of a painter for his canvas which … I'm the baker so, of course my cupcakes and cookies, and all my sweet desserts are my canvas. I think I'm going to do something with, maybe, a banana.

Faith Lapidus: Bree started cooking with her great-grandmother when she was five years old.

Lillie Walter (great-grandmother): Well, I've always tried to help them learn to cook.

Faith Lapidus: Bree perfected her great-grandmother's recipes and came up with her own. When she was 12, she told her mother she wanted to open a bakery.

Bree Britt: She told me to really think about, you know, the sacrifices and the things that I'll have to go through. You know … I wasn't going to be just a normal teenager … or a normal kid anymore. So, she told me to really think about it.

Charmaine Britt (Bree's mother): I thought it was going to be fly-by-night. Something that she just would get tired of eventually and once she saw how much work it would be. So my deal was we'll start online – the only way we can start making money is we'll do it online.

Faith Lapidus: It made enough money that Charmaine Britt became her daughter's business partner. They rented a shop and opened Bree's Sweet Treats. Charmaine runs the store during the day until Bree gets out of school.

Leo Harrington (customer): I guess it's going to be key lime today.

Faith Lapidus: Leo Harrington, a neighbouring barber shop owner, comes almost every day

Leo Harrington: The flavour … she has all kind … a great assortment.

Faith Lapidus: He admires what Bree's accomplished.

Leo Harrington: I watch her diligence; school and then here – baking all evening, getting ready for the next day.

Faith Lapidus: It's challenging but Bree says studying and running a business taught her how to better manage her time.

Bree Britt: It has also taught me hard work and responsibility … and it has also taught me to be more aware of people and when they come into the store, more … friendlier, that I can say. It's … it's taught me a lot.

Faith Lapidus: Whether it's vanilla or chocolate, key lime or strawberry, there is a secret behind Bree's recipes.

Charmaine Britt: Her cupcakes are made … are flavoured with fresh fruits or more of the extracts, more so than of sugar.

Faith Lapidus: But sugar or not, Bree's treats are sweet enough to keep them coming back for more.

Customer: They're so pretty!

Faith Lapidus: For writer Faiza Elmasry, I'm Faith Lapidus, VOA news.

From: Faiza Elmasry, "Teen Business Owner Creates Recipe for Success."
In: Voice of America News, *17 April 2015.*

TIPP

These text passages will help you find the correct answer:

1 "I've always tried to help them learn to cook." (l. 11)

2 "She told me to really think about, you know, the sacrifices and the things that I'll have to go through. You know … I wasn't going to be just a normal teenager … or a normal kid anymore. So, she told me to really think about it." (ll. 14–16)

3 "It made enough money that Charmaine Britt became her daughter's business partner." (ll. 21/22); "Charmaine runs the store during the day until Bree gets out of school." (ll. 22/23)

4 "He admires what Bree's accomplished." (l. 28); "I watch her diligence; school and then here – baking all evening, getting ready for the next day." (ll. 29/30)

5 "Bree says studying and running a business taught her how to better manage her time." (ll. 31/32); "It has also taught me hard work and responsibility … and it has also taught me to be more aware of people and when they come into the store, more … friendlier, that I can say. It's … it's taught me a lot." (ll. 33–35)

6 "Her cupcakes are made … are flavoured with fresh fruits or more of the extracts, more so than of sugar." (ll. 38/39)

1	How her great-grandmother influenced Bree:	taught her to cook/taught Bree to bake/taught her great-granddaughter her recipes
2	What Bree's mother advised her daughter to do:	to think about the sacrifices / to really think about it
3	What role Bree's mother has in the business today:	• Bree's business partner • runs the store during the day
4	What Leo Harrington thinks of Bree's work:	• admires what she accomplished • admires her discipline/diligence
5	What Bree has learnt through working in her bakery:	• to better manage her time • hard work / (to take) responsibility / to be more aware of people / to be friendlier
6	What ingredient makes Bree's sweets special:	fresh fruits / flavoured with fresh fruits / the extract of fresh fruits

Hörverstehen: Übungsset 2
Niedersachsen Englisch

You will hear each recording twice. After each listening you will have time to complete your answers.

Task 1: Behavioural Economics

You will hear an interview with a young psychologist on how people tend to behave. While listening, fill in the missing information. You need not write complete sentences. Unless otherwise specified, one aspect is enough. There is one example (**0**).

0	What conflicts of interests are named at the beginning to attract the listener's attention:	• no activities to lose weight • postponing paying a parking fine
1	Why humans prefer short-term benefits to long-term ones:	• •
2	What areas of our life are influenced by short-term thinking:	• •
3	What is meant by "present buyer's preferences":	
4	What advantages older children have over younger ones according to the psychologist:	
5	What classical economics is about:	
6	What behavioural economics is about:	• •
7	What is meant by "time-inconsistent preferences":	

Task 2: Robotics

You will listen to two robotics experts talking about the potential for intelligent robots to transform society. While listening, tick (✓) the correct answer (a, b or c). There is only one correct answer.

1 The first expert, Alan Winfield, holds that …

- a ☐ autonomous robots will change the world of work.
- b ☐ intelligent robots are already doing a lot of important jobs.
- c ☐ the most important jobs are not yet done by intelligent robots.

2 The robot industry still struggles to …

- a ☐ provide better learning functions for toy robots.
- b ☐ create robots which are smart enough to make the right decisions.
- c ☐ invent more autonomous robots for the education sector.

3 The second expert, Adam Afriyie, believes that …

- a ☐ it is dangerous not to know what an intelligent robot is capable of.
- b ☐ the boundaries of what we allow intelligent robots to do need looking at.
- c ☐ intelligent robots will help old people a lot in the future.

4 In general, both experts warn that …

- a ☐ technological progress usually requires a long learning process.
- b ☐ robots might soon be able to outsmart their inventors.
- c ☐ researchers need to deal responsibly with technological possibilities.

Task 3: Renting a House or Apartment

You will hear four young people talking about renting a house or apartment. Match each speaker (1 to 4) with one of the statements (A to G). There are three more options than you need.

The speaker …

A was happy that they found a cheap, cosy apartment with a spacious garden and a big office.

B had a problem with the owner of the house and told him they were moving out.

C first thought they found their dream house, but now regrets the decision to move in.

D isn't renting yet and feels as if the situation will never improve.

E did something new by renting out a flat for holiday-makers.

F found a very caring landlord who put a lot of effort into making the apartment homelike before they moved in.

G moved back home in order to be able to afford the high costs of living.

speaker	1	2	3	4
statement				

Lösung

Transkript 1 **Behavioural Economics**

Chandy Nath: How many times have you not bothered to go to the gym even though you wanted to slim up in time for the summer holidays, or not paid a parking fine on time even though you knew that by putting it off you'd pay even more? The fact is that many of us are biased in favour of what we want in the short term rather than the long term. We're impatient. We want it now and we like quick wins; and this means that we don't always make decisions in our best interests.
My name's Chandy Nath from the Parliamentary Office of Science and Technology. In this podcast we'll be finding out how short-term thinking affects all aspects of modern life from our own health and well-being, right through to pensions and global warming. We'll be talking to economists, …

Daniel Read, Economist: People have what are called present buyer's preferences. They really focus on the pleasures and pains of the moment.

Chandy Nath: … neuroscientists, …

Trevor Robbins, Neuroscientist: The sub-cortical brain will grab the immediate opportunity without thinking …

Chandy Nath: … behavioural experts …

Theresa Marteau, Psychologist: Young children have much more difficulty deferring gratification than older children.

Chandy Nath: … about what makes us short-term thinkers. And whether there's anything we can do about it. We'll also be talking to Deputy Leader of the Liberal Democrats, Vince Cable MP, to find out why this subject interests policy makers.

Vince Cable: Economics is not a science and anybody who could bring new insights to bear would seem to me very much to the good.

Chandy Nath: To help me understand all this I'm going to talk to Laura Hayns, who's a PhD student in psychology at the University of Cambridge. Now Laura specialises in behavioural economics. Laura, do you want to start just by telling me what behavioural economics is?

Laura Hayns: Basically, behavioural economics integrates findings from psychology into classical economic theory.

Chandy Nath: How does it do that?

Laura Hayns: Well, classical economics is all about how ideal people in an ideal world make rational decisions. But there's a lot of evidence now that people are actually not always rational, and the ways in which we deviate from rationality are quite systematic. So, this is where behavioural economics comes in. How do real people in a real world make decisions and what are the biases that we have when processing information?

Chandy Nath: So, in practical terms, what does that mean? Can you give me an example?

Laura Hayns: Sure. So, for example, according to classical economists our preferences should be stable across time. So, say my long-term goal is to give up smoking. Classical economists would expect that my short-term goal would be not to smoke today. However, as any smoker knows, it's actually quite difficult to resist the temptation of a cigarette. And it turns out that contrary to classical economics, our preferences are what we call time-inconsistent, so they're not stable across time – they actually change. So, even though my New Year's resolution might be to give up smoking this year, chances are in the short term, so, even, disappointingly, on New Year's Day, I might actually prefer the immediate gratification of a cigarette. I think this pattern of decision-making comes into a lot of areas of our lives.

From: Chandy Nath/Laura Hayns, Parliamentary Recording Unit.
http://www.parliament.uk/audio/scienceinparliament/behaviouraleconomics/

TIPP

These text passages will help you find the correct answer:

1 "We're impatient. We want it now and we like quick wins" (l. 5)
2 "In this podcast we'll be finding out how short-term thinking affects all aspects of modern life from our own health and well-being, right through to pensions and global warming." (ll. 8–10)
3 "People have what are called present buyer's preferences. They really focus on the pleasures and pains of the moment." (ll. 11/12)
4 "Young children have much more difficulty deferring gratification than older children." (ll. 17/18)
5 "classical economics is all about how ideal people in an ideal world make rational decisions." (ll. 31/32)
6 "So, this is where behavioural economics comes in. How do real people in a real world make decisions and what are the biases that we have when processing information?" (ll. 34–36)
7 "And it turns out that contrary to classical economics, our preferences are what we call time-inconsistent, so they're not stable across time – they actually change." (ll. 43–45)

1 Why humans prefer short-term benefits to long-term ones:	• lack of patience • we like quick wins/want things now
2 What areas of our life are influenced by short-term thinking:	*Name two of the following:* • health/well-being • pensions • global warming
3 What is meant by "present buyer's preferences":	focus on pleasures/pains of the moment

4	What advantages older children have over younger ones according to the psychologist:	They are more patient./ They can defer gratifications.
5	What classical economics is about:	ideal people in an ideal world making rational decisions
6	What behavioural economics is about:	• real people in a real world making decisions • in how far people are prejudiced
7	What is meant by "time-inconsistent preferences":	preferences change over time

Transkript 2 Robotics

Alan Winfield: The new kind of robotics that really has not yet made a big impact in society but is on the verge, if you like … on the cusp of making a big impact is called intelligent robotics. So, intelligent robots unlike those old kind of robots that make cars. Intelligent robots are capable of deciding what to do next on their own. The word that we use is "autonomous". So, the … if you like, the autonomous robot industry is new. The best examples of autonomous robots are really, so far, are toys. So, for instance, you know the Sony Aibo, which was the pet robot dog – that was a very good example of an autonomous mobile robot. Of course, I've forgotten the biggest application of autonomous mobile robots, which is, of course, robot vacuum cleaners. Most of those robots that I've just described are not learning. The toy robots do have some learning functions. One of the reasons, of course, the toy robots can be more advanced is because the scope for things going wrong is smaller. In other words, the potential for it to do harm if it does the wrong thing is much smaller than if it's a robot that's driving your car, for instance. So, typically, we find that the more serious and safety-critical the application, then the less the intelligence or the learning. One of the big challenges that we face in the robotics research community is how to figure out how to make intelligence safe; and that's a problem that we haven't yet cracked. We're just beginning to solve that problem but my guess is it'll be another 10 or 20 years before we can really build intelligent robots that we can have good confidence … are both going to do the right thing and equally importantly, not do the wrong thing.

Chandy Nath: Alan Winfield pointed out that the autonomous robots we have today aren't really that bright. So, toy robot dogs, robot vacuum cleaners – but hopefully the technologies demonstrated at the reception which Lord Salisbury just referred to were at the forefront of current research. Now, we've heard how Lord Salisbury was particularly impressed by the robot arm; Adam Afriyie, was there anything at the reception that particularly caught your eye?

Adam Afriyie: What struck me most was actually – and what Alan raises there – which actually was the ethical debate around how far does one allow robots, these new technologies to make decisions? And one of the speakers pointed out that if, for example, you've got assistive living technologies and an iPad, for example, where an older person who needs some support – maybe they've got Alzheimer's … needs some reminders, needs some medical input – how far do we allow that to go before we say … actually people need human interaction. Now I'll pick one example which is actually that, in the computer industry, computer chips actually design the next generation of computer chips. And, in fact, most technologists will admit they actually don't know how these computer chips work anymore because the … other computers have designed them. So, we're already into this vein where actually we may require those laws of robotics that Asimov first came up with to be applied. […]

Chandy Nath, Parliamentary Recording Unit. http://www.parliament.uk/about/podcasts/scienceinparliament/robotics/

TIPP

The following clues will help you find the correct answer:

1. The first expert, Alan Winfield, talks about intelligent robots that are used today, such as toy robots and vacuum cleaners but also mentions that there is still a lot of research needed until more intelligent robots can be used (cf. ll. 1–10, 18–21).
2. Alan Winfield claims toy robots have "some learning functions" (l. 11) because they cannot do a lot of harm. Before autonomous robots can be used to drive cars, for example, their actions and reactions need to be a lot more reliable as far as safety is concerned (cf. ll. 12–21).
3. The second expert, Adam Afriyie, thinks that intelligent robots can already do more than the technicians that designed them can fully comprehend. But he does not see that as a threat in itself. He just points out that this is an issue that has to be taken into consideration (cf. ll. 34–39).
4. Both experts are convinced that scientists and researchers need to use what might already be possible from the technological point of view in a responsible way (cf. ll. 18–21, 28–30).

1 The first expert, Alan Winfield, holds that …

c ☑ the most important jobs are not yet done by intelligent robots.

2 The robot industry still struggles to …

b ☑ create robots which are smart enough to make the right decisions.

3 The second expert, Adam Afriyie, believes that …

b ☑ the boundaries of what we allow intelligent robots to do need looking at.

4 In general, both experts warn that …

c ☑ researchers need to deal responsibly with technological possibilities.

Transkript 3 Renting a House or Apartment

Speaker 1: We saw the ad in the summer, in about July, I think, but we weren't really serious about moving then so we didn't even go and see it. It wasn't until November when they re-advertised it that we got in touch with the agency and had a look. They'd put the price down since the summer too, I suppose because it had been empty so long, so that made it more affordable for us which helped us make up our minds. It was perfect – a bigger garden for the kids and enough space for an office. In winter it was lovely, very cosy, in fact, which is important to me as I really feel the cold, whereas my husband will open a window when it's minus temperatures outside! Anyway, in July when summer really started and we had that heatwave, we understood why no one had wanted to rent it over summer. It was boiling! All those lovely big windows that made the flat so light and open were like a greenhouse as soon as it got warmer. From about 8 in the morning until 7 in the evening, it was like living in a sauna! We couldn't stand being at home, and weekends were especially bad. No air conditioning, of course. If only we'd gone to see it when it was first advertised in July, we'd never have moved in!

Speaker 2: I always rent apartments when I go on holiday, rather than staying in hotels. Hotels are so impersonal, aren't they? This way you get to feel like you really live in the place you're visiting. It's the first time I've done it the other way round, though, and rented out my place … but it seemed like a good way of making some extra money. The website is really easy to use and they only charge five per cent commission, which is lower than a lot of the other holiday rental sites. It's all about the photos and the reviews. Get the photos right and the place can look really upmarket and spacious, but you don't want to make it look too much better than it really is or you end up with a bad review. It's better to undersell and overdeliver so guests are pleasantly surprised and leave an extra positive review. So far, I'm averaging three stars because of one bad review that brought my average down from four and a half stars, but hopefully I'll get it back up during the busy season.

Speaker 3: Buying a house seems so far out of my reach it's almost impossible, as it is for loads of people my age these days. My parents always told me renting was throwing money away, but it was different in their day. Then people could afford to buy a house on a normal salary, but nowadays house prices are so high and no bank will look at you unless you've got a huge deposit. The problem with my dream of buying is that it's never going to come true. Not unless my parents help me out, but I've got two sisters and we're all in the same position. At least they've both got good jobs. Not good enough to buy a house, but at least they can afford to rent places of their own in nice areas. I just don't earn enough to rent around here. Even if I get promoted to manager, it'll be tough to find somewhere unless I share, and call me fussy, but there aren't that many people I want to share a bathroom and kitchen with. Some days I think I'll be stuck living with my parents forever – even renting is like a dream to me.

Speaker 4: At first our landlord was really helpful, couldn't do enough for us. You hear stories of nightmare landlords and we felt like we were really lucky, or so we thought anyway. He redecorated the whole place, from top to bottom, and let us keep all the bills in his name so we didn't have the bother of contacting all the companies ourselves. He even offered to come round and do the gardening as he knew we both worked long hours and might not have time. That's where the problems started now I look back. Then he'd pop round 'just to check everything's OK for you' once a month, then twice a month. Soon he was coming every week with some excuse or other. In the beginning we'd invite him in for tea, but it was only encouraging him, so when we realised, we'd try to have the conversation on the doorstep instead. It got so bad we pretended to be on our way out if we saw him coming up the path. We'd grab our coats and walk round the block until he'd gone. I don't know if he was just lonely or just didn't trust us not to ruin his precious house. In the end we gave our notice and found somewhere else. It's a shame because we really loved that house, but at least it's more peaceful in the new place.

Adapted from: British Council, https://learnenglish.britishcouncil.org/skills/listening/advanced-c1/renting-a-house

TIPP

These text passages will help you find the correct answer:

1 "It was perfect" (l. 6), "If only we'd gone to see it when it was first advertised in July, we'd never have moved in!" (ll. 14/15)
The speaker first mentions her positive impression of the flat (e. g. "bigger garden", "enough space", "cosy"), which could hint at statement A, but later she clearly points out that they "couldn't stand being at home".

2 "It's the first time I've done it the other way round, though, and rented out my place ..." (ll. 18/19) Here, the mentioning of "renting out" is the key to the correct solution.

3 "Some days I think I'll be stuck living with my parents forever – even renting is like a dream to me." (ll. 39/40)
The speaker still seems to live with her parents ("stuck living with my parents") and does not mention moving back in with them (as in statement G). Moreover, she is not talking about the high costs of living in general (as mentioned in statement G), but about high rents and the impossibility of buying a house.

4 "In the end we gave our notice and found somewhere else." (l. 54) Although the speaker talks about a caring landlord, which could point towards sentence F, he later talks about "problems" and that "it got so bad".

speaker	**1**	**2**	**3**	**4**
statement	**C**	**E**	**D**	**B**

Hörverstehen: Übungsset 3
Niedersachsen Englisch

You will hear each recording twice. After each listening you will have time to complete your answers.

Task 1: The Problem of Species Extinction

You will hear a recording about the problems of species extinction and climate change. VOA reporter Rosanne Skirble is talking to Kate Burns from the Al Bustan Zoological Centre and ecology professor Mark Urban.
Choose from the list (A–H) the statement that each speaker makes. For each speaker, there are two correct answers. Put the corresponding letter (A–H) into the correct box. There are two extra statements which you will not need.

A Hunting and poaching is still the number one reason why animals die out.

B Swapping animals helps to preserve the genetic diversity of species.

C If we do not reduce the emission of greenhouse gases, one in six species could die out.

D The problem of species extinction will affect all parts of the world in equal measure.

E The effects of climate change will be worst if temperatures rise 4.3 degrees above pre-industrial times.

F It is worth fighting for each individual animal.

G The extinction of some species, such as predators of crop pests, could increase the problem of hunger.

H Urbanisation and oil production contribute to the loss of biodiversity.

Speaker	Statement 1	Statement 2
Rosanne Skirble		
Kate Burns		
Mark Urban		

Task 2: Happiness by Design: Finding Pleasure and Purpose in Everyday Life

You will hear a report on what makes us happy. While listening, fill in the missing information. You need not write complete sentences. Unless otherwise specified, one aspect is enough. There is one example (**0**).

0	The two things Professor Dolan talks about in his book *Happiness by Design*:	• pleasure • purpose
1	Two things that are essential for the first client's happiness:	• •
2	How Dolan knows what makes people happy:	• •
3	What makes most people miserable:	
4	What kind of time is least valuable to most people:	
5	Why it is important how we use our time:	
6	Two instant measures of being happier:	• •
7	How to achieve happiness according to Dolan:	
8	Two activities that do not make us happier:	• •

Task 3: All-Women's Mosque Opens in L.A.

You will hear a report about the first women-only mosque in the United States. While listening, tick (✓) the correct answer (a, b or c). There is only one correct answer.

1 Interviewee Tanzila Ahmed stresses that she likes going to this mosque because she …

a ☐ prefers women-only prayer.

b ☐ appreciates meeting people from different cultural backgrounds.

c ☐ enjoys the unique spiritual experience.

2 In traditional mosques …

a ☐ women and men pray separately.

b ☐ men lead all the prayers.

c ☐ women are excluded from Friday prayers.

3 Edina Lakovic, who gave a sermon on the opening day of the all-women's mosque, felt …

a ☐ proud to stand in front of the audience.

b ☐ overwhelmed with joy because she had waited so long for this moment.

c ☐ that speaker and audience had a common goal.

4 The all-women's mosque is different to mixed-sex mosques because women …

a ☐ do not have the impression of being marginalized.

b ☐ are not harassed by male worshippers.

c ☐ have to obey a special dress code.

5 Founder and president of the all-women's mosque, M. Hasna Maznavi, was inspired by the Golden Ages in Islam when …

a ☐ women were first allowed to worship in public.

b ☐ multi-faith exchanges took place.

c ☐ many Muslim preachers promoted tolerance.

6 Islamic scholars say that it is …

a ☐ possible for women to lead other women in certain prayers.

b ☐ not acceptable for women to worship separately.

c ☐ likely other Muslim communities will soon offer all-women services.

7 The all-women's mosque allows Muslim women to focus on …

a ☐ gender issues.

b ☐ their faith.

c ☐ discussing the purpose of their existence.

Lösung

Transkript 1 The Problem of Species Extinction

Rosanne Skirble: In the United Arab Emirates, the rare bongo antelope is on the brink of extinction says Kate Burns, a veterinary nurse at Al Bustan Zoological Centre, which houses several of the animals. Burns hopes to breed more.

Kate Burns: Each individual counts. Mhmm, there is only 47 left in the wild. Mhmm, so, yeah, breeding, we need to maintain the genetic diversity of the species and that means, you know, swapping, swapping animals, swapping experience.

Rosanne Skirble: Humans are pushing this species and others to extinction. While hunting and poaching certainly play a role, so do urban sprawl and oil extraction. Climate changing emissions from power plants, buildings and transport also threaten biodiversity. Climate models predict the Earth's temperature will increase from two to six degrees Celsius this century. Experts say a 4.3-degree increase above pre-industrial times is a tipping point, which will lead to the worst impacts of climate change. Extinctions will accelerate, says University of Connecticut ecology professor Mark Urban.

Mark Urban: We reached the point where we had 16 % extinction risk for species. So one in six species could be endangered if we don't do anything about controlling greenhouse gases.

Rosanne Skirble: Urban reviewed 131 articles on species extinction for an analysis, which appears in the journal *Science*. He says some regions of the world will be harder hit than others.

Mark Urban: The small land masses play a role, places with lots of endemic species like Australia and South America. Mhmm, these are species that are already constrained to, to small ranges and so even a small shift in those ranges could endanger them.

Rosanne Skirble: Climate change will alter species and the habitats in which they live, Urban warns. Their loss will spread disease and have other unintended consequences.

Mark Urban: If you think about our food security and we have crops. Well, it's very important to understand, say, the rainfall pattern in the future, and, and the ability of those crops to still be grown. But what we're neglecting are the biotic interactions. So, what if we lose a, a really important predator of a pest in that field and suddenly that pest increases and decreases the crop yields.

Rosanne Skirble: Urban says his study gives policy makers and the public added incentive to adopt new strategies, to conserve and protect the most threatened species. Rosanne Skirble, VOA News, Washington.

From: Rosanne Skirble, Kate Burns, Mark Urban, "One in Six Species Threatened with Extinction."
In: Voice of America News, *30 April 2015.*

TIPP

This listening text contains quite a lot of background noises. Don't let them distract you and try to focus on what the speakers are saying. Also, don't worry if you do not know all the vocabulary in the text. You do not have to understand each and every word in order to be able to solve the task.

These text passages will help you find the correct answer:

A "Humans are pushing this species and others to extinction. While hunting and poaching certainly play a role, so do urban sprawl and oil extraction. Climate changing emissions from power plants, buildings and transport also threaten biodiversity." (ll. 7–10): Hunting and poaching are mentioned as two reasons among others, not as the most important ("number one") reason.

B "we need to maintain the genetic diversity of the species and that means, you know, swapping, swapping animals" (ll. 5/6)

C "one in six species could be endangered if we don't do anything about controlling greenhouse gases." (ll. 16/17)

D "He says some regions of the world will be harder hit than others." (ll. 19/20): This quote clearly shows that statement D must be wrong and therefore can't be matched to any of the speakers.

E "Experts say a 4.3-degree increase above pre-industrial times is a tipping point, which will lead to the worst impacts of climate change." (ll. 11–13)

F "Each individual counts." (l. 4)

G "If you think about our food security and we have crops. Well, it's very important to understand […] the ability of those crops to still be grown. […] So, what if we lose a, a really important predator of a pest in that field and suddenly that pest increases and decreases the crop yields." (ll. 27–31)

H "Humans are pushing this species and others to extinction. While hunting and poaching certainly play a role, so do urban sprawl and oil extraction." (ll. 7/8)

Speaker	Statement 1	Statement 2
Rosanne Skirble	H	E
Kate Burns	F	B
Mark Urban	C	G

Transkript 2 Happiness by Design: Finding Pleasure and Purpose in Everyday Life

Professor Paul Dolan: For me happiness is in our experiences of life. Things that we feel day to day, moment to moment. And I talk about pleasure and purpose. OK, so my name's Paul Dolan, I'm at London School of Economics and my book is called *Happiness by Design – Finding Pleasure and Purpose in Everyday Life.* So, happy lives are ones that contain some balance; it's not the same for everybody and it's not in equal measure. But some kind of balance between things that we find fun on the one hand and things that we find fulfilling on the other. Well, it is a subjective experience. I think everything ultimately matters because it makes us feel better, so I can describe to you I think the things that I find pleasurable and the things that I find purposeful. And I can also probably give you a good sense of how much I find them pleasurable and how much I find them purposeful. And equally, of course, things that I find painful and things that I find pointless, so I think we are now getting a better insight into the quantitative nature of those elements.

Client 1: Happiness for me is a very ethereal thing, I think. By that I mean that it is very difficult to say what it is, and it can be different, at different stages of my life. But in essence, happiness for me, as I've grown older, is quite a few intangible things, things which make me think that life is worth it, so it's spending time with the people I want to be with, it's not just living from moment to moment but actually just being in the moment and doing the things that are actually most important. So the places that are really important for me, and often, actually, it's later on that you realise the happiest times. Well, I'm getting better at that.

Professor Paul Dolan: We're getting many observations on many people over many years, and there seems to be something sensible coming through from the answers people give us. We get associations with some things that you would expect them to be associated with, you know, poverty makes people miserable but being rich doesn't make people happier. So, you know, there are some nice insights coming through from this data. Time that we spend with other people that makes us feel nice, time spent on trains and on tubes and on buses, not so nice.

Client 2: The things that make me happy are: spending time with my friends and family, going out for dinner, going to watch my football team play football, playing with my cat.

Professor Paul Dolan: Well, I think how we use our time is absolutely critical, it's the scarcest resource we've got, right? The few moments that we've been talking now, or that I've been talking now, are a few moments closer to death and it's time I won't ever get back, so I think it's incumbent on us all to think about how we use that time and just re-orientate some of it away from things that we're finding painful and pointless. And spend a bit more time, you know, with things that we find pleasurable and purposeful which would include spending more time with people that we like being with; would include spending a bit more time outdoors, maybe listening to music, all of these things, I think most of us know if we stop and think for a moment, would make us feel a bit happier. The interesting question is why we don't do more of it? And helping others, too, makes us feel nice, too. So all these things that we would get good feedback for if we paid attention to those experiences, but one of the reasons why we don't do those things more is we don't pay attention to those experiences as much as we might, we tell ourselves big stories about the things that we think should make us happy, buying more stuff, earning more money, the kind of narratives and stories that we tell ourselves or we're told by other people that sometimes deviate us off the path of using our time in those ways that make us happier. [...] But I think the important thing is that all of us could be a little bit happier by doing some more of the things that make us feel good. And the critical thing is to design environments that make it easier for us to do those things. You know, if you've got a friend that you want to speak to, plan a time in the diary that you speak to them, the same time every week, and then habits will get formed and automatically you speak to that person without having to think too hard about doing so. So all of us, wherever we start from, I think, can nudge ourselves a little bit happier.

From: Paul Dolan/Lee Millam, Pod Academy, *5 October 2014.*
http://podacademy.org/podcasts/happiness-design/

TIPP

These text passages will help you find the correct answer:

1 "But in essence, happiness for me, as I've grown older, is quite a few intangible things, things which make me think that life is worth it, so it's spending time with the people I want to be with, it's not just living from moment to moment but actually just being in the moment and doing the things that are actually most important. So the places that are really important for me" (ll. 15–20)

2 "We're getting many observations on many people over many years, and there seems to be something sensible coming through from the answers people give us." (ll. 22–24)

3 "you know, poverty makes people miserable but being rich doesn't make people happier." (ll. 25/26)

4 "Time that we spend with other people that makes us feel nice, time spent on trains and on tubes and on buses, not so nice." (ll. 27/28)

5 "Well, I think how we use our time is absolutely critical, it's the scarcest resource we've got, right? The few moments that we've been talking now, or that I've been talking now, are a few moments closer to death and it's time I won't ever get back" (ll. 32–35)

6 "And spend a bit more time, you know, with things that we find pleasurable and purposeful which would include spending more time with people that we like being with; would include spending a bit more time outdoors, maybe listening to music, all of these things, I think most of us know if we stop and think for a moment, would make us feel a bit happier. [...] And helping others, too, makes us feel nice, too." (ll. 37–42)

7 "So all these things that we would get good feedback for if we paid attention to those experiences" (ll. 42/43)

8 "we tell ourselves big stories about the things that we think should make us happy, buying more stuff, earning more money, the kind of narratives and stories that we tell ourselves or we're told by other people sometimes deviate us off the path of using our time in those ways that make us happier." (ll. 45–49)

1 Two things that are essential for the first client's happiness:	*Name two of the following:* • (spending time with) people he likes • being in the moment • places that are important
2 How Dolan knows what makes people happy:	• through observations • through people's answers
3 What makes most people miserable:	poverty
4 What kind of time is least valuable to most people:	time spent on public transport
5 Why it is important how we use our time:	scarcest resource / we won't get it back
6 Two instant measures of being happier:	*Name two of the following:* • spending time with people we like • spending more time outside • listening to music • helping others
7 How to achieve happiness according to Dolan:	paying attention to pleasurable experiences
8 Two activities that do not make us happier:	• buying more stuff • earning more money

Transkript 3 All-Women's Mosque Opens in L.A.

Elizabeth Lee: Once a month Muslim women gather inside this building for an experience unlike any other in the United States.

Tanzila Ahmed, Worshipper: I came here two months ago and it was so empowering to be surrounded by women of all ethnicities or races.

Elizabeth Lee: Unlike most traditional mosques where men and women are separated and men lead Friday prayers, the women's mosque is for women and led by a woman. Edina Lakovic gave a sermon on the opening day of the mosque.

Edina Lakovic: When I stepped up to the plate, I felt that I was connected to the women in the audience and realising that we were all there for the same reason because we wanted to reconnect to our faith, or take the next step in our faith and that we wanted to try something a little different.

Elizabeth Lee: Something a little different because some Muslim women say they've always felt like outsiders at traditional mosques.

Tanzila Ahmed: In the mosques that I've been growing up in, we were always kind of shadowed into a backroom. We weren't allowed to be in the same space as, you know, where the sermons were being held. What was empowering about this was, we didn't – I didn't even have to think about that. I didn't have to worry about the patriarchy issues that I usually have to deal with when going to a mosque.

Elizabeth Lee: The women's mosque does not have a dress code. The women pray in a multi-faith building that also houses Jewish and Christian events. Founder M. Hasna Maznavi says this was the reason she picked this place for the mosque.

M. Hasna Maznavi: Something that really inspires me is … are the Golden Ages in Islam. And this was a time when Muslims, Jews, and Christians all worked together.

Elizabeth Lee: But not everyone believes an all-women's mosque is necessary. Islamic scholars say while it is acceptable for women to lead other women in prayer, they question whether that should include the shortened midday Friday prayer or the sermon. The discussion about women's role in Islam is not a new one, says Brie Loskota at the University of Southern California.

Brie Loskota: The women's mosque itself is not an isolated event. There have been a lot of critiques of women's roles and the limited and narrowed nature of many of those roles in Muslim institutions for many decades. And that has come to a head especially with sort of the gen-next millennium Muslim women.

Elizabeth Lee: Loskota says the women's mosque is a response to this critique with the uniquely American characteristics.

Brie Loskota: There is a large focus on interreligious dialogue. There is a great focus on pluralism and how do you exist in a plural context. There's a great focus of diversity.

Elizabeth Lee: And for these women: a focus on spirituality. Elizabeth Lee for VOA News, Los Angeles.

From: Elizabeth Lee, "Unconventional All-Women's Mosque Opens in Los Angeles."
In: Voice of America News, *3 April 2015.*

TIPP

These text passages will help you find the correct answer:

1 "I came here two months ago and it was so empowering to be surrounded by women of all ethnicities or races." (ll. 3/4)

2 "Unlike most traditional mosques where men and women are separated and men lead Friday prayers" (ll. 5/6)

3 "When I stepped up to the plate, I felt that I was connected to the women in the audience and realising that <u>we were all there for the same reason</u> because we wanted to reconnect to our faith, or take the next step in our faith and that we wanted to try something a little different." (ll. 8–11)

4 "Something a little different because some Muslim women say they've always <u>felt like outsiders at traditional mosques</u>." (ll. 12/13); "In the mosques that I've been growing up in, <u>we were always kind of shadowed into a backroom</u>. We weren't allowed to be in the same space as, you know, where the sermons were being held." (ll. 14–16)

5 "Something that really inspires me is … are the Golden Ages in Islam. And this was a time when <u>Muslims, Jews, and Christians all worked together</u>." (ll. 22/23)

6 "Islamic scholars say while <u>it is acceptable for women to lead other women in prayer</u>, they question whether that should include the shortened midday Friday prayer or the sermon." (ll. 24–27)

7 "And for these women: a <u>focus on spirituality</u>." (l. 38)

1 Interviewee Tanzila Ahmed stresses that she likes going to this mosque because she …

b ☑ appreciates meeting people from different cultural backgrounds.

2 In traditional mosques …

a ☑ women and men pray separately.

3 Edina Lakovic, who gave a sermon on the opening day of the all-women's mosque, felt …

c ☑ that speaker and audience had a common goal.

4 The all-women's mosque is different to mixed-sex mosques because women …

a ☑ do not have the impression of being marginalized.

5 Founder and president of the all-women's mosque, M. Hasna Maznavi, was inspired by the Golden Ages in Islam when …

b ☑ multi-faith exchanges took place.

6 Islamic scholars say that it is …

a ☑ possible for women to lead other women in certain prayers.

7 The all-women's mosque allows Muslim women to focus on …

b ☑ their faith.

Sprachmittlung

Aufbau des Prüfungsteils „Sprachmittlung"

In der Abiturprüfung werden Ihnen **ein oder mehrere Ausgangstexte auf Deutsch** vorgelegt. Ihre Aufgabe besteht darin, den Inhalt des Texts bzw. der Texte **auf Englisch zusammenzufassen**. Eine Sprachmittlung ist also keine wörtliche Übersetzung – vielmehr sollen Sie die Kernaussagen eines Texts **sinngemäß** in die andere Sprache übertragen. In der Regel ist die Aufgabenstellung in einen **Kontext** eingebettet, d. h., es ist genau vorgegeben, für wen, zu welchem Anlass und in welchem Textformat Sie den deutschen Text zusammenfassen sollen. Wichtig beim Verfassen einer Sprachmittlung ist also nicht nur, dass Sie alle inhaltlich relevanten Aspekte in die Fremdsprache übertragen, sondern dass Ihre Lösung genau an die Situation und den Adressatenkreis angepasst ist.
Für die Bearbeitung der Sprachmittlungsaufgabe haben Sie **60 Minuten** Zeit.

Vorgehen in der Prüfung

Lesen Sie sich zunächst die Aufgabenstellung und den Ausgangstext (bzw. die Ausgangstexte) einmal ganz durch, um sich einen **groben Überblick** über den Inhalt zu verschaffen. Gehen Sie dann folgendermaßen vor:

Schritt 1 Aufgabenstellung genau lesen

Analysieren Sie die Aufgabenstellung in Hinblick auf die folgenden Aspekte:

- In welcher Form sollen Sie den Text wiedergeben (**Textsorte**)? Damit sind in der Regel bereits bestimmte formale Vorgaben verbunden. Bei einer E-Mail müssen Sie beispielsweise eine passende Anrede- und Schlussformel verwenden, ein Artikel weist immer eine Überschrift auf usw.
- Für wen sollen Sie den Text zusammenfassen (**Zielgruppe/Adressat*in**)? Das hat u. a. Auswirkungen auf den Sprachstil, den Sie verwenden.

- In der Regel enthält die Aufgabenstellung einen sogenannten **Operator**. Dabei handelt es sich um ein Aufforderungsverb, an das bestimmte formale Vorgaben geknüpft sind. Bei den Operatoren „sum up“ oder „outline“ etwa sollen Sie knapp und präzise die Kernaussagen bzw. wesentlichen Aspekte wiedergeben. Manchmal sind auch mehrere Operatoren miteinander kombiniert – dann müssen Sie die Vorgaben jedes einzelnen Operators berücksichtigen.

Operator	Dos and Don'ts	Beispiel
write [+ text type]	textsortenspezifische Vorgaben beachten (siehe Tabelle auf der folgenden Seite)	*[…] Using the information from the text,* ***write an article*** *for the English project website in which you present the drawbacks of digital language assistants such as Alexa. (ÜA 2)*
sum up / summarise / outline / present	• die wichtigsten Aspekte knapp und präzise zusammenfassen • ggf. kulturspezifische Aspekte erklären	*[…] Using the information from the text, write an article for the English project website in which you* ***present*** *the drawbacks of digital language assistants such as Alexa. (ÜA 2)*
explain	• Zusammenhänge darlegen • ggf. kulturbezogene Unterschiede miteinbeziehen	*[…] write an article for the project website in which you* ***explain*** *how and why more and more Germans have changed their consumer behaviour. (2017-5)*

- Manchmal müssen Sie nicht den Text als Ganzes zusammenfassen, sondern sollen sich nur auf bestimmte Teilaspekte fokussieren (beispielsweise die Nachteile bestimmter Entwicklungen). Achten Sie also genau auf den **inhaltlichen Fokus** der Aufgabenstellung.

Schritt 2 Schlüsselstellen markieren und Notizen machen

Lesen Sie sich nun den Ausgangstext noch einmal aufmerksam durch und markieren Sie sich die für die Aufgabenstellung relevanten Textstellen. Machen Sie sich neben den Stellen Notizen (idealerweise bereits auf Englisch).

Schritt 3 Notizen strukturieren

Gehen Sie Ihre Notizen noch einmal durch und bringen Sie sie in eine logische Reihenfolge – beispielsweise, indem Sie sie nummerieren. Fertigen Sie anschließend aus Ihren Notizen und den Überlegungen zur geforderten Textsorte eine Grobgliederung an.

Schritt 4 Lösung ausformulieren

Formulieren Sie Ihre Lösung anhand der Grobgliederung aus. Ihr Text sollte dabei deutlich kürzer sein als der Ausgangstext. Führen Sie sich noch einmal vor Augen, welche Zieltextsorte gefordert ist und welche formalen und sprachlichen Aspekte es dabei zu beachten gilt. Eine Übersicht über die Merkmale der häufigsten Zieltextsorten finden Sie in der folgenden Tabelle.
Denken Sie außerdem daran, ggf. **kulturspezifische Ausdrücke und Phänomene**, die einer englischsprachigen Person vielleicht nicht geläufig sind, zu **erklären**. Das können Begriffe aus der deutschen Medienlandschaft sein (z. B. „... *Tatort*, a very popular TV crime series"), technische Termini (z. B. „... cars have to pass the *TÜV* – an inspection to ensure that they meet the safety requirements") usw. Auch dieser Aspekt – also Ihre Fähigkeit, zwischen Kulturen zu vermitteln und verbale Brücken zu bauen – fließt in die Bewertung der Sprachmittlung mit ein.

Textsorte	Aufbau	Sprachstil
Artikel	• Überschrift • Einleitung mit Hinführung zum Thema • klar gegliederter Hauptteil (z. B. Vor- und Nachteile, Chancen und Risiken)	• neutrales Register • bei jugendlicher Zielgruppe nicht zu förmlich
E-Mail	• passende Anrede • Einleitung mit Bezugnahme zum Kontext • klar gegliederter Hauptteil • evtl. abschließender Satz mit Bezugnahme zum Kontext • Schlussformel und Name	• formelle E-Mails: sachlich-nüchtern; meist Verwendung von Langformen • persönliche E-Mails: umgangssprachlich; Verwendung von Kurzformen
Blogeintrag	• Überschrift (+ ggf. mehrere Zwischenüberschriften) • Anrede der Leserschaft mit Bezugnahme zum Kontext / Anlass des Schreibens • klar gegliederter Hauptteil • kurze Abrundung (z. B. mit Aufforderung zum Kommentieren o. Ä.)	• oft eher umgangssprachlich; bei Blogs von Organisationen o. Ä. etwas sachlicher • häufig Verwendung der 1. Person Singular („I") • meist direkte Anrede der Leserschaft („you")

Auf der folgenden Seite finden Sie eine Liste mit hilfreichen Wendungen für die Sprachmittlungsaufgabe. Weitere Formulierungshilfen enthalten übrigens die digitalen „**MindCards**".

Wenn Sie mit dem Formulieren Ihrer Lösung fertig sind, lesen Sie sich Ihren Text noch einmal in Ruhe durch und verbessern Sie Rechtschreib- und Grammatikfehler.

Hilfreiche Wendungen – Strukturieren eines Artikels/Blogeintrags etc.

Aspekte aufzählen	*First of all, … / To begin with, …* *Firstly, … Secondly, … Thirdly, …* *In addition, … / Moreover, … / Furthermore, …* *Finally, … / Lastly, … / To conclude, …*
Gründe angeben	*As … / Since …* *… because …* *Due to …*
Folgen aufzeigen	*Thus, … / Therefore, …* *As a result, … / As a consequence, …*
zusammenfassen	*To conclude, … / To sum up, … / All in all, …*

Hilfreiche Wendungen – E-Mails

formelle E-Mail	Anrede und Schluss, wenn man die Ansprechperson nicht kennt: *Dear Sir or Madam,* *[…]* *Yours faithfully,* *[first and last name]* Anrede und Schluss, wenn man die Ansprechperson kennt: *Dear Mr Smith, / Dear Mrs Smith, / Dear Ms Smith,* *[…]* *Yours sincerely,* *[first and last name]*
persönliche E-Mail	Anrede und Schluss: *Dear Sam, / Hi Sam, / Hello Sam,* *[…]* *Yours, / Take care, / All the best, / Hugs,* *[first name]*

Hilfreiche Wendungen – Blogeintrag

die Leserschaft einbeziehen	*Did you know …? / Have you ever …? / Would you …?*
um Kommentare bitten	*Tell us about your experiences in the comment section.* *Please leave a comment below and let me know what you think.* *I'd love to hear what you think about this topic. Please leave a comment below.*

Sprachmittlung: Übungsaufgabe 1

Mit Schritt-für-Schritt-Anleitung

Aufgabenstellung

Your English friend Jake is planning to spend a year abroad in Recife, a town in the northeast of Brasil. He has heard that flying kites is a very popular pastime in Brasil, and is looking forward to trying it out himself. You have read the following two articles about this sport. You think it is interesting, but are also a bit worried about your friend.

Write an e-mail to your friend, outlining the main features of kite flying as well as its positive and problematic aspects.

Text 1 **Kampf der Drachenläufer**

In Brasilien beginnt die Hochsaison für ein seltsames Hobby

Sommerferien in Brasilien. Hochsaison der Drachenläufer, der kleinen und der großen. Die einen stehen auf einer freien Wiese, andere lassen ihre Drachen hoch oben über den Dächern der Favelas steigen. Wo man hinsieht, flattern bunte Papierdrachen am Himmel. Meiner ist aus verblasstem, rotem Seidenpapier mit einem lilafarbenen Totenkopf drauf. Er hängt im Schrank, und ich traue mich nicht, ihn endlich mal steigen zu lassen, weil ich mir sicher bin, nach ein paar Minuten wäre er weg.

Auf Anfänger wie mich nehmen die Profis an den Drachen nämlich keine Rücksicht. Sie kappen alles, was an einer Schnur durch die Luft weht [...].

Noch ein Grund, warum ich meinen Drachen erst gar nicht startklar machen muss: Das Drachen-Steigen-Lassen ist in Brasilien in fester Männerhand. Frauen und Mädchen sieht man selten inmitten der begeisterten Drachenläufer. Das Ziel ist einfach, jedenfalls beim Wettstreit mit den Drachen: Je mehr Exemplare eines anderen Teams gekappt und eingesammelt werden können, desto besser. Dafür werden die Drachenschnüre sogar ordentlich frisiert. Sie werden durch eine klebrige Masse gezogen, das so genannte Cerol. Es ist eine Mischung aus Leim, Zahnpasta und vielen fein gemahlenen Glassplittern. Danach schneidet so eine Drachenschnur wie ein Messer. Nicht selten liest man in brasilianischen Zeitungen von Unfällen mit den fast kaum zu erkennenden Schnüren, die über hunderte Meter auch Straßen kreuzen. Motorräder haben in Brasilien extra eine Art Antenne am Lenker, die die Drachenschnüre durchtrennen, bevor sie den Motorradfahrer verletzen.

Doch nicht immer dienen die Papierflieger nur dem Vergnügen. Eben weil sie so ein gewohntes und unauffälliges Bild am brasilianischen Himmel sind, haben die Drogengangs früh begonnen, sie für ihre Zwecke zu nutzen. Die Drachen werden teilweise als Kommunikationssystem genutzt, mit dem sich Drogenhändler untereinander verständigen. Drachen kündigen die Ankunft einer neuen Ladung Kokain an, warnen vor der Polizei oder melden Fremde in der Favela. Wer die Zeichen der Papierdrachen zu deuten weiß, ist schneller und sicherer informiert als mit jedem Funkspruch.

Dass das Drachenstiegen vor allem bei den unteren Einkommensklassen so populär ist, hat seinen Grund: Neben dem hohen Spaß- und Wettkampffaktor ist das Hobby mit den Papierdrachen sehr kostengünstig. Für zwei Euro bekommt man die komplette Ausrüstung mit Schnur und Drachen. Hunderttausende gehen pro Saison über die Ladentheken der kleinen Geschäfte. […]

Der starke Küstenwind in Rio de Janeiro und die schnellen Manöver mit den Drachen verlangen jedem Mitspieler vollen Einsatz ab, und das heißt, fest zupacken, auch wenn die Schnur voller Glassplitter ist. Gelingt es, einen gegnerischen Drachen zu kappen, muss auch noch einer aus dem Team hinterherhetzen und ihn einsammeln. Wenn es dabei über Gräben, Mauern und Flüsse geht – Pech gehabt, da muss ein echter Drachenläufer durch. […]

Quelle: Solveig Flörke, „Kampf der Drachenläufer", in: DIE WELT, *Springer A. Berlin. http://www.welt.de/print/die_welt/sport/article123940300/Kampf-der-Drachenlaeufer.html*

Text 2 Drachen für alle

Für den normalen Touristen gibt es in Brasilien viel zu sehen. Diejenigen von ihnen, die mehr über die brasilianische Kultur herausfinden wollen und sich nicht mit den ausgetretenen Pfaden zufriedengeben, können besonders viel entdecken. Dies gilt im speziellen für den Bereich der Jugendkulturen. Eine sehr beliebte Freizeitbeschäftigung für Kinder und Jugendliche ist Drachen steigen lassen. Gerade bei gutem Wetter kann man sehr viele Drachen, auf Portugiesisch Papagaios oder Pipas, über brasilianischen Vorstädten fliegen sehen. […]

Überall auf der Welt lassen Kinder Drachen steigen, aber in Brasilien machen dies besonders viele. Weiterhin die Frage nach dem wieso? Es ist sicherlich ein billiges Vergnügen und kann somit von vielen Kindern ausgeübt werden. Es mag auch des Menschen Streben nach dem Unmöglichen, einem vogelgleichen Fliegen ausdrücken. Für manchen kann es die Verbindung der Erde oder des selbst zu etwas im Himmel oder dahinter darstellen. All dies oder nichts davon mag es sein, aber es gibt weitere Erklärungsversuche. Wenn brasilianische Großstädte aus der Fernsicht von Google Earth betrachtet werden, ist unschwer zu erkennen, dass sie sehr zugebaut sind, viel mehr als vergleichbare westliche Großstädte. Beispielsweise hat Sao Paulo weniger als ein Prozent Grüngebiete. Da bleibt für Kinder nicht viel zu entdecken. Der einzige Freiraum, der noch bleibt, ist der Raum über ihren Köpfen. Diesen erobern sie sich mit ihren Pipas. […]

Quelle: Peter Michalski. Artikel: „Claiming the Sky", in: Graffiti Magazine, *S. 4–8, https://issuu.com/graffiti-magazine/docs/graffiti-magazine6*

1 Analyse the task. What do the text form, addressee, command term ("operator"), and focus mean in terms of the structure or language of your mediation? Write your notes in the grid below.

Write an e-mail to your friend, outlining the main features of this pastime, its positive and problematic aspects.

text form: e-mail	**target group / addressee: friend**	**"operator": outline**	**focus: main features, positive and negative aspects**
⇩	⇩	⇩	⇩

2 Read the texts again carefully, highlight relevant passages and take notes. You may want to use different colours or symbols such as "~" for general information on flying kites, "+" for positive aspects and "–" for problematic aspects.

3 Use your notes from tasks 1 and 2 and sort them to get a rough structure for your e-mail.

4 Use your rough structure and write your e-mail in complete sentences.

Lösungsvorschlag

1 **TIPP**

If you are having difficulties, read the information in the introductory chapter again ("Vorgehen in der Prüfung").

text form: e-mail	**target group/ addressee: friend**	**"operator": outline**	**focus: main features, positive and negative aspects**
⇩	⇩	⇩	⇩
proper address and salutation; reference to year abroad, worries	friendly, informal tone	short/concise, no unnecessary details, no quotations	main body could be divided into three parts

2+3 **TIPP**

The example answer also contains line references, so that you can compare them with the passages you highlighted in task 2.

Hi Jake,	address
Happy to hear about year abroad/interest in flying kites; bit worried	introduction
~ kites called "pipas" or "pagagaios" (T2, l. 6) ~ mainly done by men/boys (T1, ll. 10/11)	main features of flying kites
+ cheap (T1, ll. 29–31; T2, ll. 9/10) + not much space left in cities → claim sky (T2, ll. 14–19) + feeling like flying (T2, ll. 10–13)	positive aspects
– very competitive: aim to cut strings/collect trophies (T1, ll. 7/8, ll. 11–14) – strings prepared with glass, very sharp, invisible → often accidents (T1, ll. 14–20) – used as a means of communication by drug dealers (T1, ll. 22–27)	problematic aspects
Sure about it? Please take care!	conclusion
Hugs,	salutation
Kristin	name

4 **TIPP**

Your rough structure is meant to guide you through the process of writing. You may want to re-read some passages in the texts if you are not sure how to express a certain aspect.
Remember that you are writing to a friend. Your language should thus be rather informal and you can also use short forms. Don't forget that you are meant to express worries about your friend's decision to try out kite flying. In the end, go through your e-mail again, check it for spelling or grammar mistakes and correct them.

Hi Jake, — **address**

It was very exciting to hear about your plans for your year abroad in Recife. Your enthusiasm about becoming a "pipa guy" was contagious and so I informed myself about this interesting hobby. What I read left me a bit worried, so I'd like to give you some information I've found in two German newspaper articles.

introduction: reference to year abroad, interest in kite flying, worries

In summer, the Brazilian sky is full of kites, also called pipas or papagaios. Mainly men or boys, particularly the youngsters from poor areas, are into pipas.

main part: main features

It's a cheap hobby so everyone can afford it. Furthermore, there's not much natural space left to explore for poor kids in Brazilian cities and that's why they claim the sky. You might even feel like a part of the elements, or flying yourself, when using the kite.

positive aspects

Still, for some people, it's the competitive factor they like best: This means cutting the strings of as many other kites as possible and collecting the trophies. And this is where my concerns come in. The competitors take flying kites too seriously: they are ruthless and strengthen their strings by gluing bits of broken glass to them so that they're razor-sharp! I think it's awful that non-participants are exposed to the nearly invisible strings, which frequently cause accidents in the streets. Besides, I really dislike the thought that drug dealers also use kites as a quick and efficient means of communication.

problematic aspects

Are you sure this is the right hobby for you? I wish you'd think it over again – at least take care, please.

conclusion: worries

Hugs, — **salutation**

Kristin — **name**

Sprachmittlung: Übungsaufgabe 2
Niedersachsen Englisch

Aufgabenstellung

You are taking part in an international youth project on “The Impact of Digitisation and AI”.
Using the information from the text, write an article for the English project website in which you present the drawbacks of digital language assistants such as Alexa.

Text

Experten warnen vor Sprachassistenten: Diese Risiken birgt Alexa für Kinder

Minderjährige geben Alexa, Siri und ähnlichen Sprachassistenten zu viel von sich preis, zeigt ein Gutachten. Auch Datenschützer äußern Kritik.

Ein Junge, sechs Jahre alt, wünscht sich ein Kinderlied, ruft „play Digger, Digger“ ins Mikrofon. Und was tut Amazons Sprachassistentin „Alexa“? Sie schlägt ihm verschiedene Porno-Titel vor. Diese Geschichte ist nicht die einzige Panne vergangener Jahre, die Eltern schockiert. Zu sehen auf Youtube. Jetzt warnt sogar der Wissenschaftliche Dienst des Bundestags.

In einem Gutachten wird bemängelt, dass Kinder und Jugendliche persönliche Informationen von sich preisgeben oder eben Inhalte abrufen können, die sie nicht hören sollten. Außerdem stelle sich die Frage, was eigentlich mit Besuchern sei, die nicht wüssten, dass die Software gerade ihre Sätze aufzeichnet. Amazon dürfte der Pflicht zur Informationsvermittlung bei der Datenerhebung von Nutzern zwar ausreichend nachkommen, heißt es – „offen bleibt jedoch, wie unbeteiligte Dritte und Minderjährige von der Datensammlung ausgeschlossen werden können“.

Mit Blick auf die USA sei außerdem unklar, „zu welchen weiteren Zwecken Amazon seine Daten zukünftig nutzen könnte“. Dass sich Kriminelle Zugriff zu den Daten in der Cloud verschaffen könnten, sei ebenfalls nicht auszuschließen.

Eine Reihe von Kritikpunkten. Das Bundesinnenministerium fühlt sich in der Sache aber nicht zuständig. Ein Sprecher erklärte auf Anfrage der Deutschen Presse-Agentur: „Die Nutzung der Sprachassistenten betrifft Datenverarbeitungen durch nichtöffentliche Stellen.“ Für diese lasse die Datenschutz-Grundverordnung der EU den nationalen Gesetzgebern so gut wie keinen Regelungsspielraum.

„Wir müssen darauf dringen, dass die Einwilligungserklärung für den Nutzer auf die Gefahren und Möglichkeiten hinweist, die mit der Übertragung und Nutzung der Daten sowie der Daten von Dritten, die sich zufällig im Raum befinden, hinweist“, meint hingegen der fraktionslose Bundestagsabgeordnete Uwe Kamann. Dies müsse detailliert erfolgen, „und nicht indem man nur einmal ein Häkchen für alles setzt“.

Kamann war es, der die Frage aufgeworfen hatte, ob es zulässig ist, dass Amazon die Spracheingaben der „Alexa"-Nutzer auswertet. […]

Der Hamburgische Datenschutzbeauftragte Johannes Caspar ist ebenfalls empört. Er teile die Befürchtungen des Wissenschaftlichen Dienstes des Bundestags. Probleme würden sich „aus der hohen Zahl von Fehlaktivierungen bei automatischen Sprachassistenten" ergeben.

Diese führten dazu, dass Gespräche immer wieder übertragen werden, weil das System das Aktivierungswort fälschlicherweise verstehe. „Von diesen Datenerhebungen sind ausnahmslos alle Personen im Haushalt betroffen, ohne dass die relevanten rechtlichen Vorgaben vorliegen dürften", sagte Caspar zu Tagesspiegel Background Digitalisierung & KI.

Insbesondere dürften „Kinder kaum einwilligungsfähig sein". Ein weiteres Problem ist aus seiner Sicht „die fehlende Zugriffskontrolle durch eine personalisierte Steuerung, mit der eine Nutzung des Sprachsystems durch dritte unbefugte Personen verhindert werden könnte".

Amazon bietet den Nutzern zwar neuerdings mit dem Befehl „Alexa, lerne meine Stimme" die Möglichkeit, ein persönliches Stimmprofil einzurichten. Diese werden nach Angaben eines Amazon-Sprechers aber nur genutzt, „um das individuelle Nutzererlebnis zu verbessern". Auf den Befehl „Computer, spiele Musik!" hin würden für verschiedene Profile unterschiedliche Titel abgespielt. Das Gerät für Kinder zu sperren, erlaubt die neue Stimmerkennung nicht. […]

Der Sprachassistent wird nicht zum ersten Mal als Übel für Kinder angesehen. Im vergangenen Jahr veröffentlichte die britische Childwise Agency eine Untersuchung mit dem Ergebnis: Da Alexa Anweisungen ohne Wörter wie „bitte" oder „danke" ausführt, fürchten Experten, dass Kinder zu unhöflichen Wesen heranwachsen, die bloß noch befehlen.

Alexa, lies mir eine Gute-Nacht-Geschichte vor! Alexa, ich will …! Im April 2018 brachte Amazon tatsächlich eine Version für Kinder auf den Markt. Diese formuliert ihre Antworten kindgerechter, sagt der Hersteller. Außerdem bekamen Kinder ein Lob, wenn sie bitten und sich bedanken.

Ein anderes Alexa-Problem untersucht nun die Otto-von-Guericke-Universität Magdeburg. Nicht einmal jede vierte KI-Fachkraft sei eine Frau. Daraus ergebe sich die Frage, ob sich dies auch in Denkmustern bei der Künstlichen Intelligenz widerspiegele. Die Unesco hatte bemängelt, dass Siri und Alexa Gender-Stereotype reproduzieren.

Demnach seien sie unterwürfig, gehorsam und stets freundlich. Vor dem Hintergrund, dass Kinder mit der Technologie aufwüchsen und Sprache ein Geschlechtsmarker sei, bestehe die Gefahr, dass bestimmte Vorstellungen von Frauen transportiert würden – als dienende Maschinen.

Quelle: Sonja Álvarez, Marie Rövekamp: „Experten warnen vor Sprachassistenten – Diese Risiken birgt Alexa für Kinder", Tagesspiegel *vom 09. 07. 2019, https://www.tagesspiegel.de/wirtschaft/experten-warnen-vor-sprachassistenten-diese-risiken-birgt-alexa-fuer-kinder/24573516.html*

Lösungsvorschlag

TIPP

To solve the task, you should start by analysing the assignment in order to find out which formal requirements your solution must fulfil and which aspects you have to focus on:

- text form: article → interesting heading, several well-structured paragraphs
- target group: participants of an international youth project
  → style: should show expertise, but not be overtly formal
- "operator": "present" → give a concise account of the main aspects
- focus: disadvantages and problems mentioned in connection with Alexa, Siri and other digital language assistants

The following aspects could come up in your solution:

- two main points of criticism: data protection issues and dangers Alexa and other similar devices might pose to children
- child protection and educational issues:
  - children could be presented with inappropriate content (cf. ll. 1–3, 7/8)
  - children's data are saved and used without them giving their consent (cf. ll. 6/7, 11/12, 37, 45/46)
  - children learn that commands yield the desired results → their language becomes impolite (cf. ll. 49–51)
  - children learn gender stereotypes because language assistants have female names and reproduce an image of women as obedient servants (cf. ll. 59–64)
- data protection issues in general:
  - indiscriminate recording of everyone (with or without explicit permission), especially because activation of technologies is prone to errors (cf. ll. 8–12, 32–35)
  - insecurity as to what happens with the recorded data (cf. ll. 13–15)
  - lack of legal data protection framework in Germany for private commercial providers (cf. ll. 16–20)

Is Alexa a danger for children as well as for data security?

heading

In many German households, digital language assistants like Siri or Alexa have become a part of everyday life. While they might make some tasks easier, some experts also regard them with growing suspicion.

introduction

One of the most pressing issues is data protection. A voice assistant records thousands of pieces of information and so far there are no clear-cut rules as to what happens with these. Criminals potentially accessing the data are only the tip of the iceberg. With a private company involved in the data collection, many of Alexa's potentially unauthorised uses are not even considered in European data protection laws.

data protection issues: no legal framework, potentially criminal uses of data

Voice assistants do not limit their data collection to those who have explicitly given their permission. Instead, as soon as the assistant is activated – a process that despite experiments with voice recognition is still prone to errors –, everyone in the vicinity is recorded indiscriminately.

lack of consent of those being recorded

This is especially relevant in connection with child protection laws. Children cannot be considered to have given their permission to be recorded. Additionally, Alexa might inadvertently provide them with content that is inappropriate for their age.

child protection and educational issues: no consent, inappropriate content

There are further concerns when it comes to Alexa's educational side effects: Alexa does what you want her to do without being asked politely. This might lead to children becoming used to a commanding and impolite language.

communicating by giving commands

Secondly, Alexa, Siri and co. could reproduce harmful gender stereotypes: with their female names and their obedient behaviour, they could convey an image of women as docile servants.

gender stereotypes

Thus, for all her alleged progressiveness and user-friendliness, Alexa might also be a danger lurking in your living room.

conclusion

Sprachmittlung: Übungsaufgabe 3
Niedersachsen Englisch

Aufgabenstellung

You are doing an internship with a non-governmental organisation that runs the blog "letsgetfair.blogging.com". Using the information from the text below, write an entry for this blog in which you inform consumers about the negative consequences of "fast fashion".

Text **Unsere zweite Haut**

Schön, wenn die Bluse nur zehn Euro kostet. Nicht gut, wenn dafür die Umwelt leidet und Arbeiter ausgebeutet werden. […]

Beutestück Nummer zwei ist roséfarben und glänzt. Die junge Frau hält das Kleid in die Kamera, dreht und wendet es, Metallic-Optik sei das und habe 5,99 Euro gekostet. Ein Hammerpreis, sagt Funnypilgrim, wie sie sich auf YouTube nennt. Die weiteren Eroberungen der Shoppingtour: noch ein Kleid, ein Pulli, fünf Hosen, ein Oberteil, eine Strickjacke und ein Gürtel. Willkommen im Polyester-Paradies. […]

Die Konsumenten, die Polyesterkleidchen für 5,99 Euro und ebenso billige Baumwoll-T-Shirts kaufen, sind Teil des Systems Fast Fashion. Viele tragen ihre Kleider nur ein paar Mal, dann muss etwas Neues her – weil die Mode sich geändert hat oder die Teile schlicht kaputt sind. Modeketten produzieren Kleidung in immer kürzerer Zeit und bringen ständig neue Stücke in die Läden. Die Billigproduktion und der schnelle Modezyklus gehen zulasten von Arbeitern, Umwelt, Klima und der Gesundheit derjenigen, die die Kleider am Ende tragen. […]

Die Produktionsstrecke vom Entwurf bis zum ausgelieferten Kleidungsstück dauert heute nur noch wenige Wochen. Neue Kollektionen kommen nicht mehr wie früher zweimal pro Jahr in die Läden, es treffen kontinuierlich neue Kleider ein. So signalisieren die Anbieter den Kunden, dass sie ständig ihre Garderobe erneuern sollten – und machen dies möglich, indem ein T-Shirt oft kaum mehr kostet als ein Kaffee. Wer bei Billiganbietern wie H&M, Zara oder der gerade expandierenden irischen Kette Primark kauft, kann bei allen Trends mitmachen, ohne viel Geld auszugeben. Die Kunden spielen da gerne mit. Wegwerfen und Neukaufen wird zum Prinzip.

„Je mehr Kleidung hergestellt wird, desto größer wird auch die Belastung für die Umwelt", sagt Kirsten Brodde, Textilexpertin von Greenpeace. Bei der Produktion werden Hunderte verschiedener Chemikalien eingesetzt – Farbstoffe, Färbebeschleuniger und Bleichmittel, zusätzlich Substanzen, die dafür sorgen, dass Kleider griffiger werden, weniger knittern, mehr glänzen oder dass Leder nicht schimmelt. Gerade in Ländern wie China, Indien und Bangladesch, aus denen ein großer Teil unserer Textilien kommt, sind gefährliche Stoffe verfügbar. Greenpeace analysierte das Abwasser chinesischer Fabriken, die auch deutsche und multinationale Textilunternehmen beliefern, und fand langlebige giftige Chemikalien.

Die Menschen, die in solchen Fabriken unsere Kleidung herstellen, gefährden ihre Gesundheit. Bei der Sandstrahl-Methode etwa – mit der neue Jeans behandelt werden, damit sie abgetragen aussehen – atmen die Arbeiter Quarz ein, das die Lunge angreift. Nach heftiger Kritik verpflichteten sich H&M und das Jeanslabel Levi Strauss dazu, die Technik nicht mehr anzuwenden. Insgesamt haben sich die Sozialstandards jedoch kaum verbessert, obwohl die Zustände in den Fabriken lange bekannt sind. Die Organisation „Kampagne Saubere Kleidung" kritisiert niedrige Löhne und mangelnde Sicherheit. Bei einem Brand in einer Textilfabrik in Pakistan, die unter anderem für KiK produzierte, starben im September mehr als 250 Arbeiter.

20 Kilogramm Textilien pro Jahr

Auch hierzulande sorgt das Prinzip Fast Fashion für Umweltprobleme – in Form von Müll. Der durchschnittliche Europäer verbrauche im Jahr 20 Kilogramm Textilien, der Amerikaner sogar 35, schreibt Textil-Experte Andreas Engelhardt in seinem Buch *Schwarzbuch Baumwolle*. Der weltweite Fasermarkt umfasste nach Angaben der Bremer Baumwollbörse 1990 ein Volumen von 38 Millionen Tonnen, im Jahr 2000 von knapp 50 Millionen und 2012 sogar von 75 Millionen Tonnen. Etwa die Hälfte dieser Fasern wird für Kleidung genutzt, schätzt Engelhardt.

Die vielen chemischen Zusätze in Textilien schaden vor allem den Arbeitern, womöglich aber auch den Käufern. Einige der Textil-Chemikalien können Kontaktallergien auslösen, zum Beispiel Formaldehyd. Damit werden Kleider behandelt, damit sie weniger knittern und ihre Form behalten. Zinnorganische Verbindungen, die Kleidung während des Transports vor Pilzbefall schützen, könnten nach Einschätzung des Bundesinstituts für Risikobewertung (BfR) die Fruchtbarkeit einschränken und das Nervensystem angreifen. Sie sind in der EU verboten. Andere Substanzen stehen im Verdacht, das Krebsrisiko zu erhöhen, zum Beispiel einige Azofarbstoffe. Nach Angaben des BfR verzichtet die deutsche Industrie schon lange auf die gefährlichen Mittel, nur wird ja kaum noch Kleidung in Deutschland hergestellt. „Man muss davon ausgehen, dass in einigen importierten Textilien, insbesondere aus Nicht-EU-Staaten, solche problematischen Farbstoffe enthalten sein können", schreibt das BfR. […]

Quelle: ZEIT Wissen, *Nr. 1/2013. Von Susanne Schäfer.*
http://www.zeit.de/zeit-wissen/2013/01/Nachhaltige-Kleidung

Lösungsvorschlag

TIPP

Begin by analysing the assignment so as to know which type of text you have to write, to whom it is addressed, and what its style and main focus should be:

- text form: blog entry → catchy headline, several well-structured paragraphs, direct address to readers and invitation to leave their comments
- organisation that runs the blog: NGO fighting for fair trade;
  target group: consumers (presumably in richer countries)
  → style: meant to convince consumers that sustainably and fairly produced clothes are the only alternative to fast fashion
- focus: negative consequences of "fast fashion"

The following aspects should come up in your solution:

- introduction: short explanation what "fast fashion" is (cf. ll. 6–10)
- negative consequences in low-wage countries:
  - use of toxic substances that pollute the environment and endanger the workers' health (cf. ll. 21–34)
  - low wages (cf. l. 36)
  - lack of safety measures in factories (cf. ll. 36–38)
- negative consequences in consuming countries:
  - increasing amount of waste because clothes are thrown away quickly (cf. ll. 40–46)
  - health risks (e. g. allergies, fertility problems, risk of cancer) due to chemical substances (cf. ll. 48–54)

Bloody clothes – Fashion victims cause victims of fashion

catchy headline

Have you ever wondered how it is possible to buy a dress for only € 5.99? Western consumers are trapped in the vicious circle of "fast fashion" that makes us buy new clothes constantly, only to replace them quickly after some time because they are not up-to-date anymore.

introduction: direct address to readers, definition of fast fashion

But someone has to pay the price for our craving for the biggest bargain: In this case, it is the workers who produce cheap fashion in India, China, Bangladesh and Pakistan. Due to lack of safety measures, hundreds of workers have already died e. g. when a fire broke out in their factory. In China and Bangladesh, toxic substances used in production endanger the workers' health and pollute the underground water. Workers run huge risks in the sweatshops of Western fashion labels, for example, but cannot be paid appropriate wages as the big companies would then not be able to sell their products as cheaply as they do now.

consequences in low-wage countries: lack of safety

use of toxic substances → health risks, pollution

low wages

But in the long run, we as consumers have to face the consequences of our greed. More and more waste is produced due to our endless hunger for fashionable clothing. Chemical substances used to prevent clothes from wrinkling or becoming mouldy can damage our health severely, threaten fertility and even enhance the risk of cancer.

consequences in consuming countries: waste, health risks

The good news is: You can help put an end to all that: Start shopping for fair trade clothes and feel better instantly.

Have you already tested fair trade stores? Tell us about your experiences …

conclusion: direct address to readers, invitation to comment

Sprachmittlung: Übungsaufgabe 4

Niedersachsen Englisch

Aufgabenstellung

You are taking part in an international school project about "visions of the future". Based on the text below, write an article for the project website in which you describe current problems in cities and how they could be solved in the future.

Text **Wie die Städte der Zukunft aussehen**

[...] Immer mehr Menschen leben in Städten. Seit dem Jahr 2007 ist ihre Zahl weltweit sogar größer als diejenige aller Landbewohner – ein Novum in der Geschichte der Menschheit. Bis 2030 werden sich nach Schätzung der Vereinten Nationen rund fünf Milliarden Städter auf unserem Planeten drängeln, das sind rund zwei Milliarden mehr als heute. Selbst im stark urban geprägten Deutschland, wo bereits drei Viertel der Bevölkerung in Städten wohnen, wachsen die Ballungszentren und Metropolen weiter, obwohl die Gesamtbevölkerung insgesamt zurückgeht.

Längst drohen vielerorts Verkehrsinfarkte, Staus und Parkplatznot gehören zum Alltag. Vor allem Megacities verbrauchen Unmengen an Energie, Rohstoffen und Fläche. Auf der anderen Seite produzieren sie Massen an Schadstoffen, Abwasserströme und Müllberge.

„So wie bisher wird es in Zukunft nicht funktionieren, die Urbanisierung ist in eine Sackgasse geraten“, warnt Steffen Braun vom Fraunhofer-Institut Arbeitswirtschaft und Organisation (IAO) in Stuttgart. Das Institut koordiniert maßgeblich die Fraunhofer-Initiative „Morgenstadt“, die Konzepte und Technologien entwickelt für die Vision einer klimafreundlichen und lebenswerten Stadt.

Um sinnvolle Lösungen zu finden, erklärt Braun, sei es notwendig, verschiedene Bereiche wie Energie, Verkehr oder Gebäudetechnik miteinander zu vernetzen. Beispiel: Mobilität in der Stadt. „Die gegenwärtigen Fahrzeuge durch Elektroautos zu ersetzen, reicht allein nicht aus. Zusätzlich sind neue Konzepte notwendig, zum Beispiel das der gemeinschaftlichen Nutzung von PKWs. "Denn dadurch verringert sich auch der Energieverbrauch und es entsteht Platz – auf den Straßen und auf Parkplätzen. Den notwendigen Strom erhalten die Elektroautos dann nicht mehr an öffentlichen Tankstellen, sondern zu Hause. Das birgt weitere Einsparmöglichkeiten. Laden Privatbesitzer ihr Fahrzeug in der heimischen Garage auf, lässt sich der Energiebedarf des Autos mit dem Energiehaushalt des Gebäudes abstimmen.

Wenn aber tatsächlich irgendwann überwiegend Elektroautos unterwegs sind, hat das weitere Auswirkungen. Zum Beispiel steigt die Luftqualität und die Lärmbelastung geht zurück. „Das bedeutet, dass dann eventuell wieder mehr Wohnraum entlang von Hauptstraßen entstehen könnte“, sagt Braun. Insofern haben Veränderungen bei der Automobil-Technik durchaus auch Auswirkungen auf die Stadtplanung.

Schallschutz und Luftqualität lassen sich zudem noch auf andere Weise verbessern: So könnte man Fassaden derart beschichten, dass sie Schall absorbieren oder den Schadstoffgehalt in der Luft mittels Nanotechnik reduzieren. Auch wäre es möglich, die Gebäudeoberflächen so zu gestalten, dass beispielsweise aus einem Wohn- oder Bürohaus eine Art Minikraftwerk wird. Algen, in durchsichtigen Modulen an der Fassade angebracht, könnten Biogase erzeugen. Und Membranüberdachungen würden das Prinzip Photovoltaik noch viel stärker in die Architektur integrieren, als das bislang der Fall ist. […]

Auch im Wohnbereich selbst ließe sich einiges optimieren. In einem Beitrag im Wissenschaftsmagazin *Science* entwirft Diane Cook von der Washington State University in Pullman (USA) die Vision eines „Smart Home". Künstliche Intelligenz könnte demnach im Haus viele energiesparende und lebenserleichternde Lösungen möglich machen: von Fenster- und Türkontrollsystemen oder der Lichtsteuerung via Sensoren bis hin zur automatischen Bewässerung des Gartens und Fütterung des Haustiers. Immerhin verbrauchen die Haushalte in den meisten Ländern mehr als 40 Prozent der insgesamt benötigten Energie.

Für saubere Straßen und Parks könnten in Städten der Zukunft Roboter sorgen. Wie Michael O'Grady und Gregory O'Hare vom University College Dublin in *Science* berichten, seien schon viele technologische Grundlagen dafür vorhanden. Das europäische Dustbot-Projekt habe gezeigt, dass Roboter in urbaner Umgebung autark Müll sammeln können. Die „Schmutzroboter" navigieren per GPS, sie sollen telefonisch bestellt werden können und den aufgesammelten Unrat eigenständig zur Deponie bringen.

„Das technologische Potenzial für die Stadt der Zukunft existiert bereits", bestätigt der Fraunhofer-Experte Braun. Was noch fehle, sei die weiträumige Anwendung in der Praxis. Und da könne Deutschland eine Leitfunktion einnehmen. „Die Probleme, die wir heute in Deutschland haben, gibt es beispielsweise in zehn bis 20 Jahren in China." Was in den Städten hierzulande funktioniere, könnte dann auch andernorts in der Welt Anwendung finden. Natürlich unter Berücksichtigung der jeweiligen Verhältnisse vor Ort, auf die Konzepte und Technologien abgestimmt werden müssten.

Quelle: Harald Wiederschein, „Wie die Städte der Zukunft aussehen", Focus Online, *19. 04. 2012, https://www.focus.de/wissen/technik/tid-25536/neue-studien-wie-die-staedte-der-zukunft-aussehen_aid_739009.html*

Lösungsvorschlag

TIPP

First, analyse the assignment:
- text form: article → heading, several well-structured paragraphs
- target group: participants of international school project
  → style: should show expertise, but not be overtly formal
- focus: current problems in cities and how they could be solved

Your text should contain the following information:
- current problems in cities:
  - worldwide, urban living is increasing rapidly (cf. ll. 1–7)
  - current urban development is not sustainable: traffic problems, enormous need for resources, huge amounts of waste (cf. ll. 8–11)
- possible solutions:
  - connect different areas, such as energy, traffic and building construction (cf. ll. 17/18)
  - change urban mobility: use communal cars and electric cars (cf. ll. 19–31)
  - construct buildings that absorb noise, improve air quality and produce energy (cf. ll. 32–39)
  - use artificial intelligence in private homes to save energy (cf. ll. 40–47)
  - employ robots to clean public spaces (cf. ll. 48–53)
- conclusion: technology exists, but application is missing
  → Germany could take the lead (cf. ll. 54–60)

Cities of the Future

heading

Urban living is rapidly increasing throughout the world. In Germany, for example, three-quarters of the population live in built-up areas. Traffic jams, congestion and the lack of sufficient parking spaces are the daily problems of urban areas. The growth of megacities, though, results in large amounts of energy, raw materials and ground space being needed, and huge amounts of waste being produced. Urban areas developing as they currently are have no future; there is an urgent need to change and adapt.

current problems: increasing urbanisation → traffic problems, need for resources, waste

The solution to many problems is to connect areas together, such as energy, traffic and buildings, because one thing alone is not sufficient. Electric cars, for example, will not improve the problems of saving energy, reducing traffic and the parking problem by themselves. If communal car use was introduced, too, then an improvement would be seen. Electric cars would improve air quality and reduce noise, resulting in living spaces near main roads becoming attractive and usable, influencing urban planning.

possible solutions: connection of different areas; mobility: communal cars and electric cars

Building construction can alleviate many problems, too, with surfaces absorbing noise, reducing pollutants or producing power, for example.

building construction

Lives can be improved by using artificial intelligence in the home to operate lights, water the garden and even feed pets. It can also be used for cleaning public spaces: robots are able to collect rubbish and dispose of it.

artificial intelligence / robots

The technology for change exists but the application of it is missing. Germany could take the lead in urban development with countries like China following a decade later.

conclusion

Textaufgabe

Aufbau des Prüfungsteils „Textaufgabe“

In der Abiturprüfung werden Ihnen **zwei Textaufgaben zur Auswahl** gestellt. Als Prüfungstexte kommen sowohl **Sach- als auch literarische Texte** infrage (Umfang: maximal 1 000 Wörter), die theoretisch durch weitere Materialien (etwa einen Cartoon oder eine Statistik) ergänzt werden können. Die Texte werden Ihnen in der Prüfung erstmals vorgelegt, d. h., sie entstammen nicht den Unterrichtslektüren. Eventuell wird aber in einer der Teilaufgaben verlangt, einen Bezug zwischen dem Prüfungstext und den **Pflichtlektüren bzw. -filmen** herzustellen. Mit dem „**AbiturSkript Englisch Niedersachsen 2023**“ (Bestell-Nr. 3546S3) können Sie sich darauf optimal vorbereiten. Es enthält knapp zusammengefasst alle wichtigen Informationen zu den verpflichtenden Materialien.
Sie haben in der Prüfung **30 Minuten Zeit**, um sich die Texte und Aufgaben durchzulesen und sich für einen der beiden Vorschläge zu entscheiden. Wählen Sie am besten denjenigen Vorschlag, zu dem Ihnen spontan mehr einfällt und dem Sie sich auch sprachlich am besten gewachsen fühlen. Für die eigentliche Bearbeitung der Textaufgabe stehen **210 Minuten** zur Verfügung. Achten Sie darauf, sich die Bearbeitungszeit sinnvoll einzuteilen. Planen Sie etwa die letzten 45 Minuten für das Korrekturlesen ein. Verteilen Sie die restliche Arbeitszeit sinnvoll auf die Einzelaufgaben (einen Anhaltspunkt dafür gibt Ihnen die prozentuale Gewichtung der jeweiligen Teilaufgabe).

Die **Aufgabenstellung** besteht in der Regel aus drei Teilen, die dem folgenden Schema entsprechen:

- Teilaufgabe 1: Textverständnis
- Teilaufgabe 2: Textanalyse/Vergleich o. Ä.
- Teilaufgabe 3: Transfer (Stellungnahme oder kreative Aufgabe)

Auf den folgenden Seiten finden Sie nützliche Hinweise zur Vorgehensweise bei jeder der drei Teilaufgaben – mit „Dos and Don'ts“, Formulierungshilfen und vielem mehr. Zusätzlich stehen Ihnen auf der **Plattform MyStark** sechs **Lernvideos** zur Verfügung, in denen das Vorgehen am konkreten Beispiel eines Sach- und eines literarischen Texts gezeigt wird (Zugangscode vgl. vorne im Buch).

Vorgehen bei Teilaufgabe 1

Mit der ersten Teilaufgabe soll überprüft werden, ob Sie den Text wirklich verstanden haben. Häufig wird daher von Ihnen verlangt, dass Sie den Text (oder bestimmte Aspekte daraus) **in eigenen Worten zusammenfassen**. Am besten gehen Sie dabei nach dem Schema vor, das Sie bereits aus dem Kapitel zur Sprachmittlung kennen:

Schritt 1 Aufgabenstellung genau lesen

Lesen Sie zunächst die Aufgabenstellung aufmerksam durch:

- Wichtig ist zum einen der **Operator** (also das verwendete Aufforderungsverb), da damit bestimmte formale Vorgaben verbunden sind, die Sie befolgen müssen. In der folgenden Tabelle sind die häufigsten Operatoren für die Textverständnisaufgabe zusammengefasst.

Operator	Dos and Don'ts	Beispiel(e)
sum up/ summarise/ outline/ state	• die wichtigsten Aspekte knapp und in eigenen Worten zusammenfassen • keine Zitate oder Zeilenangaben • keine persönliche Wertung	• *Summarise the text.* • *Outline the author's view on social media. (Video-Set 1)*
describe	bestimmte Aspekte detailliert wiedergeben	*Describe what happens in the Watson-Crick laboratories. (ÜA 2)*

- Als Zweites sollten Sie auf den **inhaltlichen Fokus** der Aufgabenstellung achten, also ob Sie den Text als Ganzes zusammenfassen müssen oder sich nur auf bestimmte Teilaspekte konzentrieren sollen (etwa „the author's view on social media").

Schritt 2 Schlüsselstellen markieren und Notizen machen

Gehen Sie den Text noch einmal durch, unterstreichen Sie die für die Aufgabenstellung relevanten Passagen und machen Sie sich dazu Notizen. Wenn Sie eine Zusammenfassung des ganzen Texts schreiben sollen, unterteilen Sie den Text in Sinnabschnitte und versuchen Sie, den Inhalt jedes Abschnitts in wenigen Worten zusammenzufassen.

Schritt 3 Notizen strukturieren

Sehen Sie sich nun Ihre Notizen (und ggf. die markierten Textstellen) noch einmal an und überlegen Sie, in welcher Reihenfolge Sie die Aspekte in Ihrem Text anführen möchten. Oft können Sie sich in Ihrer Lösung an der **Textchronologie** orientieren. Manchmal macht es aber auch Sinn, bestimmte **Aspekte zu bündeln** oder sie in der Lösung umzustellen. Dann können Sie die Aspekte z. B. entsprechend nummerieren und haben so bereits eine Art Grobgliederung für das anschließende Ausformulieren der Lösung.

Schritt 4 Lösung ausformulieren

Verwenden Sie Ihre strukturierten Notizen und Unterstreichungen im Text als Grundlage und formulieren Sie daraus Ihre Lösung in ganzen Sätzen.

- Beginnen Sie Ihren Text am besten mit einem sogenannten **Basissatz**. Darin nennen Sie den Autor bzw. die Autorin, den Titel des Texts, das Erscheinungsdatum (und ggf. den Erscheinungsort) sowie das zentrale Thema.
- Achten Sie in Ihrem Hauptteil darauf, Ihre Notizen sinnvoll miteinander zu verknüpfen, etwa durch **Konjunktionen**.

Hilfreiche Wendungen

Basissatz formulieren	*In his/her article "...", published in ... on ..., the author deals with/focuses on/describes/criticises/... .* *The extract from the novel/short story "...", written by ... and published in ..., deals with/is about ...*
die Sicht des Autors/der Autorin wiedergeben	*According to the author, ...* *The author emphasises/points out/...*
Aspekte aufzählen	*First of all, ... / To begin with, ...* *Firstly, ... Secondly, ... Thirdly, ...* *In addition, ... / Moreover, ... / Furthermore, ...* *Finally, ... / Lastly, ... / To conclude, ...*
Gründe angeben	*As ... / Since ...* *... because ...* *Due to ...*
Folgen aufzeigen	*Thus, ... / Therefore, ...* *As a result, ... / As a consequence, ...*
Gegensätze herstellen	*However, ... / Yet ...* *While ...* *..., whereas ...* *Although ...* *On the one hand ... On the other hand ...*

Weitere hilfreiche Wendungen finden Sie in den digitalen „**MindCards**“.

Vorgehen bei Teilaufgabe 2

Im zweiten Teil der Textaufgabe müssen Sie sich detaillierter mit dem Text auseinandersetzen. In der Regel wird hier eine **Analyse** verlangt (Operatoren „analyse" oder „examine"): Sie sollen dabei nicht nur wiedergeben, **was** im Text gesagt wird, sondern auch **wie** und **warum**, also welche Funktion oder Wirkung bestimmte Textelemente haben. Weitere mögliche Aufgabenstellungen in diesem Teil der Prüfung sind **Vergleiche** oder **Gegenüberstellungen**. In seltenen Fällen kann es auch vorkommen, dass Sie einen Bezug zwischen dem Prüfungstext und einer bestimmten Pflichtlektüre (oder allgemein „materials studied in class") herstellen sollen.

Gehen Sie auch bei der zweiten Aufgabe nach dem gewohnten Schema vor:

Schritt 1 Aufgabenstellung genau lesen

- Auch hier gibt Ihnen der **Operator** wieder Aufschluss, was Sie genau tun müssen. Besonders wichtig bei allen unten genannten Operatoren ist, dass Sie Ihre Untersuchungsergebnisse durch **Textbelege** untermauern.

Operator	Dos and Don'ts	Beispiel
analyse/ examine	bestimmte Textmerkmale oder Aspekte detailliert untersuchen	*Analyse the means the author uses to convey his attitude and the effect they have on the reader. (Video-Set 1)*
compare	Unterschiede und Gemeinsamkeiten aufzeigen	*Compare the protagonist's situation with the situation of immigrants depicted in materials studied in class.*
contrast	Unterschiede zwischen zwei oder mehr Dingen herausarbeiten	*Contrast the authors' views on immigration.*
explain	Zusammenhänge verdeutlichen / Ursachen und Wirkungen aufzeigen	*Explain the protagonist's inner conflict.*
illustrate	etwas anhand von Beispielen erklären	*Illustrate how the author criticises the lack of ethical standards in science.*

- Achten Sie außerdem auf den **inhaltlichen Fokus** der Aufgabenstellung, d. h., ob bestimmte Aspekte genannt werden, auf die Sie in Ihrer Lösung zwingend eingehen müssen (z. B. „the **means** the author uses […] and their **effect on the reader**").

Schritt 2 Schlüsselstellen markieren und Notizen machen

Gehen Sie den Text noch einmal systematisch in Hinblick auf die in der Aufgabenstellung genannten Aspekte durch.

- Angenommen die Aufgabenstellung lautet folgendermaßen (vgl. Video-Set 1, Teilaufgabe 2):

  Analyse the means the author uses to convey his attitude on social media and the effect they have on the reader.

  Überlegen Sie sich als Erstes, welche Haltung der Autor gegenüber sozialen Medien zum Ausdruck bringt (das „**was**" des Texts). Machen Sie sich dann neben dem Text Notizen, welche sprachlichen Mittel diesem Zweck dienen, und wie genau sie das tun. Sie können auch auf einem separaten Blatt eine **Stoffsammlung** anlegen – z. B. eine Tabelle mit den Spalten „attitude", „means (+ Zeilenverweise)" und „effect". Zu „means" zählen beispielsweise Aufbau des Texts, Wortwahl oder rhetorische Mittel. Eine Übersicht über häufig verwendete rhetorische Mittel finden Sie auf der übernächsten Seite.
- Wenn Sie einen **Vergleich** anstellen sollen (Operator „compare"), suchen Sie nach Gemeinsamkeiten und Unterschieden und kennzeichnen Sie diese z. B. durch entsprechende Symbole (z. B. = und ≠) oder legen Sie sich ebenfalls eine Tabelle an. Bei einer **Gegenüberstellung** (Operator „contrast") reicht es, wenn Sie sich auf die Unterschiede konzentrieren.

Schritt 3 Notizen strukturieren

Gehen Sie Ihre Notizen noch einmal durch und überlegen Sie sich davon ausgehend, wie Sie Ihre Lösung aufbauen könnten:

- Bei einer Analyseaufgabe haben Sie meist mehrere Möglichkeiten. Manchmal bietet es sich an, der **Textchronologie** zu folgen. Im erwähnten Beispiel könnten Sie z. B. auch sprachliche Mittel aus verschiedenen Textpassagen **bündeln**, die eine ähnliche Wirkung auf die Lesenden haben.
- Bei einem Vergleich können Sie Ihre Lösung oft in **zwei große Blöcke** unterteilen und zunächst alle Gemeinsamkeiten beschreiben, dann alle Unterschiede. Oder Sie gehen anhand einzelner **Vergleichspunkte** vor und arbeiten jeweils heraus, ob sich hier eine Ähnlichkeit oder ein Unterschied feststellen lässt.

Schritt 4 Lösung ausformulieren

Wenn Sie Ihre Notizen strukturiert und sich einen groben Aufbau überlegt haben, können Sie an das Ausformulieren Ihrer Lösung gehen. Untergliedern Sie Ihren Text in **Einleitung**, **Hauptteil** und **Schluss**.

- In der **Einleitung** nehmen Sie kurz auf die Aufgabenstellung Bezug. Im bereits genannten Beispiel sollten Sie also erwähnen, welche Haltung der Autor gegenüber sozialen Medien einnimmt („was?“) und dann zu Ihrer Analyse der sprachlichen Mittel („wie?“) und deren Wirkung („wozu?“) überleiten:

  In his article, the author Matt Haig assumes a rather negative attitude on social media. He employs different means to warn the reader of its dangers and make them adopt his critical stance.

- Im **Hauptteil** führen Sie der Reihe nach Ihre **Untersuchungsergebnisse** aus. Orientieren Sie sich dabei an Ihren strukturierten Notizen. Nennen Sie zu Beginn jedes neuen Absatzes zunächst eine Ihrer **Thesen** und untermauern Sie diese anschließend mit einem **Beispiel** bzw. **Textbeleg**. Als Textbelege eignen sich wörtliche Zitate oder Zeilenverweise.

Firstly, Haig uses rhetorical devices such as metaphors.	These
He compares social media to the fast food and tobacco industries (cf. ll. 46/47) and claims that its effects can be as harmful as “secondhand smoke or a bad diet” (l. 50).	Beleg(e)
Since most readers would agree that smoking and eating junk food can be dangerous, they are likely to agree with his argument.	Schlussfolgerung (hier: *effect*)

- Im **Schlussteil** runden Sie Ihre Lösung ab, indem Sie noch einmal kurz auf die Aufgabenstellung eingehen.

  In sum, through his clever use of rhetorical devices […], Haig manages to convince the reader of his argument and make them reflect critically on their own stance on social media.

Hier noch einmal zusammengefasst einige Tipps zum richtigen Zitieren:

Textbeleg	Dos and Don’ts	Beispiel
direktes Zitat	• in Anführungszeichen, mit Zeilenangabe dahinter in Klammern • wenn in den Satz eingebunden: auf grammatikalische Richtigkeit achten • Änderungen oder Auslassungen durch eckige Klammern kenntlich machen	*The author stresses that “[i]t’s high time we realised the consequences of our […] behaviour” (ll. 8/9).*
indirektes Zitat	• Inhalt der Textstelle in eigenen Worten paraphrasieren • Zeilenangabe in Klammern mit „cf.“ (steht für „confer“ = vergleiche)	*The author urges us to be aware of the effects of our way of living (cf. ll. 8/9).*

Die folgende Tabelle bietet Ihnen einen Überblick über häufig verwendete Stilmittel. Achten Sie bei einer Analyse darauf, die Stilmittel nicht einfach nur zu benennen, sondern ihre Funktion und Wirkung im jeweiligen Kontext zu erläutern.

Stilmittel	Definition	Beispiel
alliteration	Mehrere Wörter beginnen mit dem gleichen Laut.	*[...] face the fire at freedom's front.* (Ronald Reagan)
antithesis	Gegenüberstellung gegensätzlicher Begriffe und Gedanken	*To err is human, to forgive divine.* (Alexander Pope)
ellipsis	Auslassung eines Wortes oder Satzteils	*Mastercard accepted.*
euphemism	Beschönigung; Unangenehmes mit angenehmen Worten sagen	*early retirement = unemployment*
hyperbole, exaggeration	Übertreibung	*He nearly died laughing.*
irony	Man sagt das Gegenteil von dem, was man meint.	*You broke that window really well!*
metaphor	Wort in übertragener Bedeutung; Bild, Vergleich (ohne „as" oder „like")	*All the world's a stage.* (Shakespeare, *As You Like It*)
parallelism	gleichartiger Satzbau	*What a day may bring, a day may take away.*
paradox	scheinbar falsche Aussage	*Fair is foul and foul is fair.* (Shakespeare, *Macbeth*)
personification	Vermenschlichung, Verkörperung (in Gestalt einer Person)	*The day has eyes, the night has ears.*
pun	Der witzige Effekt beruht auf der Doppeldeutigkeit des gebrauchten Wortes.	*We shot two bucks, but that was all the money we had.* (*buck* = 1. Bock; 2. Dollar)
repetition	mehrmaliges Aufführen desselben Wortes /Ausdrucks zur Verstärkung einer Aussage	*Tomorrow and tomorrow and tomorrow.* (Shakespeare, *Macbeth*)
rhetorical question	Scheinfrage, auf die keine Antwort erwartet wird	*How is it that a country that prides itself on its economic success could have so many very poor people?*
simile (comparison)	Form des Bildes; direkter Vergleich (mit Vergleichswort)	*My love is like a red,red rose.* (Robert Burns)

Die folgenden Formulierungen können Sie für „klassische Aufgabenstellungen“ wie Analysen und Vergleiche einsetzen:

Hilfreiche Wendungen – Textanalyse und Vergleich	
Stilmittel benennen	*The author uses/employs ...* *The author refers to ... /provides examples of ...* *This is shown by.../is further exemplified by.../becomes apparent in ... / becomes obvious in .../manifests itself .../is hinted at ...*
Funktion/Wirkung auf die Leserschaft beschreiben	*This serves to illustrate/emphasise/add credibility to the argument/ convince the reader/evoke the readers' sympathies ...* *The author wants to make the reader aware that ...* *The reader is made to feel ...* *The author appeals to the reader to ...* *The text is like a wake-up call ...* *By directly addressing the reader, ...*
Vergleiche anstellen	*Compared to/with ... / In comparison to/with ...* *Similarly, ...* *By contrast, ...* *In contrast to ... / Unlike ...*
Beispiele anführen	*For example, ...* *..., for example. / ..., for instance.* *..., such as ... / ..., e. g. ...*

Theoretisch ist es auch möglich, dass Ihnen in der Prüfung neben einem Text zusätzliches Material vorgelegt wird – etwa in Form eines Cartoons oder einer Statistik. Das kann in Teilaufgabe 2 der Fall sein, aber auch in anderen Teilaufgaben. Bei der Auswertung helfen Ihnen die folgenden Ausdrücke und Wendungen:

Hilfreiche Wendungen – Cartoon	
das Dargestellte beschreiben	*The cartoon shows ... / In the cartoon, you can see ...* *In the background ... / In the foreground ... / In the centre of the cartoon ...* *On the left ... / In the top right-hand corner you can see ... / The left half shows ...* *The cartoon has a/no caption ...* *The caption reads ...*
die Botschaft interpretieren	*The cartoonist/artist illustrates .../wants to express the fact that ...* *The cartoonist/artist makes clear/criticises/emphasises ...* *The cartoon is a reference to .../refers/alludes to .../is a criticism of ...* *The message of the cartoon is ... / The cartoon might suggest that ...* *To get across this message, the cartoonist ...*

Hilfreiche Wendungen – Statistik

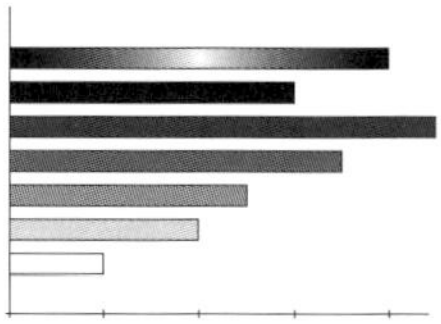

bar chart/graph (Balken-, Säulendiagramm)

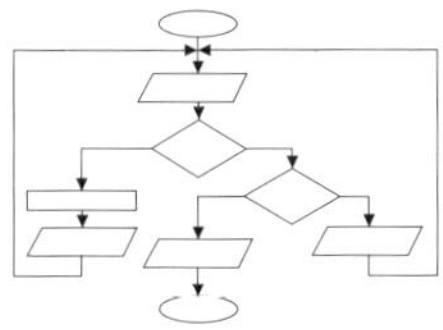

flow chart (Flussdiagramm)

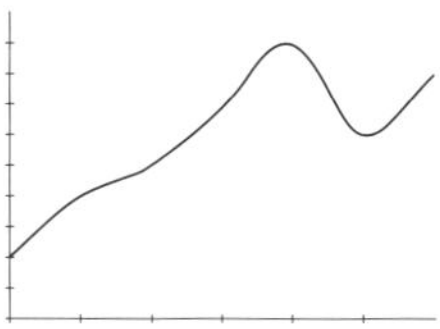

line graph (Kurvendiagramm)

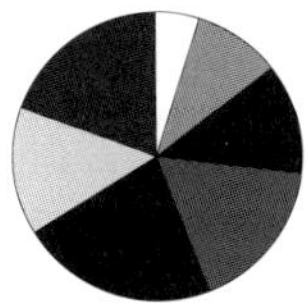

pie chart (Kreisdiagramm, Kuchendiagramm)

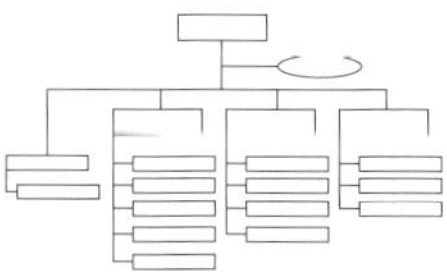

organisation(al) chart (Organigramm)

Thema / Modulreihe	12.1 The Challenge of Individualism	12.3 Tradition and Change
GK verb.	Presentations	Presentations
GK verb.	I USA	Work and Industrialization
GK verb.	II Science and Technology	United Kingdom
GK fakultativ	III Them and Us	Extreme Situations

table (Tabelle)

Statistiken allgemein beschreiben	*The pie chart shows/compares …* *As you can see from the line graph …* *The bar graph demonstrates …* *This table gives information about …* *Its most significant feature is …* *The figures in the table show that …* *The figures prove that … / This implies that …* *The statistics suggest that …* *The diagram makes it clear that …* *There is evidence that …*
eine Zunahme beschreiben	*to rise/go up/increase by … to …* *to rise/go up/increase from … to …* *an increase/a rise of …*
eine Abnahme beschreiben	*to drop/go down/decrease/fall by … to …* *to drop/go down/decrease/fall from … to …* *a drop/decrease/fall of …* *a drop/decrease/fall in …*

Weitere hilfreiche Wendungen finden Sie in den digitalen „**MindCards**“.

Vorgehen bei Teilaufgabe 3

Die dritte Teilaufgabe im Abitur schließt zwar an das Thema des Prüfungstexts an, geht aber meist über die reine Textarbeit hinaus. Sie müssen hier also einen **Transfer** leisten und entweder eine **Stellungnahme** zu (Teil-)Aspekten des Prüfungstexts schreiben oder – seltener – eine **kreative Aufgabenstellung** bearbeiten. Manchmal wird auch von Ihnen verlangt, einen **Bezug zu einer Pflichtlektüre** bzw. zu „materials studied in class" herzustellen. Gehen Sie wie folgt vor:

Schritt 1 Aufgabenstellung genau lesen

Die Aufgabenstellung in Teil 3 ist in der Regel in einen **Kontext** eingebettet – ähnlich wie Sie das auch von der Sprachmittlungsaufgabe kennen. Es wird Ihnen also eine bestimmte Situation vorgegeben, die Sie zwingend in Ihrer Lösung berücksichtigen müssen. Dabei sollten Sie auf folgende Aspekte achten:

- Welche **Textsorte** ist vorgegeben?
- Wer ist (ggf.) die **Zielgruppe** bzw. **der Adressat/die Adressatin** des Texts?
- Auf welche **inhaltlichen Aspekte** sollen Sie eingehen?
- Welcher **Operator** wird verwendet? Häufig werden auch mehrere Operatoren miteinander kombiniert – in diesen Fällen müssen Sie die Vorgaben jedes einzelnen Operators berücksichtigen.

Operator	Dos and Don'ts	Beispiel
write [+ text type]	textsortenspezifische Vorgaben beachten	*You are taking part in an international school project "Young People and Their Dreams." Your contribution is an article for the project website.* ***Write the article*** *in which you discuss whether young people should follow their dreams regardless of what their parents say. (2017-9)*
discuss / assess / evaluate	hier müssen zwingend Pro- <u>und</u> Kontraargumente angeführt werden, die zu einer begründeten Schlussfolgerung führen	*[…] Write the article in which you* ***discuss*** *whether young people should follow their dreams regardless of what their parents say. (2017-9)*
comment (on)	die eigene Meinung begründet darlegen (Argumentation kann „einseitig" sein oder Pro- und Kontraargumente umfassen)	*[…] Write a letter to the editor in which you* ***comment on*** *the author's claim that "multiculturalism has failed" (l. 8).*
justify	eine nachvollziehbare Begründung für eine Entscheidung geben	*Imagine you are the protagonist. Write an e-mail to your friend* ***justifying*** *your decision to decline her offer.*

Schritt 2 Notizen machen / Stoffsammlung anlegen

Aus der Analyse der Textsorte, Operatoren etc. in Schritt 1 ergibt sich bereits ein Grundgerüst, wie Sie Ihre Lösung aufbauen müssen. Um nun Aspekte bzw. Argumente für den Hauptteil Ihrer Lösung zu sammeln, sollten Sie eine **Stoffsammlung** anlegen: Sie können dazu beispielsweise eine **Mindmap** erstellen, in der Sie Ihre Ideen sammeln, eine **Tabelle** mit Pro- und Kontraargumenten anlegen usw.

Schritt 3 Notizen strukturieren

Gehen Sie Ihre Stoffsammlung noch einmal durch, bündeln Sie ggf. ähnliche Aspekte und überlegen Sie, in welcher Reihenfolge Sie die einzelnen Punkte anführen möchten. Wenn Sie in einer **Stellungnahme** Pro- und Kontraargumente anführen müssen (z. B. Operatoren „discuss“ oder „assess“), haben Sie zwei Möglichkeiten: Sie können Pro und Kontra entweder in **zwei separaten Blöcken** abhandeln oder jeweils **einzelne Argumente einander gegenüberstellen**. Auch wenn Sie linear argumentieren dürfen (z. B. „comment on“) kann es sich anbieten, auf mögliche Gegenargumente einzugehen und diese zu entkräften.

Schritt 4 Lösung ausformulieren

Formulieren Sie jetzt Ihren Text aus:

- Rufen Sie sich noch einmal ins Gedächtnis, welche formalen und stilistischen Vorgaben Sie in Hinblick auf die vorgegebenen **Textsorten** und ggf. **Zielgruppen** beachten müssen.
- Vergessen Sie bei einer **Stellungnahme** nicht, Ihre Argumente durch Beispiele zu untermauern. Die einzelnen Absätze Ihres Hauptteils sollten also nach dem Muster **„These – Beleg / Beispiel“** aufgebaut sein.

  One of the biggest dangers of social media is cyberbullying. — These
  According to recent studies, about half of all teenagers and adolescents have already been threatened or insulted online on platforms such as Instagram or Facebook. This can have serious consequences on their mental or physical health, performance in school, etc. — Beleg / Beispiel

- Achten Sie bei **kreativen Aufgabenstellungen** (z. B. „write an interiour monologue“) besonders darauf, aus welcher **Perspektive** Sie schreiben sollen bzw. an welche **Informationen aus dem Ausgangstext** Sie anknüpfen können.

Textsorte	Aufbau	Sprachstil
Artikel / Essay	• Überschrift • Einleitung mit Hinführung zum Thema • klar gegliederter Hauptteil	• neutrales Register • bei jugendlicher Zielgruppe nicht zu förmlich
E-Mail	• passende Anrede • Einleitung mit Bezugnahme zum Kontext • klar gegliederter Hauptteil • evtl. abschließender Satz mit Bezugnahme zum Kontext • Schlussformel und Name	• formelle E-Mail: sachlich-nüchtern; Verwendung von Langformen • persönliche E-Mail: informell / umgangssprachlich; Verwendung von Kurzformen
Leserbrief	• Anrede • Nennung des Artikels, auf den man sich bezieht • klar gegliederter Hauptteil • Name und Wohnort	• meist eher förmlich
Rede	• Begrüßung des Publikums • strukturierter Hauptteil • Verabschiedung / Dank	• direkte Anreden • Verwendung rhetorischer Mittel • Stil je nach Thema und Zielgruppe emphatisch / locker / aufrüttelnd / …
innerer Monolog	• assoziativer Aufbau (Gedankenstrom) • Bezugnahme auf Themen oder Ereignisse, die im Ausgangstext oder der Aufgabenstellung genannt wurden	• 1. Person Singular (Ich-Perspektive) • mündlicher Stil • Sprache muss zur Figur passen
Fortsetzung / Ende einer Geschichte	Wiederaufgreifen von Handlungssträngen und Figurendarstellung des Ausgangstexts	• Erzählperspektive / Sprachstil wie im Ausgangstext
Dialog zwischen zwei Figuren	Wiederaufgreifen von Handlungssträngen und Figurendarstellung des Ausgangstexts	• jeweils Name der Figur, gefolgt von direkter Rede • mündlicher Stil • Sprache muss zu den Figuren passen

Hilfreiche Wendungen – Leserbrief	
Anrede	*Sir/Madam, / Dear Sir or Madam, / Dear Editor,*
Bezug nehmen	*I am writing in reference to the article …* *In the article …, the author wrote about …*
Meinung ausdrücken	*I would like to congratulate you on the article …* *I (wholeheartedly) agree with the author that …* *However, the author fails to mention that …* *What the author does not take into account is …*

Hilfreiche Wendungen – Rede	
Publikum begrüßen	*Ladies and gentlemen,* *Good evening, / Good afternoon,* *It's an honour and privilege to speak to you today….* *I am proud to stand here in front of you today …*
sich bedanken	*Thank you for your attention.*

Weitere nützliche Formulierungen für verschiedene Zieltextsorten finden Sie im Kapitel zur Sprachmittlung sowie in den digitalen „**MindCards**".

Textaufgabe: Lernvideos
Mit Schritt-für-Schritt-Anleitung

Auf **MyStark** (www.stark-verlag.de/mystark) stehen Ihnen sechs **Lernvideos** zur Verfügung, in denen die Vorgehensweise bei der Textaufgabe an konkreten Beispielen gezeigt wird. Die Texte und Aufgabenstellungen finden Sie ebenfalls auf MyStark. Am besten lesen Sie sich die Texte zunächst einmal genau durch und überlegen sich bei jeder Teilaufgabe, wie Sie sie lösen würden. Erst danach sollten Sie sich das zugehörige Video ansehen.

Video-Set 1: Sachtext

Text: "I used to think social media was a force for good. Now the evidence says I was wrong" by Matt Haig

Aufgabenstellung

1 **Outline** the author's view on social media. *(Video 1)*

2 **Analyse** the means he uses to convey his attitude and the effect they have on the reader. *(Video 2)*

3 **Write** a **letter to the editor/blog entry/speech** expressing your own opinion on the chances and dangers of social media. *(Video 3)*

Video-Set 2: literarischer Text

Text: *The Hate U Give* by Angie Thomas (extract from the novel)

Aufgabenstellung

1 **Describe** the night of the shooting as it is presented in the interview and as Starr remembers it. *(Video 1)*

2 **Characterise** the police officer as he is presented in this abstract. Take into account the narrative perspective. *(Video 2)*

3 "'His life always matters more!' […] 'That's the problem!'"
Discuss the statement referring to the general situation of African Americans in the US. *(Video 3)*

Textaufgabe: Übungsaufgabe 1
Niedersachsen Englisch

Aufgabenstellung

1 Describe Job's living conditions in London/England.

2 Analyse the atmosphere created in this excerpt taking into account the narrative perspective employed.

3 You are taking part in a creative writing course on "Migration Experiences" and have dealt with the excerpt from Craig's novel *Hearts and Minds*. Your task is to put yourself in the shoes of the protagonist, Job, who regularly sends money and letters to his sister in Harare/Zimbabwe.
Write Job's letter after his encounter with Polly.

Text **Excerpt from Amanda Craig, *Hearts and Minds***

Job left his home country Zimbabwe because of the cruel regime of President Robert Mugabe. Now he lives in London illegally. Polly Noble, a single mother, works as a human rights lawyer and defends undocumented immigrants who try to get a residence permit. Job, who works as a mini-cab driver, earns some extra money by driving Polly's son Robbie to and from school.

Job has a little more money these days, thanks to the regular work of picking Robbie up from school. He likes the boy, with his unmistakable look of a child who is loved, and he likes Polly, who always looks so anxious. She is one of those Englishwomen who is like a small bird, all softness and busyness. Job is sorry for her because she has no husband to help her.

"I just wish, I could find this girl," she says from the back seat. "It's maddening."

"May I ask, madam, why you are seeking her?"

"She used to work for me, and she's disappeared."

"I too have lost someone", Job says, nodding. "My wife."

"Have you told the police?"

"No," he says, sighing. "She has disappeared in Harare."

"Mine was my au pair," says Polly.

"I do not know this word."

"She is someone who lives in your home and looks after it and your children for a few hours every day in return."

"Ah. Like a maid?"

"Yes, I suppose so."

Job thinks of how, little by little, his mother had become bitter because they did not even have running water in their hut, like the Wisdens in their big house. It was different for Job, in the beginning, because he and his sister had been allowed to play with Beth. Such dear little piccaninnies, the white people had called them, and although he remembered the phrase he had been too innocent to register the insult, though his mother had. She was old enough to remember the wars, and the way white people had tried to prevent Independence, while all Job and Miriam cared about was having fun. But then, when he was twelve, it had all changed. He had grown up, and become the size he is now, and the Wisdens didn't want him to play with Beth any more.

Polly is saying, "Au pairs come from abroad, and aren't trained, so they – well, they cost a lot less, but they learn English and live in your house as part of the family. I thought I had a really good one, only she's disappeared."

"I am missing my wife," says Job. "I do not know if she is dead or alive. We have a very bad president in my country."

"I know."

"That, there, is where I live now."

Polly looks out at the tall, shabby grey concrete building he points to. "Oh, I know this place!" she exclaims.

"You have been there?"

"Er – no, not exactly. I can see it from my house, that's all."

"One day, perhaps, you might like to visit me," Job says.

"One day, perhaps," she replies.

He knows that she never will, though they pretend to each other, in the way of the British, that they are equals. It's one of those polite English fictions of equality that are like grease on a wheel shaft. She talks to him in a friendly, interested way; she's surprised to find that he reads Dickens and Shakespeare. Perhaps the kind of Africans she defends are not like him, though he tells her that people in his country learn English now in order to read these authors.

Poor people do live differently in Britain. They have so many things that it seems to drive out thought. Job would never have dreamt he could one day drive a car like the one he leases from Mo, for instance. Nor would he have believed that he might have a TV set, thrown out because it was an old, bulky design instead of the flatscreen ones everyone expects. Also, there is so much culture available for free. Job has walked, amazed, round every museum he can find on Sundays, where people from all over the globe wander in to enjoy the most beautiful paintings, inventions, buildings. He can't join a public library, but the cheapness of second-hand paperbacks on stalls and in charity shops almost makes him weak. There is an abundance of everything – food dropped half-eaten on the pavement that goes to feed birds or rats – and yet a consciousness of nothing. He thinks of the city conjured for him by Dickens; that foggy, dark place riddled with crime and yet suffused with kindness and courage. He had been a little disappointed when he arrived to find the soot had been scoured away during the last century, and no horse-drawn carriages. Yet there were still men like Bill Sikes, with their dogs and violence. He sees them right outside his home.

Home for Job is now a tiny room with only a sink to drink from and wash in, and the noise of police sirens and traffic wailing and sighing in a continuous susurration below. Damp blooms on the walls, outlining new continents – as if those who live here, in the perpetual stench of urine, beer, sour milk and cinders, need any more reminders of what they have lost. Job's own room is sub-let from another foreigner, in a kind of food chain of privation and opportunism. There is a whole family next to Job, sleeping on a floor that is all a heaving, twanging mattress. He doesn't even know where they are from because they speak no English, but he suspects it is the Gambia. On his other side are two sisters from Turkey, and then a young couple from somewhere in the Indian subcontinent. Intimately acquainted with each other's bowel movements and cooking smells, his fellow tenants mind their own business, and when they pass each other silently on the stairs or in the corridor they keep their heads down. They bang on his door when he shouts out from his nightmares and he bangs on theirs if they quarrel or fail to quieten a baby, but otherwise they pretend not to exist, which is another polite English fiction. But the worst of all are the other sounds – the sounds couples make together, when alone in the dark. Job can't stand listening to them, and being reminded of his wife. His stomach is full, but his heart is empty.

Excerpt from: Amanda Craig. Hearts and Minds. *London: Little, Brown, 2009.*

Annotations

43 Dickens: Charles Dickens (1812–1870) is a famous English writer.
48 Mo: Job is a taxi driver who leases his car from a man called Mo.
59/60 Bill Sikes: an aggressive and vicious character in Charles Dickens' novel *Oliver Twist*
62 susurration: (poet.) a soft rustle *(leises Rascheln)*

Lösungsvorschlag

1 **TIPP**

In this assignment you have to describe in detail what you learn about the conditions under which Job lives in England.

- Job works as a taxi driver → earns some money
- regularly picks up a boy called Robbie from school → earns extra money
- has immigrated from Zimbabwe
- is obviously living in GB illegally as he cannot join the public library
- worries about his wife
- misses his home
- lives in a shabby, run-down building in a tiny, mildewed room with only the bare necessities, there is little to no privacy
- obviously lives in a rough part of London (as he meets violent men outside his home)
- though he is poor, he owns some material goods, e. g. an old TV set
- enjoys the cultural offers in London

introduction: reference to source

Job, one of the protagonists in Amanda Craig's novel *Hearts and Minds*, published in 2009, is an undocumented immigrant from Zimbabwe.

main part: Job's living conditions

He lives in a rough part of London where he meets violent men outside the house he lives in. In this run-down house, Job has a very small and mildewed room, only fitted with the bare necessities. There is next to no privacy there because everybody hears the most intimate sounds of their neighbours. He misses his home country and his wife, whom he worries about because he does not know if she is still alive in Zimbabwe.

Job works as a taxi driver and earns some extra money by picking up a boy called Robbie from school on a regular basis. Therefore, he can afford some small luxuries like second-hand books, which enrich his life immensely. He also owns some material goods like a TV set that has been discarded by others. Job also enjoys the cultural abundance he finds in London.

2 **TIPP**

For this task you have to observe the atmosphere in this extract. To do so, you need to have a look at how people, objects and places are described. Which words are used and what do these words evoke? You must also take into account the narrative perspective in this situation and how this affects the readers and their perception of everything described.

- the atmosphere is ambivalent: hopeful and depressing
- the third-person narrator tells the story from Job's perspective: the reader shares his feelings and thoughts (cf. e. g. ll. 2–5), which are ambivalent, too
- hopeful:
  - Job earns more money
  - he likes Polly (who is compared to a bird, cf. l. 4) and her son Robbie (who looks like a child who is loved, cf. l. 2)
  - Polly is friendly and interested in Job (cf. l. 42)
  - poor people in England live a better life than in Zimbabwe (cf. ll. 46–56)
  - there is an abundance of material wealth, food, culture (cf. ll. 46–56)

  depressing:
  - Job misses his wife and worries about her (cf. ll. 30/31)
  - Job remembers the discrimination he faced in Zimbabwe (cf. ll. 18–20)
  - the place he lives in is bleak and depressing (cf. ll. 34, 61–75)
  - there is no privacy and the sounds of his neighbours' lovemaking make him miss his wife even more (cf. ll. 75–77)
  - Job feels emotionally crippled ("his heart is empty", l. 77)
  - the notion of equality is just a pretence (cf. ll. 40–42)
  - people in England are superficial (cf. l. 56)
  - the atmosphere of Charles Dickens' *Oliver Twist* is evoked (cf. ll. 56–60)

introduction: thesis, reference to assignment

The atmosphere the author evokes in this extract is ambivalent as it is both hopeful and even a little enthusiastic, but also depressing. This atmosphere is created by the choice of a particular narrative situation and by an ambivalent description of characters and places.

main part: narrative technique – third-person narrator, limited point of view

In this extract the story is told by a third-person narrator who sees the events through Job's eyes (cf. e. g. ll. 2–5), which are the eyes of an African immigrant, who has a different perspective on life in London than a Londoner. On the one hand, Job is fascinated by the abundance he finds in London. On the other hand, he is depressed by his private situation and how superficial Londoners are.

ambivalent general atmosphere

The description of Polly and her son makes a positive impression at first. Robbie is described as "a child who is loved" (l. 2) and Polly "is like a small bird, all softness and busyness" (l. 4). Thus, an air of love and softness is evoked. However, this is immediately modified into a negative evaluation of her living conditions when Job feels "sorry for [Polly] because she has no husband to help her" (ll. 4/5). Also, her explanation of what an au pair is, reminds Job of his early experiences of discrimination by White people in Zimbabwe (cf. ll. 18–26), which spoils the atmosphere.

ambivalent impression of the city and its inhabitants

The relationship between Job and Polly is also ambivalent. Job's perception of both Polly and her son indicates that he cares for her. The fact that he invites her to his place and that she accepts, even though in a very non-committal way, creates a positive atmosphere as some sort of friendship seems to develop. Again, however, the additions made from Job's perspective suggest that true friendship will never arise between the two of them as they only "pretend to each other [...] that they are equals" (ll. 40/41). The next sentence generalises this situation when the narrator observes that equality is "one of those polite English fictions [...] that are like grease on a wheel shaft" (ll. 41/42). Thus, the English in general are discredited as polite but dishonest, which spoils the atmosphere considerably.

Furthermore, the English are also depicted as very superficial people. "They have so many things that it seems to drive out thought" (ll. 46/47). The "abundance of everything" (l. 54) results in a "consciousness of nothing" (l. 56). This description ruins the impression of London, which was very positive and even enthusiastic just some lines before when Job's visits to museums are described. There, Job is "amazed" (l. 51) by the amount of culture and enjoys "the most beautiful paintings, inventions, buildings" (l. 52).

reference to contrasts in Charles Dickens' novel *Oliver Twist*

Very important for the atmosphere created in this excerpt is the reference to Charles Dickens' novel *Oliver Twist*, which has made a lasting impression on Job. When he came to London, he expected a "foggy, dark place riddled with crime and yet suffused with kindness and courage" (ll. 56/57). Here again, the ambivalence is apparent as darkness opposes kindness and crime opposes courage. However, it seems that along with "the soot" (l. 58) and "horse-drawn carriages" (l. 59), kindness and courage have disappeared. All that remains are "men like Bill Sikes, with their dogs and violence" (ll. 59/60); the atmosphere is thus perceived as dangerous and threatening.

depressing atmosphere of Job's home and personal situation

This is all the more true because Job observes these frightening people in front of his home (cf. ll. 59/60). Even without them, the description of his house creates a depressing atmosphere, as it is a "shabby grey concrete building" (l. 34). The inside is even worse because "[d]amp blooms on the walls, outlining new continents – as if those who live here, in the perpetual stench of urine, beer, sour milk and cinders, need any more reminders of what they have lost" (ll. 63–65); in Job's case, his wife and his home country represent his losses. He feels the loss of his wife all the more because in his flat he hears the sounds of his neighbours' lovemaking (cf. ll. 75–

77). As a consequence, he feels emotionally crippled ("his heart is empty", l. 77). As these are the last words of the excerpt, the reader is left with a very depressing impression, which is, however, softened by the poetic language used to describe the scene. The traffic wails and sighs "in a continuous susurration" (l. 62) and "[d]amp blooms on the walls" (l. 63).

To conclude, the narrative perspective chosen largely influences the ambivalent atmosphere. Due to this perspective, the readers are invited to share Job's point of view, who assesses the people and places in a very level-headed way, seeing both the positive and the negative aspects. **conclusion**

3 **TIPP**

In this assignment you need to write Job's letter to his sister after his encounter with Polly. To prepare for this task, you should try to put yourself into Job's shoes. This is probably not his first letter home, so you should focus on what has recently happened in his life. Your notes for task one will help you here. Consider what you find out about his sister in the excerpt (called Miriam, childhood experiences). As this is a personal letter, you should use everyday English but you need also take into account that Job tends to use poetic language and no crude words.

- Ask Miriam how she is and express worries for her safety.
- Ask for news about your wife (make up her name, e. g. Zadie).
- Tell her about Polly and her son and the extra money you earn.
- Tell her that you remembered childhood experiences.
- Tell her about the invitation and your impression that equality is only a pretence.
- Relate the fact that Polly was surprised you knew Shakespeare and Dickens.
- Maybe add that she is a human rights lawyer.
- Tell her about a recent visit to a museum or a book you bought and read.

9 September 2009 — date

Dear Miriam, — greeting

How are you and your family? I hope this letter reaches you in a safe place. I'm often worried sick about your and Zadie's safety and wish you could all be here with me. — introductory sentences

Here in London I still work as a taxi driver and drive around in this big car I have leased from a man called Mo. Lately, I've earned some extra money because I regularly pick up a boy called Robbie from school and take him home. Robbie is a nice boy, who looks like he is loved. On our way to his home, he chatters about his day at school — account of events and experiences and I enjoy his company because he is still so innocent and treats me like a friend.

Robbie's mum, Polly, is nice and friendly, too. She really worries about a girl who used to look after her son but who has disappeared. She calls her an "au pair" and it reminded me of our mother's work at the Wisdens and how they called us "dear little piccaninnies" until I seemed to be a threat to Beth. But Polly really seems to care about her au pair and doesn't seem to be racist. Still, I know that we will never be real friends. She pretends that we are equal but this is just the way of the English. Equality is a polite English fiction, which will never come true. The other day we realised that we live quite close to each other, so on the spur of the moment, I invited her to come to my place one day and she accepted the invitation in a very non-committal way, so I knew at once that she would never come. She was surprised to learn that I have read Shakespeare and Dickens, as if Africans were all illiterate people. Maybe that is her impression from the people she meets at work. She is a human rights lawyer and helps illegal immigrants to obtain a residence permit. Maybe when you come here, too, she can help both of us to stay in England. Wouldn't that be great? encounter with Polly

When I'm not working, I walk a lot through London. I've already told you about the abundance of culture in this city in my last letter, but it keeps amazing me. There are all these beautiful buildings with even more beautiful things inside. Many museums are for free. Last Sunday I visited the Tate Modern Gallery. Just imagine that you don't have to pay an entrance fee to see the most beautiful paintings and exhibits inside. I'm sure you would love it. impression of London

Londoners don't seem to see the beauty around them. They rush past and don't acknowledge people or places. There is such an abundance of culture and material wealth, they can't appreciate it any longer. What a pity for them. impression of Londoners

Dear Miriam, with this letter I'm sending you some of the extra money I earn from Polly. I hope it will help you and Zadie and hopefully, one day, I will have sent you enough money so you can both come to London, too. I miss you so much. closing sentences

Take good care of yourself. I hope to hear from you soon.

Love,

Job

Textaufgabe: Übungsaufgabe 2

Niedersachsen Englisch

Aufgabenstellung

1 Describe what happens in the Watson-Crick laboratories.

2 Examine the protagonists' attitudes towards the research that goes on at Watson-Crick.

3 You are taking part in an international workshop on "The Ethics of Science". Write a speech in which you discuss the questions Jimmy asks himself in l. 65 ("How much is too much, how far is too far?").
Refer to your background knowledge about genetic engineering as well as to the novel *Frankenstein*.

Text **Excerpt from Margaret Atwood, *Oryx and Crake***

Oryx and Crake*, a dystopian novel by Canadian author Margaret Atwood, is set in a post-apocalyptic world inhabited by genetically manipulated organisms. Jimmy, who seems to be the only human being not wiped out by a pandemic, reflects on his life before the catastrophe. In this extract, a meeting between him and his friend Crake, a brilliant scientist, is portrayed. Crake studies bio-engineering at the Watson-Crick Institute, where the two friends meet.*

1 […] "On day one they toured some of the wonders of Watson-Crick. Crake was interested in everything – all the projects that were going on. He kept saying "Wave of the future," which got irritating after the third time.

[…] they went to NeoAgriculturals. AgriCouture was its nickname among the students. They had to put on biosuits before they entered the facility, and scrub their hands and wear nose-cone filters, because what they were about to see hadn't been bioform-proofed, or not completely. A woman with a laugh like Woody Woodpecker led them through the corridors.

"This is the latest," said Crake.

What they were looking at was a large bulblike object that seemed to be covered with stippled whitish-yellow skin. Out of it came twenty thick fleshy tubes, and at the end of each tube another bulb was growing.

"What the hell is it?" said Jimmy.

"Those are chickens," said Crake. "Chicken parts. Just the breasts, on this one. They've got ones that specialize in drumsticks too, twelve to a growth unit."

"But there aren't any heads," said Jimmy. He grasped the concept – he'd grown up with sus multiorganifer, after all – but this thing was going too far. At least the pigoons of his childhood hadn't lacked heads.

"That's the head in the middle," said the woman. "There's a mouth opening at the top, they dump the nutrients in there. No eyes or beak or anything, they don't need those."

"This is horrible," said Jimmy. The thing was a nightmare. It was like an animal-protein tuber. "Picture the sea-anemone body plan," said Crake. "That helps." "But what's it thinking?" said Jimmy.

The woman gave her jocular woodpecker yodel, and explained that they'd removed all the brain functions that had nothing to do with digestion, assimilation, and growth.

"It's sort of like a chicken hookworm," said Crake.

"No need for added growth hormones," said the woman, "the high growth rate's built in. You get chicken breasts in two weeks – that's a three-week improvement on the most efficient low-light, high-density chicken farming operations so far devised. And the animal-welfare freaks won't be able to say a word, because this thing feels no pain."

"Those kids are going to clean up," said Crake after they'd left. The students at Watson-Crick got half the royalties from anything they invented there. Crake said it was a fierce incentive.

"ChickieNobs, they're thinking of calling the stuff."

"Are they on the market yet?" asked Jimmy weakly. He couldn't see eating a ChickieNob. It would be like eating a large wart. But as with the tit implants – the good ones – maybe he wouldn't be able to tell the difference.

"They've already got the takeout franchise operation in placc," said Crake. "Investors are lining up around the block. They can undercut the price of everyone else." […]

"This is BioDefenses," said Crake. "Last stop, I promise." […]

They were standing in front of a series of cages. Each contained a dog. There were many different breeds and sizes, but all were gazing at Jimmy with eyes of love, all were wagging their tails.

"It's a dog pound," said Jimmy.

"Not quite," said Crake. "Don't go beyond the guardrail, don't stick your hand in."

"They look friendly enough," said Jimmy. His old longing for a pet came over him. "Are they for sale?"

"They aren't dogs, they just look like dogs. They're wolvogs – they're bred to deceive. Reach out to pat them, they'll take your hand off. There's a large pit-bull component." "Why make a dog like that?" said Jimmy, taking a step back. "Who'd want one?"

"It's a CorpSeCorps thing," said Crake. "Commission work. A lot of funding. They want to put them in moats, or something."

"Moats?"

"Yeah. Better than an alarm system – no way of disarming these guys. And no way of making pals with them, not like real dogs."

"What if they get out? Go on the rampage? Start breeding, then the population spirals out of control – like those big green rabbits?"

"That would be a problem," said Crake. "But they won't get out. Nature is to zoos as God is to churches."

"Meaning what?" said Jimmy. He wasn't paying close attention, he was worrying about the ChickieNobs and the wolvogs. Why is it he feels some line has been crossed, some boundary transgressed? How much is too much, how far is too far?

"Those walls and bars are there for a reason," said Crake. "Not to keep us out, but to keep them in. Mankind needs barriers in both cases."

"Them?"

"Nature and God."

"I thought you didn't believe in God," said Jimmy.

"I don't believe in Nature either," said Crake. "Or not with a capital N."

Annotations

17 sus multiorganifer, pigoons: genetically altered pigs designed to grow human organs
54 CorpSeCorps: a security service corporation guarding security facilities like bio-engineering labs

Lösungsvorschlag

1 **TIPP**

In this task, you have to describe (i. e. give a detailed account of) what happens at Watson-Crick Institute. Make sure you remain neutral and avoid Crake's enthusiasm as well as Jimmy's doubts about the research going on at the labs. Use your own words as far as possible.

- general information about the Watson-Crick Institute:
  - genetic laboratory
  - very progressive research
  - very risky; high-security equipment needed
  - students get a share of the profits for their inventions
- "ChickieNobs":
  - genetically manipulated animals
  - no elaborate brain functions → feel no pain
  - allows efficient production of chicken parts
- "Wolvogs":
  - look friendly, like normal pet dogs
  - highly aggressive
  - used as guard dogs

introduction: source and topic

In the extract from Margaret Atwood's *Oryx and Crake*, the narrator describes the genetic laboratories at the Watson-Crick Institute.

main part: general information about the laboratory

The Institute seems to be made up of different departments where very progressive research is being conducted. As Crake explains, the students working there are highly motivated because they get a share of all the profits as soon as their inventions go on the market. Since the research at Watson-Crick is extremely advanced as well as risky, visitors have to wear protective clothing like biosuits and nose-cone filters in order to avoid contamination and infection, and are hindered from approaching the genetically manipulated organisms too closely.

"ChickieNobs"

The first project Jimmy and Crake visit is the development of the "ChickieNob" in the department of NeoAgriculturals. The ChickieNob is an attempt at growing marketable chicken parts more efficiently by modifying the growth rate and the structure of the organism. The genetically manipulated animals are compared to sea anemones or hookworms because they live only to feed, lacking elaborate brain functions and the means and desire to move. The improvement mentioned is that mass production of chicken parts will be more efficient without coming into conflict with animal welfare supporters, since the ChickieNobs do not have any sensual perception.

The second project, which they visit in the department of BioDefenses, is a special dog breed commissioned by the CorpSeCorps, a security service. These wolvogs look like normal pet dogs but, due to their dominant pit-bull traits, are highly aggressive and intended for use as guard dogs. "Wolvogs"

2 **TIPP**

In this assignment, you are required to take a closer look at Jimmy's and Crake's attitudes towards the things they see. Explain in what aspects they differ. Do not only concentrate on the obvious points but also try to find out what is implied, for example in Crake's statements on "Nature" and "God" (cf. ll. 61–71). It helps to structure your text by dealing with one person at a time. Give lines to support your arguments.

- Crake's attitude:
  - fascinated by and proud of scientific progress (cf. ll. 1–3)
  - matter-of-fact, purely scientific point of view (cf. ll. 14/15, 23, 27)
  - interested in economic aspects (cf. ll. 33–35, 40/41, 54)
  - thinks mankind should be in control of nature (cf. ll. 57–71)
- Jimmy's attitude:
  - expresses doubts about the research (cf. ll. 14–21)
  - reacts emotionally, is shocked by what he sees (cf. ll. 13, 16–18, 22–24)
  - rather disgusted by ChickieNobs (cf. ll. 37–39)
  - worries about safety (cf. ll. 59/60) as well as about moral and ethical implications (cf. ll. 63–65)

introduction

Crake's and Jimmy's attitudes obviously differ widely. While Crake is enthusiastic about the research, Jimmy has many doubts about it.

Crake's attitude: fascination / pride

Crake is fascinated by the scientific progress achieved by the students, while at the same time being pragmatic and mainly interested in the monetary profits to be gained. His language reflects this attitude: On the one hand, he expresses his pride in the new developments, even irritating Jimmy with his repetition of "Wave of the future" (ll. 2/3). On the other hand, he tries to employ a neutral tone and often counters Jimmy's worries with short, fact-based replies, as in lines 14/15 where he states matter-of-factly, "Those are chickens, [...]. Chicken parts. [...] They've got ones that specialize in drumsticks too, twelve to a growth unit." He sees everything from a purely scientific point of view, such as when he compares the ChickieNobs to a "sea anemone" (l. 23) and a "hookworm" (l. 27) and is convinced that that concept "helps" (l. 23) to dispel Jimmy's worries.

purely scientific point of view

Another aspect of great interest to Crake is the economic gain possible through the new inventions. He repeatedly talks about money

interest in economic aspects

(cf. ll. 33–35, 40/41, 54) and calls it a "fierce incentive" (l. 35) driving the students' ambition.

The wolvogs do not seem to worry him either. Again, he uses short simple sentences to counter Jimmy's fears and is completely convinced that "they won't get out" (l. 61). His utter reliance on the controllability of nature is expressed strikingly in his metaphorical comparison that "Nature is to zoos as God is to churches" (ll. 61/62). What he means is that both God and Nature might be agreeable concepts, but they should never be able or allowed to dominate human life (cf. ll. 66/67). In his final statement of not believing in Nature (l. 71), he sounds almost arrogant in his conviction that man is above and in control of both God and Nature.

man in control of nature

In contrast to Crake's confidence and pragmatism, Jimmy seems to both doubt and even fear the new inventions' implications. He is shocked rather than impressed when he sees the ChickieNobs, which is shown by his horrified question, "What the hell is it?" (l. 13). Furthermore, he cannot keep his emotional distance the way Crake seems to be able to. His question of what the ChickieNobs are thinking (cf. ll. 23/24) illustrates his tendency to humanise them and his thoughts of being in a "horrible" (l. 22) place and seeing "a nightmare" (l. 22) emphasise his state of horror.

Jimmy's attitude: emotionality, shock

While Jimmy seems to be accustomed to genetically modified organisms up to a certain degree (cf. ll. 16–18) and even has to admit that "as with tit implants [...] maybe he wouldn't be able to tell the difference" (ll. 38/39) between eating a ChickieNob and "real" chicken, this thought freaks him out and disgusts him. His comparison to "eating a large wart" (l. 38) illustrates that.

disgust with ChickieNobs

His emotional side becomes apparent again when he is confronted with the wolvogs. He is attracted to them at first and has always wanted a pet (cf. l. 48). When he learns their secret, he is all the more taken aback and asks shocked questions, like "Why make a dog like that?" (l. 52) or "Who'd want one?" (ll. 52/53).

emotionality, shock

That he is truly worried, even frightened, is further exemplified by his subsequent, partly elliptical questions, "What if they get out? Go on the rampage? Start breeding, then the population spirals out of control [...]?" (ll. 59/60).

worries about safety

However, Jimmy's worries are not limited to safety issues. He has moral and ethical concerns, expressed in fundamental questions like, "Why is it he feels some line has been crossed, some boundary transgressed?" (ll. 64/65) and "How much is too much, how far is too far?" (l. 65). As they remain unanswered, Jimmy is revealed to be rather helpless in the face of the rapid technological developments.

moral and ethical concerns

3 **TIPP**

Write a speech in which you debate the question of how far progress should go. In a speech, it is important that you remember certain conventions, like addressing your audience, structuring your arguments convincingly and using stylistic devices, e. g. rhetorical questions, to keep the listeners interested. The style can be quite emphatic and should contain elements of spoken language.
The operator "discuss" means that you have to take into consideration different perspectives, i. e. to weigh the advantages and disadvantages of genetic engineering, and come to a justified conclusion.

- advantages:
  - cure illnesses, create organs to replace diseased ones → reduce suffering
  - create plants and animals that are resistant to pests or pathogens → fight world hunger
- disadvantages:
  - consequences of tinkering with nature cannot be foreseen
  - gradual shifting of moral boundaries:
    example 1: stem cell research → embryos have to be destroyed
    example 2: creation of human-animal chimeras → raises ethical questions, e. g. about the social and moral status of these beings
- reference to *Frankenstein* → scientist's wish to play God ends in disaster
- conclusion: need for restrictions and clear rules that guide science

Dear fellow participants, — **direct address**

introduction — How much is too much, how far is too far? When I look at science and technology today, I am not ashamed to admit that I am terrified. There seem to be no boundaries at all, nothing seems to be sacred, everything seems to be possible when it comes to "our future". But I would like to appeal to your common sense that it might be exactly that future which is at risk if we do not start to act more responsibly.

advantages, but also **risks**: consequences can't be foreseen — Don't get me wrong – I do not want to stand in the way of progress, but right now we cannot foresee what impact some scientific methods will have on our lives. Of course, the advantages of science are undeniable. Take genetic engineering, for example: We can cure diseased organs or replace them with working ones, we can optimise plants for better yield or immunity, but at what price? And will we stop at "optimising" human beings in the same way?

Genetically enhanced crops might offer enough to save the starving world because we will be able to modify plants to almost any climate or need. But on the other hand, there are simply too many things we do not yet know about them: What impact will these plants have on our ecosystem? How will they affect us, our bodies, our health? So far, there are no reliable studies on what happens to biodiversity or our organism. The same applies to animals, such as genetically enhanced chickens or pigs that are more resistant to any kind of pathogens. I personally do not fancy eating them without knowing the consequences.

But besides these environmental and health issues, one of the biggest questions is an ethical one: Once we are familiar with modifying plants and animals, why stop at the human race? Like I said, it is great to grow organs which can save lives, it might be even better to eradicate genetic defects beforehand, but are there no moral boundaries?

shifting of moral boundaries

For the growth of human organs, for example, we need embryos to harvest the cells from, by which process they are normally destroyed. Don't they count as human beings as well? Shouldn't we have a moral responsibility to protect all life forms?

example: stem cell research

Recently, scientists have managed to create human-animal chimeras by injecting human stem cells into the embryos of other species (such as monkeys). So far, the chimeras live for only a few days, but it is only a matter of time until they will survive for longer. This kind of research raises profound ethical questions: first of all, isn't it cruel to experiment with animals and humans in this way? And what will the social and moral status of these chimeras be – will they be treated like animals or like human beings? I think we are crossing a dangerous line here by tinkering with nature in this way.

example: creation of human-animal chimeras

As early as the 19th century, the writer Mary Shelley warned against what might happen if scientists become too ambitious and try to play God. The title character of her novel *Frankenstein* is obsessed with the wish to create a living being from dead body parts. Once he has finished his work, however, he is overwhelmed by the ugliness of his creature and leaves it to itself. Feeling rejected by its creator and the other people it meets, the "monster" becomes embittered and finally turns evil, killing several innocent people.

reference to *Frankenstein*

I think this dystopian story is an admonishment that scientists should think very carefully about the consequences of their research and that they also have a responsibility towards their creation. Arguably, the real monster in the novel is not the being created out of dead body parts, but the scientist, Viktor Frankenstein, himself, who simply abandoned his creation.

Call me backward, but I think that we literally need to put our foot on the brake for a while – slowing down the radical und irreversible progress of genetic engineering in order to understand what exactly we have altered already. So, for now, we need restrictions and for the future, we need strict rules to make sure that the power of science is used responsibly – for our own good and that of life on our planet in general. Thank you.

conclusion: need for clear rules

thanks

Textaufgabe: Übungsaufgabe 3

Niedersachsen Englisch

Aufgabenstellung

1 Outline the development of segregation since the 1960s.

2 Analyse the author's attitude towards the segregation that influences her private life and how it is conveyed.

3 Imagine you read the article below on *The Guardian*'s website.
Write an entry for the comment section in which you express your own thoughts as to the current state of segregation in the US and to Allen's opinion about it.

Text — Our 21st-Century Segregation: We're Still Divided by Race

Even now, there are two Americas: one for brown people, one for whites. The difference is that we choose it today.

Many Americans don't want to admit it, but I'll say it: segregation is still around. Sometimes by design. And sometimes by choice.

Let me be clear, this isn't the segregation of my parent's era. It's not a legally mandated and enforced system backed by public figures like former Alabama George Wallace, who famously said, "Segregation today. Segregation tomorrow. Segregation forever," to resounding applause, in 1963. The "whites only" signs have ceased to lurk over water fountains, bathrooms, and restaurant counters.

Yet, 21st-century segregation exists overtly in our school systems, communities, and prisons. It also permeates our society in ways we don't even realize.

We need to continue the conversation about the shocking segregation in our schools and neighborhoods. According to a study last year, 43 % of Latinos and 38 % of blacks go to schools where less than 10 % of their peers are white. But beyond that, we often fail to talk about how segregation impacts us personally. How it permeates not only many of our public and private institutions, but American culture at large. We less easily talk about cultural or social segregation, an area that we have control over, via the restaurants we patronize, the bars we drink at and the places where we worship.

It's time for us to face the reality that for many Americans, even if we live and work around "diversity", our best friends and spiritual leaders, the people we invite into our lives and homes, often look like we do, reinforcing a de facto segregation. This social and cultural segregation isn't restricted to "uneducated" people living in the country. It is equally prominent in environments where smart, educated people are supposed to "know better". People who have studied race, spent months abroad in India or Africa, tasted the best fufu and mofongo, read Ralph Ellison, James Baldwin and Pablo

Neruda, and who may even have black "friends" or lovers, still too often manage to have a community that doesn't reflect diversity in their broader city or nation.

[…]

My knee-jerk reaction is to blame racism and discrimination. To complain about all the times that I've felt odd being the only brown face in the crowd. To get mad about how all the television shows that have casts that look like my family are segregated to the so-called "cable ghettos". To get angry at all the bouncers who say they have a racial quota in hotspots. And to wonder why all the books I like are sitting in a "separate" section … until of course, I realize, I'm guilty of many of the same offenses: I segregate, too.

I think about all the nights I plan out that were based on the racial and ethnic make-up of the crowd I am going out with. If I am hanging with black friends, I likely go to an all-black establishment, where I know my friends will like the music, and the mating potential. If I am hanging out with an all-white crowd, I immediately cross all black locations off the list, not wanting anyone to feel uncomfortable. Instead, I relegate myself to being one of a few blacks in the crowd. If it's going to be a night with mixed company, the venue would be more likely to be up for grabs. But an all-black locale still would probably be out of the question.

This isn't secret intel: many blacks, whites, Latinos, and Asians seem to stick to these same guidelines, too, particularly in New York City, America's supposed great melting pot. There are still two Americas: one for brown people and one for whites, and both are heavily segregated.

If our social worlds were more integrated, perhaps we would see it trickle down to the way we govern and the way we dispense justice. Having some sort of connection, a shared experience is the only way I believe that we can get politicians, police officers, and everyday citizens […] to truly understand race.

It may seem silly to connect major state and federal policies to something as simple as a night on the town, but our experiences are shaped not just by legalese and policy, but also by understanding and interacting with each other. Segregation in the 21st century is not just about being legally and physically separated, but about a cultural separation that still feels like it divides more than it binds.

From: Reniqua Allen, "Our 21st-century segregation: we're still divided by race",
on: theguardian.com, *3 April 2013.*
http://www.theguardian.com/commentisfree/2013/apr/03/21st-century-segregation-divided-race

Annotations

6 to lurk: to wait quietly or secretly for sth to happen or sb to appear, usually with bad intentions
9, 13 to permeate: to be present everywhere
27 knee-jerk reaction: way of automatically responding to sth
42 intel: short for intelligence, "insider" information acquired by well-informed sources
47 to dispense justice: to decide whether or not sb is guilty of a criminal act and how this person should be punished
51 legalese: all the special words and expressions that belong to the terminology of judges and lawyers

Lösungsvorschlag

1 **TIPP**

In this task, you are supposed to outline a development, which means that you should summarise it concisely. It might be helpful to structure your text by contrasting the state-enforced segregation of the 1960s with the "voluntary" cultural and individual segregation that the author claims exists today.

- segregation in the 1960s:
  - prescribed by law
  - Black and White people separated spatially
- segregation today:
  - overt segregation in institutions
  - self-imposed segregation in personal lives
    → more implicit, often not admitted
  - tendency to surround oneself with people from same ethnicity
    → impact on social and cultural life
  - could be overcome through more interaction with people from other backgrounds

introduction: source and topic

The article "Our 21st-Century Segregation: We're Still Divided by Race" by Reniqua Allen was published on the website of *The Guardian* in April 2013 and is about segregation in the US. According to the author, segregation still exists in the 21st century but it is a culturally motivated separation that people choose freely.

main part: segregation in the 1960s

Up until the 1960s, segregation was prescribed by law: Black and White Americans were not allowed to eat at the same places or use the same toilets, for example.

segregation today

While it is no longer state-enforced, the author claims that segregation is still found in public institutions, such as schools or prisons. Even more importantly, however, it exists in people's private lives, impacting society and culture. The reason for this is that people tend to surround themselves with members of their own ethnicity and go to places where they are among "their own". As this new segregation comes from the inside rather than the outside, people are likely to deny it because by admitting to its existence, they would have to admit that they contribute to the phenomenon as well.

On the other hand, the author claims that it could be overcome through individual effort, by means of common experiences and more social interaction with people from other racial backgrounds.

2 **TIPP**

This analysis task is twofold: You should both present Reniqua Allen's attitude towards segregation and explain how she conveys it. It is probably a good idea to structure your answer with regard to content (her general assessment of segregation, her initial angry reaction, her blaming of herself) and substantiate each point with evidence from the text.

- personal attachment to the subject:
  - use of first-person pronoun; reflection on her position as a Black person (cf. e. g. ll. 38/39)
  - repetition of "permeate" (ll. 9, 13) to show the all-pervasiveness of the topic
- wish to raise awareness and call for change
  - address to readers to take action (cf. ll. 10, 17)
  - reference to a study about school segregation (cf. ll. 11/12) → further increases credibility
  - dismantling of politically correct behaviour as a mere pretence: interest in other cultures (cf. ll. 17–25), foreign foods (cf. l. 23) and literature about race/ethnicity (cf. ll. 23/24), but segregation in private life
- anger about modern segregation, but also self-criticism
  - examples of her own experiences with segregation (cf. ll. 27–32)
  - repetition/enumeration of verbs (ll. 27–31) → underlines frustration
  - use of verb "to segregate" in active rather than passive voice (l. 33) → stresses individual responsibility
  - examples of how she segregates, too (ll. 34–41)
- conclusion: call for more interaction (cf. ll. 46–54)

introduction

The author's attitude towards the modern kind of segregation is conveyed in different ways.

main part: personal attachment

First of all, Allen writes in the first-person singular, which emphasises how deeply she is affected by the subject of racial segregation. Being Black herself (cf. e. g. ll. 38/39), her private life is as much influenced by segregation as the society she lives in; that this influence is extensive is hinted at by the repeated use of "permeate" (ll. 9, 13). Like everybody else, she claims not to have been particularly aware of the presence of segregation in everyday life (cf. l. 9), which makes it very difficult to fight against. The result is a society that lacks the diversity it officially ensures.

wish to raise the readers' awareness

Now that the author has realised that there are "two Americas" (l. 44) existing next to each other without overlapping very often, she wants to make society aware of the lie many Americans are living: her article is like a wake-up call to make her fellow citizens see what they refuse to acknowledge (cf. l. 1). She urgently wants to force them to take action now. Thus, she writes that "[w]e need to continue the conversation about the shocking segregation in our schools"

(l. 10) and "[i]t's time for us to face [...] reality" (l. 17). To prove that this is not just her own possibly prejudiced perception of the world, she refers to a study conducted recently that revealed that schools are still heavily segregated (cf. ll. 11/12). Before talking about her own experiences, the author reveals the politically correct behaviour of the educated US middle class as a mere pretence: people talk about "diversity" (l. 18) and show interest in other cultures without really mixing with them in their private lives (cf. ll. 17–25). She enumerates foreign-sounding foods (cf. l. 23) and intellectually demanding authors who deal with the subjects of race and ethnicity (cf. ll. 23/24). Through her description of how "smart, educated people [who] are supposed to 'know better'" (ll. 21/22) include these in their lives, while still staying in their own small, segregated world, she further exemplifies this pretence.

anger about modern segregation

The author does not exclude herself from sharing the responsibility for segregation, although her metaphorical "knee-jerk reaction" (l. 27) – in other words her first impulse – would be to feel victimised. Her fury at the injustice and the fact that people do not seem to have learned from history is still perceptible when she lists her personal experiences (cf. ll. 27–32). That anger is especially emphasised by her use of language: she starts her sentences with the infinitives "[t]o complain about", "[t]o get mad about", "[t]o get angry at", "[a]nd to wonder why" (ll. 27–31) to let off steam about the everyday segregation she is confronted with.

self-criticism

However, she counters that enumeration of verbs which express her anger and frustration by blaming herself, using the half-sentence, "until of course, I realize, I'm guilty of many of the same offenses" (l. 32) and the simple, but impressive statement, "I segregate, too" (l. 33). While the verb "to segregate" is normally not used in the active voice, this personalisation of its use underlines her main point: She herself and most Americans are responsible on a very individual level; they get angry but stay passive and fail to change anything. In the subsequent lines (ll. 34–41), she provides examples of her own "offenses" of segregation. Obviously, she leads a very active social life with friends of different races and carefully selects locations according to the ethnic background of the people she meets. The reasons she gives for her choices are that she does not want non-Black people to feel uncomfortable in an all-Black crowd and that she is rather willing to be the outsider instead (cf. ll. 37–41).

conclusion: call for more interaction

Especially in the light of her own experiences, her final conclusion becomes understandable: change must come from the individual level and "trickle down" (l. 46) to state institutions. In other words, Reniqua Allen believes that political and legal guidelines are only theory as long as they are not based on real-life, multiracially shared experience. By including examples from her own life and her own mistakes, Reniqua Allen makes her article an appeal to herself and others to be that driving force for change.

3 **TIPP**

In this task, you are free to express your own ideas as to the subject of ongoing racial segregation. However, you should pay attention to the characteristics of a comment entry, which you are supposed to write. Therefore, you should clearly refer to Reniqua Allen's point of view by agreeing with her, by opposing some of her arguments and by making further suggestions etc.
Possible arguments:
- agreeing with Allen on the progress achieved through the Civil Rights Movement, but also on the de facto ongoing segregation and inequality
- approving of her point that segregation is mainly happening in people's minds
- however, to change that, politics and especially the media have the responsibility to present positive role models
- subconscious prejudices have to be broken down
- tightrope act between affirmative action and discrimination

points of agreement: progress through Civil Rights Movement

First of all, thank you very much, Ms Allen, for your enlightening article. I would say that I wholeheartedly agree on most points. As you correctly point out, segregation should be a thing of the past by now. The Civil Rights Movement has achieved so much and legally there is no reason why people of different skin color should still lead "separate, but equal" lives. Discrimination has been outlawed, we even elected an African American as President of our country and yet it would be too simplistic to interpret all these positive developments as ending inequality.

inequality still persists

Statistics speak a different language and it simply cannot be denied that there still is blatant inequality between Black and White when it comes to wealth, education, housing, the criminal justice system etc. And if no discriminatory laws can be blamed for these conditions, as was the case in the 1960s, what or who is to blame?

necessity to overcome barriers in the mind

Once more, I wholeheartedly agree with you that it is not enough to point an accusing finger at others, while in our own minds we all continue to categorise people according to their skin color, their religion, their sexual orientation or what have you. So, we have to break down those boundaries in our minds in order to effect the real change in our society that is overdue.

As to how to break down these boundaries, I slightly disagree with your opinion, however. You wrote that people interacting with people from other ethnic backgrounds in a natural and "color-blind" way would influence larger political decisions. In an ideal world I would agree, but in an ideal world, people would not even have to write articles like yours to bring the ongoing prejudices to the world's attention. The differences between various social and ethnic groups would not even be noticed and people would not categorise establishments as either "Black" or "White".

points of disagreement: idea of colourblindness too idealistic

Unfortunately, however, we do not live in an ideal world. That is why I think politics and especially the media have a duty to act as positive role models for the society at large. In my opinion, it will not work the other way round. Of course, I admit that strategies like affirmative action, racial quotas or politically correct discourse are often tightrope acts because they might lead to an even more strained atmosphere between different social or ethnic groups. Yet, I think they are necessary in order to overcome our subconscious fears of what is unknown and foreign.

politics and media must be agents of change

All in all, I believe that only by giving people time, by facilitating multiracial encounters and especially by constantly showing them as something positive can the segregation in our minds be overcome. Through your article, you have made the first important step in the right direction by addressing the problem and facing reality instead of pretending that an ideal world with no differences has already arrived.

conclusion

Textaufgabe: Übungsaufgabe 4

Niedersachsen Englisch

Aufgabenstellung

1 State why the author claims that Shakespeare does not belong in the classroom.

2 Analyse the way the author uses argumentative techniques and language to persuade the readers of his view.

3 You have been invited to take part in an international workshop on Shakespeare's plays. Your task is to write an essay evaluating Powell's view that "most of the kids have no concept of the vitality of [Shakespeare's] youth" (ll. 8/9). Refer to materials studied in class, such as the play *Hamlet*.

Text **Kill Bill: Why We Must Take Shakespeare out of the Classroom**

Shakespeare wrote to put money in his pocket, food on the table and fire in the bellies of his audiences, not strike modern teenagers with fear. Most of Shakespeare's audiences were illiterate. His words were chosen to be spoken or heard, not to be read and deadened behind a desk – they wither when performance is removed.

Our schools are full of Shakespeare, but often in completely the wrong places. Old uncle Bill has become the relative that we invite to family gatherings out of habit, not because we actually want to. He sits there in the corner sharing his stories with anyone who'll listen; the adults lend a patient ear out of a sense of duty and most of the kids have no concept of the vitality of his youth.

Even before, and most definitely since, the recent <u>plummet</u> in drama's status as a specialist subject in schools, many young people's first experience of Shakespeare is in an English classroom taught by enthusiastic purveyors of imagination, but primarily non-theatre practitioners. It's an English teacher's remit to analyse language, but pick apart every word of Shakespeare and you've dissected the butterfly – pretty in parts but a nonsensical whole and certainly unable to fly.

A well-meaning English teacher can take a student through the meaning of every word in a sentence and it soon becomes a drawn out and confusing process. Shakespeare's audience didn't know the meaning of every word uttered (uncle Bill was busily making new ones up) but the sounds and pictures they created kept viewers enthralled for hours.

English teachers agree that Shakespeare's language isn't intended to be desk-bound; it's crafted for stage. Simple. Well, not so simple these days. Recent governments have decreed that Shakespeare is so key to our national identity and intelligence that he should be studied by all the children in a specific year group. Great, you might say, but it's not.

Over the past few years I've welcomed fewer and fewer school groups to our theatre. The planning and paperwork involved is prohibitive. Consider as well the amount of staff needed to accompany such a group and the knock-on cost of cover needed back at school. Don't forget the travel time to get to a theatre for what is often a three hour show, plus travel time back. Trips can rarely happen in a school day because of other "core" subjects missed, and teachers can't be relied upon to give up their evenings to deliver what has become a luxury.

If a teacher does manage to get kids to a theatre for a rare visit, it's not always useful. Students who are inexperienced theatregoers think that a particular director's version is how Shakespeare intended his play to be done, when actually the personal interpretations can be brave, boring or bad enough to put a child off theatre for life. So, a teacher keeps the class in school and tries hard to explain the play.

Teachers are supposed to have all the answers, but dramatic literature is a playground of opinions: why does Juliet say this? Why would Macbeth do that? The real answer is that we don't know, but teachers are not encouraged to say just that: "I don't know." Their own suppositions are often reported back in essays as facts. Plays aren't meant to be taught like this. They are meant to be explored on their feet. Actors and audiences are supposed to argue over meaning, finding multiple ways of delivering word and deed.

Our BTEC acting course has just started work on *The Tempest*. These are engaged, talented young people from a range of secondary schools who auditioned to be on the course, but the majority expressed disdain, dislike and hatred for poor uncle Bill. They had all experienced him separately in schools, behind desks. Shakespeare had made them feel stupid rather than empowered.

Let's give English teachers a break, give drama teachers a boost and give young people an important sense of equality. You don't need an expensive education to understand the words, but you do need the luxury of time, space and specialism to put his words on their feet and try them out.

Powell, Mark: "Kill Bill: why we must take Shakespeare out of the classroom." In: The Guardian, *Copyright Guardian News & Media Ltd 2018*

Annotations

10 plummet: Since 2012 various decisions in educational policy have severely decreased the status of drama as school subject.

45 BTEC (Business and Technology Education Council): it provides secondary school leaving qualifications and further education qualifications

Lösungsvorschlag

1 **TIPP**

Here you are meant to report the reasons the author gives for not dealing with Shakespeare in the usual school context.

- Shakespeare's plays are to be seen and heard but not to be read
- it has become more difficult to take school groups to the theatre for organisational reasons
- it is more of a duty than a real desire to study and teach Shakespeare
- decisions in educational policy have decreased the importance of drama as a school subject
- teachers analyse Shakespeare's words, which deprives the plays of their entertainment and may even lead to confusion
- teachers are believed to know how to interpret Shakespeare's plays but that is not true because there is no one truth about them, their meaning needs to be discussed
- dealing with Shakespeare in class makes students feel ignorant

introduction: reference to source, topic

In his article "Kill Bill: Why We Must Take Shakespeare out of the Classroom" published in *The Guardian*, Mark Powell argues that Shakespeare's plays should no longer be taught in school.

main part: reasons

The most important reason he gives is that these plays are not to be read but to be seen and heard in a theatre. This, however, is becoming more and more difficult as the regulations for taking school groups to the theatre are getting stricter and stricter according to the author. Moreover, he complains that decisions in educational policy have decreased the importance of drama as a school subject in its own right.

Furthermore, Powell holds the view that Shakespeare is taught more out of a sense of duty than a real desire to deal with the playwright. He adds that English teachers tend to analyse Shakespeare's words and thus deprive his plays of their entertainment. Actually he claims that this approach to Shakespeare makes it more difficult for students to understand the text and thus leads to even more confusion.

Finally, teachers are believed to know how to interpret Shakespeare's plays. As a result, the plays' meaning or, even better, meanings are not discussed but students just convey their teachers' understanding of the plays in their papers. Consequently, Powell's experience shows that students hate Shakespeare because he makes them feel ignorant.

So, Powell argues that plays should not be taught by English teachers but by drama teachers, who teach their students how to stage Shakespeare's plays.

2 **TIPP**

In this task you need to analyse how the author tries to persuade the readers of his view that Shakespeare should be removed from the classroom. You are meant to focus on argumentative techniques such as stating facts and displaying authoritative knowledge as well as on language, for example figurative speech, allegory, imperatives and contrasts. Make sure to not just describe what you find in the text but also to interpret how it affects the readers.

- argumentative techniques: Powell bases arguments on …
  - historical facts (cf. ll. 1–4) → stresses differences between Elizabethan age and the present
  - authoritative knowledge → refers to recent decisions in educational policy (cf. ll. 10/11, 22–25); explains why fewer and fewer classes go to the theatre (ll. 26–32)
  - personal experience (ll. 45–49) → students want to put Shakespeare on stage even though most of them learned to hate him at school

  Powell anticipates the readers' reaction and contradicts (cf. ll. 24/25) → refutes counterarguments
- Language (examples): Powell uses …
  - numerous contrasts to underline the difference between Shakespeare's plays as they were intended and received in the Elizabethan age and today (cf. e. g. ll. 1–4, 21/22)
  - figurative speech:
    - his plays "wither" (l. 4) like flowers without water if they are not performed → stresses importance of seeing the plays in a theatre
    - analysing Shakespeare is like "dissect[ing] the butterfly" (l. 14) → easier for the reader to imagine the detailed approach that is taken to deal with Shakespeare; also implies that the butterfly is dead; imagination can't fly
    - students have to explore Shakespeare "on their feet" (ll. 42, 53) → stresses importance of drama teachers
    - allegory (ll. 5–9) → the reader can easily imagine the situation described
  - imperatives / parallelism / enumeration in ll. 50–53 to underline the demand to have drama teachers teach Shakespeare and not English teachers
  - an enumeration of reasons why less and less school groups come to the theatre (cf. ll. 27–32) → it is virtually impossible to take students to the theatre
  - alliteration, enumeration (l. 36) → if one manages to take students to a play, it might even be a poor performance
  - enumeration ("disdain, dislike and hatred", l. 47) → studying Shakespeare in school makes students hate the bard
  - contrast ("stupid rather than empowered", l. 49) → Shakespeare makes them feel ignorant

introduction:
thesis / reference to assignment

The author stresses his view that Shakespeare should be removed from the classroom by employing different argumentative techniques which are supported by stylistic devices such as contrasts, figurative speech, allegory and imperatives.

main part:

argumentative technique
→ reference to historical facts

language
→ contrasts

Throughout the whole text Powell emphasises that Shakespeare cannot be taught without acting his plays out, or at least seeing them in a theatre. To prove this assertion, he describes what Shakespeare intended to achieve with his plays when he wrote them 450 years ago, namely to "put […] fire in the bellies of his audiences, not strike modern teenagers with fear" (ll. 1/2). The contrast underlines the counter-productive effect Shakespeare's plays have when taught inside today's classrooms. Further contrasts which stress that the plays belong on stage can be found for example in lines 3/4 and 21/22.

language
→ figurative speech

The author also claims that Shakespeare's plays are dead if their language is analysed and they are not put "on their feet" (l. 42). When he makes this point, he uses figurative speech. For instance, he employs the verb "wither" (l. 4) to describe what happens to the words "when performance is removed" (l. 4) and compares the analysis of the plays' language to "dissect[ing] the butterfly – pretty in parts but a nonsensical whole and certainly unable to fly" (ll. 14/15). The comparison to the butterfly allows the readers to vividly imagine the detailed approach that is taken when dealing with Shakespeare in the English classroom. Furthermore, most people probably would not want to dissect a butterfly as the beauty of the creature is slowly destroyed leaving but parts of a dead body. So it can be deduced that they would not want to analyse Shakespeare word by word either.

→ enumeration, contrast

Powell uses different stylistic devices to stress the effect this approach has on the students. He employs an enumeration to show that students are left feeling "disdain, dislike and hatred" (l. 47) for the poet. Using a contrast he points out that dealing with Shakespeare's plays makes students "feel stupid rather than empowered" (l. 49). Thus, it seems entirely counterproductive to teach Shakespeare at school.

→ allegory

Additionally, the author argues that Shakespeare is only dealt with out of tradition and not out of enthusiasm. To stress this argument Powell employs an allegory in which he calls Shakespeare "[o]ld uncle Bill" (ll. 5/6) and compares him to a relative who we invite "out of habit, not because we actually want to" (ll. 6/7). The reader can easily relate to this situation as it is a typical experience many families share.

Powell argues that the situation gets worse due to recent decisions in educational policy. Dealing with Shakespeare has become obligatory for students "in a specific year group" (l. 24). Powell assumes that many readers might agree with that decision and therefore he anticipates what readers might think and contradicts. "Great, you might say, but it's not" (ll. 24/25). Thus, he can refute possible counter-arguments. The problem he perceives is that the status of drama as a subject in its own right has decreased. The word "plummet" (l. 10) emphasises the seriousness of the situation. To make things worse it also becomes harder and harder for teachers to take their students to a theatre because of the "planning and paperwork involved", which he calls "prohibitive" (l. 27). The adjective stresses the hopelessness of the situation. Furthermore, Powell lists numerous other reasons why less and less students come to the theatre (cf. ll. 26–32). On the rare occasion that a group attends a performance, they even risk seeing a poor one. Here Powell uses an enumeration and alliteration to make his point ("brave, boring or bad", l. 36). The readers readily believe the author as he has first-hand experience (cf. ll. 26–32) and therefore radiates authority. Increasing the importance of Shakespeare for the national curriculum while at the same time weakening drama as a subject in its own right, does not seem to make much sense.

argumentative technique

anticipates readers' reaction, refutes counter-arguments

language
→ choice of words

lists reasons

→ enumeration, alliteration

argumentative technique
→ radiates authority

Finally, the author uses imperatives (cf. l. 50) and an enumeration (cf. l. 52) to summarise his demands in a nutshell. As he does so in the last paragraph of his comment, the readers can easily keep his demands in mind.

language
→ imperatives, enumeration

To sum it up, Powell uses the historical perspective, a humorous allegory and his personal experience to support his most important argument for taking Shakespeare out of the classroom: the fact that a play without performance is pointless.

conclusion

3 **TIPP**

Choose a suitable heading for your essay. You should start your evaluation by explaining the meaning of the given quotation. Afterwards you need to balance the pros and cons to finally form your own opinion.

- explanation: young people do not understand that Shakespeare's plays are still relevant
- pros:
  - their language is outdated
  - Shakespeare made up new words, which may be difficult to understand
  - characters and their values are old-fashioned (e. g. role of women)
- cons:
  - performing scenes themselves allows students to step into the shoes of the characters and better relate to their situation
  - discussing complex philosophical and moral questions can be very engaging for students
  - watching modern film or theatre adaptations (e. g. Michael Almereyda's film version of *Hamlet*, set in present-day New York City) invites students to draw parallels between Shakespeare's world and our own
- conclusion: young people do recognise the relevance of Shakespeare's plays if the works are dealt with in an interesting way

Shakespeare – Our Contemporary? **heading**

introduction: explanation of quote

In an article for *The Guardian*, the author Mark Powell claims that young people today fail to see that Shakespeare's plays are still relevant. According to him, they are bored by the plays because they do not grasp the energy and enthusiasm that is inherent in them. Whereas it is certainly true that it is difficult to fill young people with enthusiasm for Shakespeare, it is not impossible.

main part: pros outdated language

The major reason why it is hard for young people to accept that Shakespeare's plays are still relevant is probably their language. These plays were written about 450 years ago in Elizabethan English and many of their words are outdated like "thee" and "thou". Also, Shakespeare made up many words, some of which have become part of everyday language but sometimes their meaning is difficult to grasp. Therefore, this language is hard to understand for British teenagers and all the more so for students who learn English as a second language. They need to decode the meaning of Shakespeare's words, which often means hard work, before they can grasp the ideas he wants to convey.

outdated role models

Some of his characters and their values also seem old-fashioned. In particular, the role of women has changed considerably. These days they usually are not dominated by their father or husband.

However, in my experience, a lot of students do recognise the relevance of Shakespeare's works if the plays are dealt with in an engaging way. Even a very long and complex play such as *Hamlet* can fascinate young people if the scenes are not just read in silence and "dissected" in class, but if the students are made to perform some of the scenes themselves, for example. This can make it easier to step into the shoes of the characters and relate to their experiences. The particular situation Hamlet is in – the question if and how to seek revenge for his father's murder – may be quite removed from the everyday realities of most teenagers. His self-doubt and the feeling of being overwhelmed by conflicting emotions and therefore finding himself unable to act, however, is something quite a few young people can relate to, at least to a certain extent. Moreover, young people's curiosity to deal even with complex philosophical and moral questions, such as whether "to be or not to be", should not be underestimated. Like Hamlet, they might have wondered what compromises they need to make to live a life worth living. They might have been in situations where they were worrying and thinking critically about something but did not really dare to act. If students are invited to bring their own perspectives and interpretations to the play, dealing with Shakespeare in the classroom becomes a very stimulating experience.

cons

activities that allow students to relate to Shakespeare's ideas → reference to *Hamlet*

Watching film or theatre adaptations can be another good means to give students an understanding of the modernity of Shakespeare's plays. Michael Almereyda's film version of *Hamlet* (starring Ethan Hawke), for example, is set in the present but still uses Shakespeare's words. The action takes place in New York City (rather than the Danish court) and Claudius does not inherit the crown, but a big company named Denmark Corporation. Comparing this version to the original play and discussing in how far this "translation" of the plot into contemporary times is convincing invites young people to look for parallels between Shakespeare's world and our own.

use of modern film versions (to show parallels to students' reality)

All in all, I believe that it is not generally true that young people have no concept of Shakespeare's vitality. A lot of students will readily accept the relevance of his plays if the works are dealt with in an interesting way – be it by performing scenes themselves, by discussing philosophical questions in class and relating them to their own experience, or by watching or comparing film adaptations.

conclusion

PRÜFUNGSAUFGABEN

HÖRVERSTEHEN

You will hear each recording twice. After each listening you will have time to complete your answers.

Task 1: The situation in the labor market (1 BE)

Hinweis: Aus lizenzrechtlichen Gründen wurden der in der Original-Prüfung verwendete Hörtext und die zugehörige Aufgabe durch einen ähnlichen Text / eine Aufgabe im Stil der Prüfung ersetzt.

Listen to the introduction of a report about the US labor market. While listening, tick (✓) the correct answer (a, b, c, or d). There is only one correct answer.

The report is about

a ☐ a large number of people looking for work.
b ☐ a shortage of university graduates.
c ☐ a lack of applicants with suitable qualifications.
d ☐ the problem of joblessness among young Americans.

Task 2: Economic mobility – the opportunity to move to a higher social class (16 BE)

Listen to a radio report about a research project on the economic mobility of young British and American citizens. While listening, fill in the missing information. You do not need to write complete sentences.

Introduction to the research project		
1	**One** surprising result of the research	
2	**One** question to be answered by the research	
Research procedure		
3	Pairs of people chosen	

4	Time span covered	
5	**One** source used	
6	Characteristic feature of persons chosen	
Research findings on economic mobility		
7	US: 19th century	
8	UK: 19th century	
9	After World War II	
10	UK: 1970s	
Explanations for the research results		
11	Economic development in the US a) 19th century b) 20th century	 a) b)
US and UK in the 1930s and 1940s		
12	How Americans saw them-selves and their society	
13	How the British saw themselves and their society	
14	Focus of American social policies	
15	Focus of British social policies	

Task 3: California's Central Valley

(7 BE)

Listen to a radio report about California's Central Valley. While listening, tick (✓) the correct answer (a, b, c, or d). There is only one correct answer.

1 The US president is visiting the region to talk about

- **a** ☐ a threatening food shortage.
- **b** ☐ climate change.
- **c** ☐ environmental pollution.
- **d** ☐ financial support.

2 The region is well-known for its

- **a** ☐ agricultural products.
- **b** ☐ energy policy.
- **c** ☐ environmental problems.
- **d** ☐ social programs.

3 Weather conditions force farmers to

- **a** ☐ dismiss laborers.
- **b** ☐ leave their land unused.
- **c** ☐ move away.
- **d** ☐ plant different crops.

4 The fight over water in California is

- **a** ☐ a long-standing problem.
- **b** ☐ of international interest.
- **c** ☐ about to be settled.
- **d** ☐ dividing communities.

5 The protest is about giving water to

- **a** ☐ city populations.
- **b** ☐ farm animals.
- **c** ☐ food production.
- **d** ☐ nature conservation.

6 Republicans want to

- **a** ☐ put food producers first.
- **b** ☐ invest more money.
- **c** ☐ protect endangered species.
- **d** ☐ wait and see.

7 Democrats want to

a ☐ only back environmentalists.
b ☐ fight climate change.
c ☐ find a workable solution.
d ☐ primarily support farmers.

Task 4: A conflict (7 BE)

Hinweis: Der Hörtext kann aus rechtlichen Gründen nicht abgedruckt werden und ist nicht in der MP3-Datei auf MyStark enthalten. Eine ungekürzte Fassung der Unterhaltung ist bei BBC unter folgendem Link abrufbar:
https://www.bbc.co.uk/programmes/p0239tql
Für die Bearbeitung von Task 4 sind die Minuten 00:00 – 01:38 relevant.

Listen to the following conversation between a mother and her child.
While listening, fill in the table below. You do not need to write complete sentences.

Topic they talk about		
Speakers	**Mother**	**Child**
Reasons the speakers use to support their position (3 for each speaker)		

SPRACHMITTLUNG

Aufgabenstellung

You are taking part in an international school project about current social trends. Based on the two texts below write an article for the project website in which you explain how and why more and more Germans have changed their consumer behaviour.

Text 1 Simon Frost, „Tausch dich glücklich“ (2013)

Wohin mit dem alten Toaster, wo der neue doch so viel schicker ist? Oder mit dem Schrank, der zwar noch völlig in Ordnung ist, aber einfach nicht in die neue Wohnung passt? Mit dem Internet lassen sich solche Fragen beantworten, ohne dass Toaster oder Schrank auf dem Müll landen müssen. Eine Möglichkeit sind Tauschplattformen. […]

Zusammen kommen die größten Anbieter auf einige hunderttausend registrierte Mitglieder. Eine Motivation fürs Tauschen ist der spielerische Charakter: Mal sehen, wer mir meinen alten Kühlschrank abnimmt und was er mir dafür bietet. Das macht Spaß, aber nur bis zu einem gewissen Punkt. „Wir denken automatisch, dass Dinge, die uns gehören, mehr wert sind als die anderer Menschen“, erläutert Häusel. Bei materiellen Dingen, besonders wenn es sich um Liebhaberstücke handelt, fällt einfaches Tauschen – deins gegen meins – deshalb schwerer: weil die Frage nach dem Gegenwert mehr Gewicht bekommt. Bei immateriellen Dingen wie etwa Musik- oder Videodateien und beim Tausch gleicher Gegenstände – etwa Buch gegen Buch – gibt es diese Schwierigkeiten eher nicht.

Den Machern der Tauschbörsen ist das Problem durchaus bekannt. Deshalb umgehen oder ergänzen die meisten das Eins-zu-eins-Tauschen mithilfe eines Punktesystems. Wer ein Buch anbietet, bekommt beispielsweise einen Punkt. Für einen Küchenschrank gibt es 75 Punkte. So schaffen die Marktplätze Ersatzwährungen oder teilweise auch Gutscheine, die sie in Anlehnung an ihren Firmennamen Flips, Swapy-Taler oder Tickets nennen. […]

Neben dem spielerischen Charakter und dem kapitalismuskritischen Ansatz hat für manche Tauscher auch der Umweltschutzaspekt eine große Bedeutung. Produkte, die man selbst nicht mehr braucht, könnten für andere durchaus nützlich sein. Auf diese Weise bleiben sie im Produktkreislauf und landen nicht auf einer Müllkippe, denn sie sind eigentlich ja noch voll funktionsfähig. Auf solche umweltorientierten Kunden zielt beispielsweise Netcycler. Das finnische Unternehmen hat neben den üblichen Marktplatzfunktionen des Tauschens und Schenkens auch Spendenmöglichkeiten in sein Angebot integriert. So können die Nutzer bei ihren Geschäften gleich noch Kleinbeträge zum Beispiel an Naturschützer oder Regenwaldretter spenden. *312 Wörter*

Quelle: Frost, Simon: Tausch dich glücklich. Der Tagesspiegel. *06. 05. 2013.*

Anmerkung

9 Hans-Georg Häusel: ein Marktforscher

Text 2 Haiko Prengel, „Repair Cafés: Basteln gegen die Wegwerfgesellschaft“ (2013)

Der Widerstand gegen die Wegwerfgesellschaft trifft sich in einem dunklen Hinterhof in Berlin-Kreuzberg. Dichtes Gedränge herrscht hier, auf den Tischen liegen Elektrogeräte. Es wird über Schaltkreise und Billig-Technik gefachsimpelt. Dazu gibt es Kaffee und Kuchen.

Angela hat ihren kaputten CD-Spieler mitgebracht. 20 Jahre sei das Gerät alt, nun gab es den Geist auf. „Aber ich will, dass es wieder geht“, sagt die 53-Jährige trotzig wie ein Kind. Mechaniker Mike ist ganz angetan von dem alten Discman: „Das ist ja ein schönes Teil. Kriegen wir auch wieder hin“, versichert er und greift zum Werkzeugkasten.

Mike ist Entwicklungsingenieur. Heute arbeitet er als ehrenamtlicher Mechaniker im Kreuzberger Repair Café. „Wegwerfen? Denkste!“ – unter diesem Motto kommen in Deutschland immer mehr Menschen zusammen, um gemeinsam ihre defekten Gebrauchsgegenstände zu reparieren. Die Repair-Bewegung könnte ein Trend werden, allein in Berlin eröffneten seit Jahresbeginn vier dieser Anlaufstellen zur Vermeidung von Elektroschrott. Aber Repair Cafés gibt es auch in vielen anderen Städten.

Idee der Repair-Bewegung sei es, Abfall zu vermeiden und der Konsumgesellschaft etwas entgegenzusetzen, sagt Elisa Garrote. Die 36-Jährige organisiert das Kreuzberger Repair Café. Anfang 2013 wurde das Café vom Verein *Kunst-Stoffe – Zentralstelle für wiederverwendbare Materialien* gegründet, und vor kurzem gewann es den Berliner Umweltpreis des BUND.

Es sei doch so, erklärt Garrote: Elektrogeräte gebe es heute in jedem Haushalt. Aber die Leute trauten sich nicht mehr, Dinge selbst zu reparieren oder ihre Mitmenschen um Hilfe zu fragen. Stattdessen landeten die Geräte beim kleinsten Defekt auf dem Müll. „Die Reparatur-Kultur ist fast tot“, meint Garrote.

Angela hätte sich auch von ihrem CD-Player trennen und sich einen MP3-Player kaufen können. Aber das lehnt sie ab: „Ich bin immer auf der Suche nach Dingen, die man wiederverwerten kann“, sagt die Kreuzbergerin. „Nicht um Geld zu sparen, sondern aus Prinzip.“

Mechaniker Mike hat inzwischen entdeckt, was das Problem von Angelas defektem CD-Spieler ist. „Es ist was mit der Spannung“, sagt er. Das Netzteil des Geräts sei wohl kaputt. Oder es sei ein läppischer Kabelbruch: Nichts, was sich nicht reparieren lasse.

334 Wörter

Quelle: Prengel, Haiko, dpa. Repair Cafés: Basteln gegen die Wegwerfgesellschaft. https://www.heise.de/newsticker/meldung/Repair-Cafes-Basteln-gegen-die-Wegwerfgesellschaft-2062573.html. 09. 12. 2013.

Anmerkung

20 BUND: Bund für Umwelt und Naturschutz Deutschland

TEXTAUFGABE

Von den zwei Aufgaben ist eine auszuwählen und zu bearbeiten.

Aufgabe I: Aufgabenstellung

1 Outline what DeGrazia says about Detroit and the American Dream. (30 %)

2 Analyze the means the author uses to convince the reader of his position. (30 %)

3 You are taking part in the international youth project "Aspects of Life and Culture in the US." For the project website, write an article in which you discuss whether the concept of the American Dream is a recipe for success. Refer to DeGrazia's article and to materials dealt with in class. (40 %)

Text I Emilio DeGrazia, "Our American Nightmare: Detroit" (2013)

Detroit used to be one of America's richest cities, but on July 18, 2013, it filed for bankruptcy. In an online article Emilio DeGrazia comments on Detroit and the American Dream. At the beginning of his article he uses a quote from a book called Detroit: An American Autopsy *by Charlie LeDuff.*

"Once the nation's richest big city, Detroit is now its poorest. It is the country's illiteracy and dropout capital, where children must leave their books at school and bring toilet paper from home … there are firemen with no boots, cops with no cars, teachers with no pencils, city council members with telephones tapped by the FBI, and too many grandmothers with no tears left to give." […]

So how did Detroit go so wrong so fast? Why did entire neighborhoods collapse? Why did people trash and burn their own groceries, houses and neighborhoods? Why would a city commit suicide? […]

I'll risk being denounced as anti-American here by suggesting that the American Dream has a tragic flaw that has made a nightmare of Detroit. Central to this American Dream narrative we are routinely fed at school, at work, and through the media is that America is the land of boundless opportunity. We keep repeating the myth that everyone can succeed here if they work hard enough. That they can do it on their own. That losers are losers because they're little engines that didn't try hard enough.

Tell that silly tale to a single mother with three kids and no money to pay the rent or heat. Tell it to an unemployed father whose unemployed son wanders the streets, angry and depressed. Tell it to the teenaged girls who refuse to go to school because they're afraid of what might happen there. Tell it to the thousands of Detroiters who don't go to doctors because they have no health insurance, and often no doctor willing to spend ten minutes with them.

Tell them with a straight face that they'll succeed if they try harder, without asking for help. Convince them they won't be shamed by asking for help.

That we all should be hard-working little engines is a nice idea, necessary for teachers and parents to repeat as they try to inspire individuals to live up to their potential, and also useful to successful types who feel a need to congratulate themselves. But it is not a credible groundwork for public discourse or public policy. At the core of the American Dream narrative is its tragic flaw, a cancerous radical individualism that expresses itself politically on both the right and left, especially among libertarians. The cancer lurks in one of our favorite words – "freedom" – repeated like a meaningless mantra, drearily by preachers and politicians. The American Dream fiction claims that an individual alone is responsible for his or her fate, and that the individual is "free to choose" this fate. An individual's failure, a whole city's failure, is not to be explained in terms of a failing economy, or Wall Street greed, or mismanagement of its major industries, or corrupt politicians, or drug users outside Detroit's city limits who enable those trapped inside to participate in the city's alternative and illegal economy. And certainly nobody wants to hear anyone explain Detroit's problems in terms of race. If black Detroiters fail, it's all their own fault, and they're just playing out their victim roles when they ask for help. If they can't succeed at the American Dream, they're not good enough. Why don't they leave us alone? Why don't they just go away?

The American Dream fiction, like the steady diet of melodramas we're routinely fed by Hollywood, has good guys and bad. The moral of this simplistic story is that those who make it are good, and those who don't are bad and deserve to lose. What's wrong with them?

It's this flawed narrative, widespread and profound in the many who live outside our Detroits, and invoked by those who do great damage from outside, that makes victims of so many Detroiters. What we as outsiders don't see is that we're victims too of the American Dream story we routinely tell ourselves. *641 words*

From: Emilio DeGrazia, "Our American Nightmare: Detroit", in: Twin Cities: Daily Planet, *11. April 2013. http://www.tcdailyplanet.net/our-american-nightmare-detroit/ (Zugriff: 19. 10. 16)*

Annotations

Introduction to file for bankruptcy: to ask to be declared officially bankrupt
9 to denounce sb.: to criticize strongly
11 narrative: *here:* myth
21 with a straight face: seriously, not joking
26 public discourse: discussion of political and social issues
28 libertarian: a person who believes in absolute freedom of the individual
29 to lurk: to wait in secret
41 simplistic: too simple
45 Detroits: the plural of Detroit is used as a symbol to refer to all American cities with similar problems
45 to invoke: *here:* to repeat constantly

Aufgabe II: Aufgabenstellung

1 Outline the conflict in the Petersen family. (30 %)

2 Compare this conflict with the conflicts depicted in *Billy Elliot* and "My Son the Fanatic". (30 %)

3 You are taking part in the international school project "Young People and Their Dreams." Your contribution is an article for the project website. Write the article in which you discuss whether young people should follow their dreams regardless of what their parents say. (40 %)

Text II Excerpt from David Nicholls, *Us* (2014)

The first-person narrator, Douglas Petersen, is a scientist. His wife Connie is an artist. Their seventeen-year-old son Albie has started experimenting with photography.

[Albie]'s a mumbler, a swallower of words. Despite spending the last six years in a perfectly nice part of Berkshire, he speaks in a bored Cockney drawl because God forbid anyone should think his father has done well or worked hard, God forbid anyone should think that he's comfortable and cared for and loved, loved equally by both of his parents even if he only seems to desire and require the attentions of one.

In short, my son makes me feel like his step-father.

I have had some experience of unrequited love in the past and that was no picnic, I can tell you. But the unrequited love of one's only living offspring has its own particular slow acid burn.

[…]

Albie announced his intention to devote his life to a hobby. Why, I asked Connie, could he not study a more practical subject and do the things he enjoyed at weekends and in the evenings, like the rest of us? Because that's not how an arts-based course works, said Connie; he needs to be challenged, to develop his famous 'eye', learn to use his tools. But wouldn't it be cheaper and quicker to just read the manual? I could understand if people still used darkrooms as I had as a young man, but all of that know-how was obsolete, and how could Albie hope to excel in a field where anyone with a phone and a laptop could be broadly proficient? It wasn't even as if he wanted to be a photojournalist or a commercial photographer, taking pictures for newspapers or advertisements or catalogues. He didn't want to photograph models or weddings, athletes, or lions chasing gazelles, photographs that people might pay for, he wanted to be an *artist*, to photograph burnt-out cars and bark, taking pictures at such angles that they didn't look like anything at all. What would he actually *do* for three years, apart from smoke and sleep? And what professional job could he hope for at the end of it?

'Photographer!' said Connie. 'He's going to be a photographer.'

We were pacing around the kitchen, furiously tidying up, by which I mean tidying up, furious. Wine had been drunk and it was late, the end of a long, fraught argument that, as was his way, Albie had provoked then fled from. 'Don't you see?' said Connie, hurling cutlery at the drawer. 'Even if it's hard, he has to try! If he loves it, we have to let him try. Why must you always have to stomp on his dreams?'

'I've got nothing against his dreams as long as they're attainable.'

'But if they're attainable then they're not dreams!'

'And that's why it's a waste of time!' I said. 'The problem with telling people that they can do anything they want to do is that it is objectively, factually inaccurate. Otherwise the whole world would just be ballet dancers and pop stars.'

'He doesn't want to be a pop star, he wants to take photographs.'

'My point still stands. It is simply not true that you can achieve anything if you love it enough – it just isn't. Life has limitations and the sooner he faces up to this fact then the better off he'll be!'

Well, that's what I said. I believed I had my son's best interests at heart. That was why I was so <u>*vocal,*</u> because I wanted him to have a secure professional life, a good life. Listening up in his bedroom, no doubt he had caught all of my words and none of my intention.

Still, the argument was not my finest moment. I had become shrill and dogmatic but even so I was surprised to discover that Connie was now standing still, wrist pressed to her forehead.

'When did it start, Douglas?' she said, her voice low. 'When did you start to drain the *passion* out of everything?' *646 words*

From: David Nicholls, Us *(2014, London: Hodder & Stoughton, 2015), pp. 49–53.*

Annotations

2 Cockney drawl: East London working-class accent
14 to develop one's eye: *here:* to develop a sense for the perfect photo
27 fraught: showing or producing tension or anxiety
41 vocal: outspoken

Lösungsvorschlag

HÖRVERSTEHEN

Transkript 1 The situation in the labor market

Hinweis: Aus lizenzrechtlichen Gründen wurden der in der Original-Prüfung verwendete Hörtext und die zugehörige Aufgabe durch einen ähnlichen Text / eine Aufgabe im Stil der Prüfung ersetzt.

The US labor market is currently facing a dilemma. While millions of people are unemployed, a lot of companies are having difficulties finding enough workers with the right skills. Most of the jobs that remain vacant are in so-called middle skills areas – work that requires technical understanding and on-the-job experience, but not necessarily a college degree. Labor market experts have been analyzing the reasons for the so-called "skills gap" and are now cooperating with representatives from the economic and educational sector to find solutions to this problem.

TIPP

This text passage will help you find the correct answer:
"a lot of companies are having difficulties finding enough workers with the right skills." (ll. 2/3)

The report is about

- **a** ☐ a large number of people looking for work.
- **b** ☐ a shortage of university graduates.
- **c** ☑ a lack of applicants with suitable qualifications.
- **d** ☐ the problem of joblessness among young Americans.

Transkript 2 Economic mobility – the opportunity to move to a higher social class

Hinweis: Aus lizenzrechtlichen Gründen ist die ungekürzte Original-Passage der NPR Sendung abgedruckt. Die in der Abituraufgabe nicht berücksichtigten Passagen sind durch eine kleinere Schriftgröße kenntlich gemacht und für die Bearbeitung der Aufgaben nicht relevant.

AUDIE CORNISH, *Host*: Imagine you were talking to two young men, both clearly smart and ambitious and both from working class families. Let's say one was American and the other was British. Who do you think has a better shot at moving up, out of a blue collar background? Surprisingly, we might need to start talking about the British Dream instead of the American Dream.

A fascinating academic study suggests that economic mobility has been increasing, quite dramatically, in the U.K., just as it's been shrinking in the U.S.

Adam Davidson, with NPR's Planet Money team, has been reading the paper and joins us now. So, Adam, explain this for us.

ADAM DAVIDSON, *Byline*: First off, I want to give credit to Jason Long at Wheaton College and Joseph Petrie at Northwestern. They did a huge amount of work for this. They wanted to ask a very simple question. We have this idea in America that you can have whatever economic destiny you want. But they wanted to see is that true. To what extent does your own economic future depend on what your parents did for a living?

So they found over 10,000 pairs of fathers and sons in the U.S. and the U.K., over the last 150 years, and they followed them to see to what extent do sons do what their fathers did, and to what extent do sons do something different.

CORNISH: Ten thousand, I mean, how do you follow that many people through their lives?

DAVIDSON: It's incredibly hard. They have to throw economic data, 'cause that can't really help you with this project, and they did what all of us who do family genealogy do – they went to Ancestry.com, they went to the Mormon church. And they specifically looked for men – there was very little data on women's economic lives in the 19th century – and men with unusual names. It's just a lot easier to follow, you know, Zebediah Parkinson(ph) through time than John Smith through time. And they would identify a father in, say, 1850 and then look to his sons in, say, 1880 to see are the sons doing the same thing their dad did or something different.

CORNISH: And what did they find?

DAVIDSON: So, in the 19th century in the U.S., there's unbelievable economic mobility. If your father, for example, was an unskilled laborer, sort of the lowest end of the working hierarchy, then you had an 80 percent chance of doing some more skilled, more highly paid job than your father. At the same time, in the U.K., you had about a 50 percent chance. Half the children of unskilled laborers were unskilled laborers themselves. But by just after World War II, the U.S. and U.K. are converging and the differences start to disappear. And by 1970, the U.K. has pulled ahead. So, by the 1970s, the children of unskilled laborers are more likely to do be doing something higher paying in the U.K. than in the U.S.

CORNISH: But why did that happen? I mean, why did the U.S. get less mobile?

DAVIDSON: These are economists, so, of course, they don't give any definitive answers but they raise some tantalizing suggestions. One simple thing is the U.S. in the 19th century was just a very unique economy. There's massive geographic mobility, there's enormous development. So, if you were a young, ambitious son of an unskilled laborer, there is lots of places you can go. You're a frontiersman – go to Chicago, go to the Gold Rush, go to California. There's just all this stuff you can do. By the 20th century, it's more like England, more of a mature, full economy.

Another interesting theory that they borrow from some other economists is that in the 1930s and 1940s, the U.S. and the U.K. are building the modern welfare state. And the U.S. still has this idea that we are a land of opportunity, that the American Dream is really possible here. And so, there is less attention focused in America on helping young people attain economic mobility, whereas in the U.K. that time there was enormous attention on specifically that issue because the British still felt, even though it was no longer entirely true, that they were a very immobile society, that children would be stuck in whatever job their parents had. And so while the U.S. is building Social Security and focusing on older people, the U.K. has the Education Act of 1944, greatly expanding education for young, working-class people.

And so in America the idea that we were a mobile society may have helped set the groundwork for us being a less mobile society later in the 20th century. Whereas in the U.K., where they believe we are an immobile society, may have laid the groundwork for them being a much more mobile society later on.

CORNISH: Adam, thank you so much for talking with us.

DAVIDSON: Thank you, Audie.

CORNISH: That's Adam Davidson with NPR's Planet Money team.

TIPP

These text passages will help you find the correct answer:

1 "A fascinating academic study suggests that economic mobility has been increasing, quite dramatically, in the U.K., just as it's been shrinking in the U.S." (ll. 6/7)

2 "They wanted to ask a very simple question. […] To what extent does your own economic future depend on what your parents did for a living?" (ll. 12–15)

3 "So they found over 10,000 pairs of fathers and sons in the U.S. and the U.K." (l. 16)

4 "So they found over 10,000 pairs of fathers and sons in the U.S. and the U.K., over the last 150 years" (ll. 16/17)

5 "they went to Ancestry.com, they went to the Mormon church." (l. 23)

6 "And they specifically looked for men […] and men with unusual names." (ll. 23–25)

7 "So, in the 19th century in the U.S., there's unbelievable economic mobility. If your father, for example, was an unskilled laborer, sort of the lowest end of the working hierarchy, then you had an 80 percent chance of doing some more skilled, more highly paid job than your father." (ll. 30–33)

8 "At the same time, in the U.K., you had about a 50 percent chance." (ll. 33/34)

9 "But by just after World War II, the U.S. and U.K. are converging and the differences start to disappear." (ll. 35/36)

10 "And by 1970, the U.K. has pulled ahead. So, by the 1970s, the children of unskilled laborers are more likely to do be doing something higher paying in the U.K. than in the U.S." (ll. 36–38)

11 a "the U.S. in the 19th century was just a very unique economy. There's massive geographic mobility, there's enormous development. So, if you were a young, ambitious son of an unskilled laborer, there is lots of places you can go. You're a frontiersman – go to Chicago, go to the Gold Rush, go to California. There's just all this stuff you can do." (ll. 41–46)

b "By the 20th century, it's more like England, more of a mature, full economy." (l. 46)

12 "the U.S. still has this idea that we are a land of opportunity, that the American Dream is really possible here." (ll. 49/50)

13 "the British still felt, even though it was no longer entirely true, that they were a very immobile society, that children would be stuck in whatever job their parents had." (ll. 52–54)

14 "the U.S. is building Social Security and focusing on older people" (ll. 54/55)

15 "the U.K. has the Education Act of 1944, greatly expanding education for young, working-class people." (ll. 55/56)

Introduction to the research project		
1	**One** surprising result of the research	economic mobility increasing in the U.K. / economic mobility shrinking in the U.S.
2	**One** question to be answered by the research	to what extent children's economic future depends on their parents' job / influence of parents' job on their children's economic future
Research procedure		
3	Pairs of people chosen	fathers and sons
4	Time span covered	150 years
5	**One** source used	Ancestry.com / (the) Mormon church / the internet
6	Characteristic feature of persons chosen	(men with) unusual names
Research findings on economic mobility		
7	US: 19th century	sons very likely to have better jobs than their fathers / 80 % chance of economic mobility

8	UK: 19th century	less economic mobility / 50 % chance of economic mobility
9	After World War II	U.K. and U.S. are converging / differences (start to) disappear
10	UK: 1970s	U.K. pulls ahead / youth more likely to have better-paid jobs / more economic mobility
Explanations for the research results		
11	Economic development in the US a) 19th century b) 20th century	 a) massive geographic mobility / enormous development / lots of places to go b) a more mature economy / more like in England/the UK
US and UK in the 1930s and 1940s		
12	How Americans saw themselves and their society	land of opportunity / belief in the American Dream
13	How the British saw themselves and their society	immobile society / children stuck
14	Focus of American social policies	social security / older people
15	Focus of British social policies	education of young (working-class) people

Transkript 3 California's Central Valley

Hinweis: Aus lizenzrechtlichen Gründen ist die ungekürzte Original-Passage der NPR-Sendung abgedruckt. Die in der Abituraufgabe nicht berücksichtigten Passagen sind durch eine kleinere Schriftgröße kenntlich gemacht und für die Bearbeitung der Aufgaben nicht relevant.

ROBERT SIEGEL, *Host:* From NPR News, this is ALL THINGS CONSIDERED. I'm Robert Siegel. And we begin this hour in California's farm-rich Central Valley. President Obama is there today, meeting with farmers and others who are affected by the state's historic drought. The president is announcing millions of dollars in emergency relief. It's his first visit to the area, where the drought is reigniting a political debate about how to manage the state's limited water resources and who should take priority. NPR's Nathan Rott reports.

NATHAN ROTT, *Byline:* Todd Allen takes a hand off his steering wheel and points to a field of brown, baked dirt passing by the right side of his truck.

TODD ALLEN: Here's a plot of ground that I'm not going to be able to farm. That's 160 acres.

ROTT: Allen owns a farm about an hour's drive west of Fresno, in California's Central Valley. This is where half of the country's entire produce is grown. Usually, Allen's fields contain cantaloupe, cotton, tomato and wheat.

ALLEN: But now, because of the drought, I'm going to have leave it fallow.

ROTT: Fallow or unplanted. Allen says he's going to have to do that with 450 of his 600 acres, and he's not alone. The drought is forcing hundreds of thousands of acres in the Central Valley to go unplanted this year. And many farmers, like Allen, aren't just blaming Mother Nature for that.

ALLEN: 20 to 30 percent of our water is gone because of a little fish.

ROTT: That little fish is the delta smelt. You've probably never heard of it. But in California, it's representative of a decade's old clash over water allocation. Here's the basics. There's not a lot of water in California, and there are a lot of people who want it: environmentalists, farmers, city folk. The delta smelt is just a species caught in the middle of all that debate.

ADAM KEATS: It's a convenient boogeyman. It's a scapegoat.

ROTT: Adam Keats is with the Center for Biological Diversity. He says the smelt are a key part of a complex ecosystem. That ecosystem being the Sacramento-San Joaquin River Delta, where much of the Central Valley's water comes from. That's where it gets complicated. The smelt are also on the endangered species list and that means some of the delta's water that would go to farmers like Allen is, instead, allocated to the fish. The result is a farmer versus fish controversy that's been going on for years in California. This year, that political fight has enticed Washington.

REPRESENTATIVE JOHN BOEHNER: How you can favor fish over people is something that people in my part of the world would never understand.

ROTT: House Speaker John Boehner visited California a couple of weeks ago to support a bill introduced by California's House Republicans. Its aim, to get farmers more water by rolling back environmental laws like the ones that protect the smelt. Senate Democrats countered this week with a bill that would give money for drought relief and allow more flexibility around those environmental laws without gutting them.

TOM HOLYOKE: Politicians don't want to let a good crisis go to waste.

ROTT: Tom Holyoke is a professor of water and politics at Fresno State University. He says that's especially true with mid-term elections coming up. Just turn on the TV …

(SOUNDBITE OF POLITICAL AD)

ROTT: Ads like these, which show Republican Doug Ose standing in the dried-out bottom of Folsom Lake, illustrate just how much the drought is going to be a part of this campaign season in California. Ose is trying to unseat a freshman House Democrat. Democrats are doing the same in vulnerable Republican districts, targeting the GOP's legislation that they say puts farmers' needs first.

MICHAEL HANEMANN: Saying we should re-allocate water to my constituents' doesn't require a whole lot of courage and is really an act of opportunism.

ROTT: Michael Hanemann is an agriculture and resource economics professor at UC Berkeley. He says that this type of grandstanding doesn't really accomplish anything. The state's key water users have made efforts to reconcile their differences in years past, but Hanemann says lawmakers haven't made the difficult far-ranging decisions that are needed.

HANEMANN: They have stayed away from it because it's an issue where there are going to be losers as well as winners. And the politicians don't want to touch it.

ROTT: But he says, sooner or later, they're going to have to. Barring a miracle March, this drought isn't going to go away. Nathan Rott, NPR News.

TIPP

These text passages will help you find the correct answer:

1 "President Obama is there today, meeting with farmers and others who are affected by the state's historic drought. The president is announcing millions of dollars in emergency relief." (ll. 2–4)

2 "This is where half of the country's entire produce is grown." (l. 12)

3 "But now, because of the drought, I'm going to have leave it fallow." (l. 14); "Fallow or unplanted. Allen says he's going to have to do that with 450 of his 600 acres, and he's not alone." (ll. 15/16)

4 "it's representative of a decade's old clash over water allocation." (l. 21)

5 "The smelt are also on the endangered species list and that means some of the delta's water that would go to farmers like Allen is, instead, allocated to the fish. The result if a farmer versus fish controversy" (ll. 28–30)

6 "House Speaker John Boehner visited California a couple of weeks ago to support a bill introduced by California's House Republicans. Its aim, to get farmers more water by rolling back environmental laws like the ones that protect the smelt." (ll. 34–36)

7 "Senate Democrats countered this week with a bill that would give money for drought relief and allow more flexibility around those environmental laws without gutting them." (ll. 36–38)

1 The US president is visiting the region to talk about

- **a** ☐ a threatening food shortage.
- **b** ☐ climate change.
- **c** ☐ environmental pollution.
- **d** ☑ financial support.

2 The region is well known for its

- **a** ☑ agricultural products.
- **b** ☐ energy policy.
- **c** ☐ environmental problems.
- **d** ☐ social programs.

3 Weather conditions force farmers to

- **a** ☐ dismiss laborers.
- **b** ☑ leave their land unused.
- **c** ☐ move away.
- **d** ☐ plant different crops.

4 The fight over water in California is

- **a** ☑ a long-standing problem.
- **b** ☐ of international interest.
- **c** ☐ about to be settled.
- **d** ☐ dividing communities.

5 The protest is about giving water to

- **a** ☐ city populations.
- **b** ☐ farm animals.
- **c** ☐ food production.
- **d** ☑ nature conservation.

6 Republicans want to

- **a** ☑ put food producers first.
- **b** ☐ invest more money.
- **c** ☐ protect endangered species.
- **d** ☐ wait and see.

7 Democrats want to

- **a** ☐ only back environmentalists.
- **b** ☐ fight climate change.
- **c** ☑ find a workable solution.
- **d** ☐ primarily support farmers.

Task 4 A conflict

Hinweis: Der Hörtext kann aus rechtlichen Gründen nicht abgedruckt werden. Eine ungekürzte Fassung der Unterhaltung ist bei BBC unter folgendem Link abrufbar:
https://www.bbc.co.uk/programmes/p0239tql
Für die Bearbeitung von Task 4 sind die Minuten 00:00 – 01:38 relevant.

TIPP

These text passages will help you find the correct answer:

Topic they talk about:
"we're thinking about moving you …"

Reasons (Mother):
1 "if they're true friends, you'll stay in touch."
2 "when we've come into this secondary school now they've got nothing, they've got no provision."
3 "you could be challenged more"; "you come home and you do so much, you do so much of your own learning …"

Reasons (Child):
1 "I've already had to move schools before"; "I had to leave all my friends and make new ones."
2 "I don't want to have to stay away from home."
3 "… I'm still in higher set, top set for everything"

Topic they talk about	a change of school	
Speakers	**Mother**	**Child**
Reasons the speakers use to support their position (3 for each speaker)	true friends will stay in touch	has already moved schools before / does not want to leave friends / does not want to make new friends all over again
	current school offers no provision for good students	does not want to stay away from home
	would like her child to be challenged more / her child learns so much at home / her child does so much of his own learning	is still in top set

SPRACHMITTLUNG

TIPP

In this task you are required to write an article. Do not forget to include a heading, a short introduction, a well-structured main body as well as a conclusion. The style or register of this text form is generally rather formal. However, as your article addresses an international student readership, it can also include informal or colloquial expressions.
Your text should contain the following aspects:

- geändertes Konsumverhalten in Deutschland: Trend hin zu Tauschbörsen und Repair Cafés
- Gründe für den Wandel:
  - Umweltschutzgedanke
  - Kritik am Kapitalismus und der Wegwerfgesellschaft
  - spielerischer bzw. geselliger Aspekt der Aktionen; dienen nicht nur dem Geldsparen

Swapping and repairing: How Germans challenge consumerism
Hundreds of thousands of Germans have drawn the consequences from mountains of rubbish and increasing capitalism: They challenge western consumer society by re-using or repairing things that would normally end up on a rubbish tip.
On the one hand, they increasingly use swapping platforms on the Internet where you can exchange objects which you no longer need for something you fancy. People who use these online platforms enjoy the playful character of swapping things. Using points as a kind of substitute currency counters feelings of unprofitable barters while, at the same time, the platforms still provide alternatives to wasting and open capitalism.
Another popular movement against our throwaway society are so-called repair cafés that have sprung up all over Germany. The use of electronic devices has multiplied, but people do not dare to repair them themselves when they are broken. They can bring them to a repair café, where experts working on a voluntary basis restore them. Not only can people thereby keep beloved objects, the repair cafés are also known for their relaxed atmosphere where repairing is often combined with a nice cup of coffee. This positive atmosphere and a good conscience outweigh any financial gains by far. People are not in it for the money but for the feeling of doing good.
Swapping platforms and repair cafés show that challenging consumerism and protecting the environment can be fun and rewarding at the same time.

TEXTAUFGABE

Text I **Emilio DeGrazia, "Our American Nightmare: Detroit" (2013)**

1 **TIPP**

For this task, you need to find all the important aspects concerning Detroit on the one hand and the American Dream on the other. Do not dwell on anything else, but only write down what is essential. Furthermore, you should use your own words rather than copy from the text.
Your text could include the following aspects:
- Detroit was once a large and wealthy city, but now it is run-down and bankrupt.
- The American Dream provides simplistic explanations for failure and therefore prevents a closer look at the real problems within society.
- Tragic illusion: The individual is held responsible for his or her fate.

In his online article "Our American Nightmare: Detroit", written in 2013, Emilio DeGrazia comments on the city and the concept of the American Dream. According to the author, Detroit and its citizens are in a terrible situation. Due to an ailing economy, Detroit is caught in a downward spiral and has gone from rich to poor. Literacy rates have dropped, while crime rates have soared. Public services are poorly funded. Thousands of people cannot afford adequate health care.

While portraying the people of Detroit and their lot in a rather sympathetic way, the author harshly criticises the concept of the American Dream. According to him, citizens are led to believe that the US is a country of unlimited opportunities where everybody can achieve everything if only he or she works hard enough. The author admits that this narrative is beneficial for educators who use it to boost their students' motivation and for those who are successful, but claims that it is a slap in the face for people who find themselves in a very desperate situation. DeGrazia argues that the concept of the American Dream implies that those who do not make it only have themselves to blame. As this easy explanation is the first to come to mind, the real problems, such as mismanagement, corruption or a prospering shadow economy, are not tackled at all. Thus, Detroit's failure is widely held to have been caused by individuals who have chosen their fate freely. In conclusion, it can be stated that the American Dream is a myth that keeps people from seeing the roots of problems because their only explanation of failure or success is the actions or attitudes of the individual.

2 **TIPP**

In this task, the focus of what you are writing is not on the content (i. e. what has been written by the author) but on the strategies used by the author (i. e. how he has written the text). Typically, you have to look for stylistic devices and figures of speech, although looking at certain word fields or the general tone of the article can also prove effective. Remember, however, that an analysis is an exercise in "digging deep": be precise with regard to how the author creates a certain impression and the purpose that this may serve. Take care not to overdo it: it is better to analyse some stylistic devices in depth rather than name as many as possible. You should also try to cluster: if several means serve the same purpose, just give one or two examples and concentrate on the effect this use of stylistic devices has on the reader.
Your analysis may include these means:
- The author criticises the concept of the American Dream harshly.
- The use of personal pronouns creates a feeling of community to get the reader on the author's side.
- The author asks questions to make the reader pay attention and to make it easier to follow his line of argument.
- Enumerations and repetitions leave the reader with the impression that there are numerous (social) problems all over Detroit.
- A negative light is cast on the American Dream through negative words and imaginary figures.

When reading the article, one feels sympathy with the people of Detroit, who are suffering as a result of developments beyond their control. At the same time, one cannot help but view the concept of the American Dream critically. Yet how exactly does the author succeed in achieving this?
Emilio DeGrazia instils sympathy with the people of Detroit by using the stylistic devices of hyperbole and parallelism in the first paragraph (cf. ll. 1–5). The author provides vivid examples of how poorly state-run institutions such as schools, the police and the fire brigade are equipped. The repetition of the phrase "with no" (ll. 3–5) makes the list of shortages seem endless. This dramatic picture seems exaggerated, however. It is questionable whether teachers really do not even have pencils left, for example.
The helplessness with which outsiders look at Detroit is implied by the series of questions starting with "why" (cf. ll. 6–8). Again, DeGrazia uses the stylistic device of parallelism but also an anaphora. Asking the question "Why would a city commit suicide?" (ll. 7/8), the author treats Detroit like a person, which makes the true dimensions of the catastrophe clear to the reader: this is not just another city that is short of money; this is a question of life and death.
The author subsequently presents the concept of the American Dream as the alleged answer to the question "Why would a city commit suicide?" (ll. 7/8) A simplistic explanation for the failure of the Detroiters is provided by means of a parallel sentence

structure beginning with "that" (cf. ll. 12–14) which seems highly repetitive and reminds one of a mantra. The reader cannot help but agree with the author that claiming that thousands of people did not "try hard enough" (l. 14) does not make any sense. The metaphor "little engines" for real people (cf. ll. 14, 23) makes the concept of the American Dream seem even crueller. In the next two paragraphs (cf. ll. 15–22), the sentences begin with the anaphora "tell it" respectively "tell that" to show how weak and unjust the tale of personal failure sounds in the bleak situation in which many people in Detroit are living.

In addition, the author uses several negative expressions to discredit the concept of the American Dream. He calls it "fiction" (l. 30) and a "flawed narrative" (l. 44) and finally compares its core, "radical individualism" (l. 27), to cancer (cf. l. 27). Originally, cancer is a disease which spreads quickly and potentially attacks and destroys the body's vital organs. What is more, it spreads unnoticed in the beginning and cannot be cured if it is discovered too late. By using the word "cancer" in this context, the author causes the reader to draw his or her own unspoken conclusions: The American Dream is portrayed as a deadly concept that takes possession of people's minds, thus infiltrating the whole of American society, which it will eventually destroy. The author appeals to his readership to take action to prevent this common illness from spreading any further. He remarks sarcastically that people "are routinely fed" (l. 11) this "flawed narrative" (l. 44) "at school, at work, and through the media" (l. 11). Usually, the expression "to be fed" is associated with babies. By subtly comparing the readers to mindless children, the author tries to appeal to their sense of pride so that they put an end to being spoon-fed and start thinking for themselves.

In the final paragraph of his article (cf. ll. 44–47), the author makes it clear that all readers can become "victims" (l. 46), and that Detroit is not an isolated case detached from the reader's world. The latter aspect is emphasised further by using "Detroits" (l. 45) in the plural. The rhetorical figure of metonymy implies that Detroit is just one example and that other US cities are already ailing as well. The frequent use of the personal pronoun "we" (cf. ll. 11/12, 23, 46/47) shows that the reader is part of a large group of victims who are all in the same situation and need to take action soon. In conclusion, the author employs stylistic devices and figurative language to make the readers think critically about the concept of the American Dream, and to sympathise with the people of Detroit.

3 **TIPP**

The assignment requires you to write an article for the website of an international youth project. Your article needs an introduction, a main part and a plausible conclusion as well as a headline. As you have to discuss whether the American Dream is a recipe for success, arguments for and against the matter in question are needed. Before you start writing, put the aspects you would like to mention in a logical order (weakest argument first, strongest argument last). Besides using the article at hand to provide ideas and examples, you are also asked to give evidence from materials discussed in class.

Note that you are expected to refer to more than one source of material. This could include Scott Fitzgerald's novel *The Great Gatsby* and the Declaration of Independence, for example (if you have discussed this document in class).

- Possible arguments for why the American Dream is a recipe for success:
  - The concept provides the opportunity to everybody to succeed through hard work no matter where he or she comes from.
  - It provides a maximum of freedom for the individual.
  - It is a true symbol of optimism and progress (as laid down in the Declaration of Independence, for example).
- Possible arguments for why the American Dream is not a recipe for success:
  - The concept neglects the fact that there are limitations that cannot be overcome that easily.
  - Failure is automatically associated with not trying hard enough. (This is not true for rich Tom Buchanan and poor George Wilson in *The Great Gatsby.*)
  - The concept is very materialistic and puts wealth and status above everything else. (Jay Gatsby's fate shows that material wealth is not everything.)

The American Dream – A recipe for success?

As part of our project "Aspects of Life and Culture in the US", it may be interesting to ponder on the question of how to achieve success. Many Americans grew up with what author Emilio DeGrazia calls the "narrative" (l. 11) of the American Dream. However, is the American Dream a recipe for success?

Before moving on to answering this question, the term "success" needs to be looked at more closely. Too often, success is defined in a materialistic way only: The more money you have, the closer you are to success. This seems one-sided, as when the Puritans first reached the shores of America, they were not looking for money. They wanted to be truly free, and to live their life in a self-determined way. For the Puritans, who found a maximum of freedom for the individual in the US, their idea of the American Dream proved a success.

In the Declaration of Independence, which states that "all men are created equal" and have the right to "life, liberty and the pursuit of happiness", there is another notion of the American Dream. This concept holds that every white man can succeed through hard work no matter where he came from. Emilio DeGrazia has to admit that this narrative is a strong and motivating incentive (cf. ll. 23–25) for many. The idea that one can leave one's old life behind and start from scratch still makes more than one million people immigrate to the "country of unlimited opportunities" every year.

However, as early as 1925, F. Scott Fitzgerald, the author of *The Great Gatsby,* made a very strong point that the American Dream as a concept is just a myth, and that it has been corrupted for a long time. Its problem is that it defines success in a way which is too narrow. His protagonist Jay Gatsby, the epitome of the American Dream if ever there was one, goes from rags to riches, and makes it in a material sense: He lives in a big mansion in the poshest part of town, and hosts a lot of flamboyant parties. However, for Gatsby, the road to financial success is paved with stones fraught with corruption. To him, material success is not an end in itself, but only a means to win back

the love of his life, the well-to-do Daisy Buchanan. The fate of Gatsby, who is unhappy despite his wealth because he loses Daisy's love once again and who is killed in the end due to a tragic misunderstanding, is a clear indication that Fitzgerald was puncturing the myth of the American Dream and its definition of success in life.
George Wilson, the mechanic, is another tragic figure in the novel. He works hard, yet his wife cheats on him with Tom Buchanan, an upper-class racist and bully, who has never had to work a day in his life. For Emilio DeGrazia, George Wilson and Tom Buchanan might be another perfect example to prove that the concept of the American Dream is fatally flawed. The explanation that Tom Buchanan gets what he deserves because he has worked hard and seized his chances is just as untrue as stating that George Wilson does not show enough initiative to succeed.
What are the implications of all this for young people? It is certainly never a bad idea to work hard for your dreams. The important thing to remember, however, is that these dreams should never be solely about money. Both *The Great Gatsby* and the fate of Detroit as analysed in De Grazia's article serve as a reminder that a society which has lost its ideals and aspirations, and which is slowly but gradually decaying, is not a society where people can truly "pursue happiness". The American Dream can be a recipe for success – if we understand the concept in its original sense.

Text II Excerpt from David Nicholls, *Us* (2014)

1 **TIPP**

In this task, it is important to focus on the conflict within the family – the conflict between father and son is certainly the more obvious one, but there is also a difference of opinion as far as Douglas and Connie Petersen's attitude to life in general is concerned. Whatever the case, do not sum up the whole text.
Stick to the present tense. Use your own words rather than copy from the excerpt at hand. You might want to mention the following aspects in your text:

- the core of the conflict: Douglas Petersen feels that his son Albie is not as close to him as to his wife Connie and resents having him as a father
- the trigger: Albie wants to study photography
- Connie's position: she is supportive of Albie and wants him to follow his dream
- Douglas' position: he would prefer it if photography remained Albie's favourite leisure activity, as he cannot imagine that his son could make a living out of it; he wants Albie to understand that dreams are not likely to come true
- the parents' problem: Connie's and Douglas' opinions on what makes life worthwhile differ greatly

In the excerpt from David Nicholls' *Us*, written in 2014, events are related to the reader through the first-person narrator, Douglas Petersen, who is disapproving of his teenage son Albie's plans of becoming a photographer after leaving school. His wife Connie, however, supports her son's passion, which leads to an argument between her and her husband. Yet there is more to the conflict than meets the eye. It is highly emotionally charged because it brings to the fore how different Douglas and Connie are as characters.

Douglas is a scientist and approaches life in a rather practical and down-to-earth way. According to him, photography might be Albie's favourite leisure activity, but no occupation one spends one's working life with, especially if this hobby is something that, thanks to technological progress, can be done reasonably well by anybody without a lot of knowledge or talent. To Douglas, a job or profession needs to pay the rent, and he sees it as his duty to introduce his son to this inconvenient fact of life rather than to encourage pipe dreams. Moreover, Douglas and Albie do not seem to be close to each other anyway, a circumstance for which Douglas blames his son, as Albie clearly prefers his mother to his father.

Connie, on the other hand, is a woman of the arts, which is why she cannot take the criticism of an artistic job lightly. She believes in following one's heart and trying to pursue one's dreams. What is more, she appears to have held a grudge against her husband's attitude to life for a long time. This becomes obvious when she reproaches him for his lack of passion. On the surface, there seems to be a typical conflict between a teenager and his father, although the conflict has its roots in vastly different outlooks on life and how to live it.

2 **TIPP**

In task 2 you are asked to compare the conflict in the text at hand to other problematic father-son relationships that you have read about (i. e. in Hanif Kureishi's short story "My Son the Fanatic") and seen a film about (i. e. in *Billy Elliot*). It is important to elaborate on both similarities and differences in your text. Therefore, it makes sense to think of plausible aspects of comparison first and then put them in a convincing order. After structuring your text in this way, write a short introduction and then best start off by explaining similarities first before focusing on the differences. Remember that you need to back up your points by giving evidence from the text.

The following findings could be mentioned in your text:

- Similarities between the conflict in "My Son the Fanatic" and the excerpt from *Us:*
  - both fathers neither feel understood nor appreciated by their sons
  - neither Parvez nor Douglas Petersen approves of his son's career choice
- Differences between the conflict in "My Son the Fanatic" and the excerpt from *Us:*
  - the conflict between Douglas and his son is not a religious matter but about Albie's career choice
  - Connie takes an active part in the conflict, whereas Parvez' wife remains passive

- Similarities between the conflict in *Billy Elliot* and the excerpt from *Us:*
  - both fathers want a job for their sons which they can make a living with
  - neither Jackie Elliot nor Douglas Petersen approves of his son's career choice
  - Billy Elliot and Albie Petersen both decide to work in an artistic profession
- Differences between the conflict in *Billy Elliot* and the excerpt from *Us:*
  - Albie is supported by his mother, whereas Billy does not have such a strong defender of his cause within the family
  - Billy gets support from his ballet teacher Mrs Wilkinson and his gay friend Michael
  - Billy has to overcome gender-related prejudices concerning male ballet dancers

Before elaborating on the conflicts portrayed in *Us, Billy Elliot* and "My Son the Fanatic", it needs to be emphasised that comparing the different works is more difficult than it may seem at first glance. One major problem is the perspective. Though the excerpt at hand is written from Douglas Petersen's point of view, he only focuses on the conflict with his wife *about* Albie. So while we can compare a father's attitude towards his son fairly well with that of another father, it is impossible to assess Albie's feelings. Consequently his emotional state cannot be compared to the feelings of Billy Elliot or Ali, Parvez' son, whose words and actions give the reader an impression of what is going on inside their head. As a consequence, it seems best to focus on the fathers and their conflicts with their offspring for the comparison.
Let us start with the conflict between Albie and his father: Douglas Petersen means well, which becomes obvious when he claims that he wants his son to "have a secure professional life, a good life" (ll. 41/42). In that regard, the excerpt from *Us* bears a striking resemblance to *Billy Elliot* and "My Son the Fanatic".
Parvez, the Pakistani protagonist of Hanif Kureishi's "**My Son the Fanatic**", also wants the best for his son. He puts in extra hours at work to be able to support his son financially – just as Douglas Petersen has worked hard to make life easy for his family (cf. l. 3). While Albie seems to distance himself from his father because he does not want anybody to think that he is "cared for and loved" (l. 4) and tries to adopt a working-class identity by putting on a fake accent (cf. l. 2), Ali rejects the secular life his father leads. So what both Ali and Albie have in common is that they resent their father's lifestyle. While it is clear that Ali does so for "religious reasons", Douglas implies that his son does not want to be associated with his parents' comfortable lifestyle, which is all the more frustrating for Douglas as he is certainly proud of what he has achieved and would like to get some appreciation for it (cf. ll. 2–5). Whereas the relationship between Ali and his mother does not become clear in the short story, Connie Petersen takes an active role in defending her son's career choice. She would like to mediate between father and son, while Ali's mother remains rather passive.

In the film ***Billy Elliot***, the situation is somewhat different. Being a hard-working miner and single parent, Jackie Elliot can support his son neither financially nor emotionally. Moreover, Billy is significantly younger than Ali and Parvez. While it could be argued that he disobeys his father by taking up and pursuing ballet rather than boxing, it does not mean that Billy rejects his father in a way that is comparable to Ali's or Albie's. Yet there are many similarities between Jackie Elliot and Douglas Petersen. Jackie is not a "man of the arts", which becomes apparent when he dismantles his late wife's piano because he needs firewood for his freezing family. Like Connie Petersen, Billy's late mother seems to have been the "arty" person in the family, and her tragic death prevents her from defending the instrument. Jackie does not see the artistic, let alone the emotional value of the piano, but has a rather down-to-earth approach to life. In that he resembles Douglas Petersen. Both Douglas and Jackie want their children to succeed in life. Their idea of "caring" is a rather traditional one as it focuses on "the necessities of life" such as making sure Ali Petersen has "a secure professional life" (l. 41) or making a man out of Billy (which is why Billy is ordered to take up boxing in the first place). However, both fathers fail to notice that there is a different side to "caring" which is not practical or of a material nature. It is the sort of emotional support that Connie Petersen is able to give her son. Against this backdrop, it is understandable why Albie finds it so much easier to get along with his mother, as she is the one who takes him as he is. Being the beloved child of middle-class parents, it might not even have occurred to Albie Petersen yet that he could have difficulties making a living as a photographer. It also remains more than questionable whether Billy Elliot decided to take up ballet because he wanted to earn money dancing. It is much more likely that Billy loves doing what he is passionate about. However, compared to Albie Petersen, Billy Elliot is in a much more difficult position for various reasons. As a young boy in the 1970s, a ballet dancer has to cope with typical prejudices in a traditional working-class environment. Moreover, apart from his ballet teacher and his gay friend Michael, Billy has no support for his passion – within the family, only Billy's partly demented grandmother is on his side. In addition, Billy's family is so poor that his father cannot afford to pay for public transport so that Billy could take part in an audition for the Royal Ballet School.

What all teenagers have in common is that they follow their dreams passionately. While Ali's dream of leading a strictly religious life is inspired by his rejection of his father's values, we cannot be sure whether Albie's and Billy's dreams are subconsciously founded on their rejection of their fathers' values. The fathers, however, have one thing in common: they all want the best for their children but tend to ignore the non-material things that are important to their offspring. This is the core of all the conflicts.

3 **TIPP**

The assignment requires you to write an article for the website of an international school project. Your article needs an introduction, a main part and a plausible conclusion as well as a headline (and subheadings to make the structure of the text more obvious to the reader). As you have to discuss whether young people should follow their dreams, arguments for and against the matter in question are needed. Before you start writing, put the aspects you would like to mention in a logical order (weakest argument first, strongest argument last).

- Possible arguments for why young people should follow their dreams:
  - Making your dreams come true is more motivating than doing something just because it makes sense.
  - The pursuit of happiness is one of the core desires of a human being; as you have only one life to live, it would be great if this was a happy one.
  - Working on a dream makes you self-confident and proud of yourself; it makes your life worthwhile.
- Possible arguments for why it would be better if young people listened to their parents:
  - Your parents have a lot of experience in life.
  - They know you well as a person (i. e. your strengths and weaknesses).
  - You might disappoint your parents if you do not take their advice, thus they might not want to support you if they do not understand your choices.

Dreams and Pipe Dreams

"I have a dream": These words by Martin Luther King Jr. have become so famous that almost everybody knows them. The powerful speech they appear in was delivered in the faith that segregation and racism can be overcome in the end. You simply cannot help but embrace the notion that it is right to have a dream and that no obstacle should keep you from pursuing this aim of yours. Is this why we all grow up with the idea that we have to follow our dreams? Unlike Martin Luther King Jr., one of the leading figures of the Civil Rights Movement, the participants on our international project "Young People and Their Dreams" live in a democratic society. Most of the fights we are involved in take place at home. We fight with our parents, especially if we want something with all our hearts and our parents voice their doubts.

Are dreams really just pipe dreams?

There are a lot of very good arguments why we should listen to our parents. Firstly, most parents love their children. Our parents saw us grow up. They told us not to touch a hotplate because they knew from experience that we would get hurt. They told us that we would not be able to fly to the skies if we spread our wings. Just as they protected us from touching the hotplate as a child, their advice on what job to take and how to live is still given out of love and the wish to protect us.

Secondly, parents know their children best – often much better than the children know themselves. Have you ever sat in a history class and wondered: Why did all those people have to die in that war, only to learn that shortly afterwards history repeated itself and that there was yet another war? When will people learn? It is the same thing with parents and children. Parents look back on a lot of experience, not just in life, but with you as a person – which is why they know what is best for you. They know if you are resilient and hard-working, and they know how you react to stress and setbacks. Listen to them and then you will not be prone to repeating the same mistakes over and over again.

Don't listen to them! No dream is a pipe dream

However, when Billy Elliot first began to dance, he felt a passion so strong and so intense that he would follow his instinct – regardless of the obstacles he had to face. *Billy Elliot* might be just a fictitious story, but let us imagine that he had practised hard and not been accepted at the Royal Ballet School. Would it have been wrong for him to have tried? Actually, it was not his dream to attend the famous ballet school in the first place. Instead, he just wanted to do what he genuinely loved doing, as it made him happy. Following your dreams is what makes life worth living. Even if you fail, it is always better to look back at something you have done – and maybe regret it afterwards – than wonder what could have been and only live your life in your dreams.

Furthermore, it is obvious that Billy is a talented dancer. However, besides the fact that he is truly gifted, his enormous motivation and courage might also have led to his admission to the Royal Ballet School. If someone is as motivated as Billy, they are much more likely to succeed because their positive attitude can make others believe in them. Therefore, it makes no sense at all to avoid taking a risk and always go for the safest option.

So what might Martin Luther King Jr. have said if he had decided to play it safe? Maybe something along the lines of: "I have a good idea how to organise American society, but I am not sure whether it is going to work so I'd rather not follow this idea." Even the most practically minded readers would notice that this is not good speech material. If Martin Luther King Jr. and others had not tried to make their vision a reality, human society as a whole would not have made progress. So if you as a young person have a dream, hold on to it with all your heart. It might not necessarily change the course of history, as the Civil Rights Movement did, but it might have a huge impact on what will become of your own life.

Niedersachsen Englisch ▪ Abiturprüfung 2018
Erhöhtes Anforderungsniveau

HÖRVERSTEHEN

You will hear each recording twice. After each listening you will have time to complete your answers.

Task 1: Morning News (6 BE)

You will hear six pieces of news from the morning edition of a radio show. While listening, match the headlines **A** to **G** with the speakers **1** to **6**. There is one more headline than you need.

Headlines

A Well-known sight in need of repair

B Financial incentive for political participation

C Missing object brought back

D Angry creature defends living space

E Successful genius still a teenager

F Misfortune causes chaos

G Missing vehicle sighted repeatedly

Speaker	1	2	3	4	5	6
Headline						

Task 2: Cereal Killer Café (6 BE)

Listen to a radio report by Leo Hornak about Whitechapel, London. While listening, tick (✓) the correct answer (a, b, c, or d). There is only one correct answer.

1 When Leo Hornak talks about "self-described anarchists", he is referring to people who
- a ☐ see themselves as hipsters.
- b ☐ meet in the Cereal Killer Café.
- c ☐ took part in violent demonstrations.
- d ☐ were born in the oldest part of London.

2 The Cereal Killer Café featured in the radio report
- a ☐ is part of a global chain.
- b ☐ will soon close due to high rents.
- c ☐ attracts mostly people with money.
- d ☐ serves reasonably priced breakfast.

3 "Class War" wants
- a ☐ low-cost flats.
- b ☐ social centres.
- c ☐ fewer immigrants.
- d ☐ more pubs and clubs.

4 Whitechapel, London
- a ☐ used to be a safe neighbourhood.
- b ☐ has always attracted mostly Bengalis.
- c ☐ used to be the location for newcomers.
- d ☐ was once home to workers from Southern Europe.

5 The demonstrators mentioned in the programme
- a ☐ are relatively well off.
- b ☐ throw paint at the police.
- c ☐ are of South Asian origin.
- d ☐ want the area to be redeveloped.

6 The main focus of this programme is on
- a ☐ serious crime in London.
- b ☐ urban change in London.
- c ☐ racial tensions in London.
- d ☐ violent demonstrations in London.

Task 3: Boredom

(13 BE)

Listen to an interview with psychologist Sandi Mann, who is speaking about her research on boredom. While listening, answer the questions. You do not need to write complete sentences.

1	Why might boredom be positive?	
2	What was the first thing people had to do in an experiment?	
3	What was special about this activity?	
4	What did people have to do in the second task?	
5	What was the result of this experiment?	
6	What happens when you daydream?	
7	When does boredom become a particularly unpleasant experience?	
8	What did a teacher do in meetings to overcome boredom?	
9	How does the psychologist explain behaviour like vandalizing?	
10	Which eating habits of bored people are mentioned? Name two.	a) b)
11	What is borodom often confused with?	
12	What does “positive boredom” imply?	

SPRACHMITTLUNG

Aufgabenstellung

You are a guest student at an American high school and your class is working on a project about popular fiction series. You have been asked to contribute an example from Germany.
Write an article for the project website using the information in both texts to describe the series and the reasons for its success.

Text 1 „Umsatzbringer ‚Die drei Fragezeichen': Da sieht Lady Gaga alt aus" (2013)

Seit Jahrzehnten lösen die kindlichen Krimihelden „Die drei Fragezeichen" einen Fall nach dem anderen – und es ist kein Ende in Sicht. […]

Die Superstars dieser Welt – sie alle kommen nicht gegen drei milchgesichtige Hobby-Ermittler an. Justus Jonas, Bob Andrews und Peter Shaw, besser bekannt als: „Die drei Fragezeichen". Sie stellen selbst Showbiz-Größen wie Lady Gaga in den Schatten.

Die Reihe aus Hörspielen und Büchern über die kindlichen Krimihelden bescherte dem Musiklabel Sony-Europa und dem Kosmos-Verlag seit ihrem Deutschland-Start 1968 einen Gesamtumsatz von fast einer halben Milliarde Euro, wie die *Wirtschaftswoche* am Samstag unter Berufung auf Branchenschätzungen berichtete. In Deutschland seien bislang mehr als 45 Millionen Tonträger und 16 Millionen Bücher der Reihe verkauft worden. […]

Die Geschichten funktionieren nach einem einfachen Grundprinzip: Verbrechensaufklärung mit einer Portion Grusel und einem hohen Wohlfühleffekt. *129 Wörter*

Quelle: mhe/afp, Der SPIEGEL Online *vom 30. 11. 2013, http://www.spiegel.de/kultur/literatur/die-drei-rekordumsatz-mit-den-kindlichen-krimihelden-a-936500.html.*

Text 2 „Kinderbuch als Bühnenshow: Die Live-Hörspiele der ‚Drei ???' befördern den Kult um sie. Ein Interview mit Jens Wawrczeck" (2015)

Drei Jugendliche, die in Kalifornien Kriminalfälle lösen: Justus Jonas, Peter Shaw und Bob Andrews sind Helden für jede Generation von Kindern in Deutschland seit 1968 – damals erschien der erste Band von „Die drei ???" in <u>deutscher Übersetzung</u>. Die Reihe wird wegen ihres Erfolgs hierzulande weitergeführt, obwohl sie in den USA 1994 eingestellt worden ist. Zur Popularität tragen die Hörspiel-Adaptionen der Krimis bei. Seit 2002 treten die Sprecher Oliver Rohrbeck (Justus), Jens Wawrczeck (Peter) und Andreas Fröhlich (Bob) zudem mit „Drei ???"-Bühnenshows auf. Dabei verwandeln sie jede noch so schnöde Halle in den fiktiven Sehnsuchtsort Rocky Beach.

Herr Wawrczeck, warum schreibt sich der Erfolg der „Drei ???“ derart fort?

Jens Wawrczeck: Wir werden vererbt. Menschen, die mit uns Kindheitserinnerungen verbinden, möchten uns in ihrem Leben behalten. Das klappt, wenn sie ihre Kinder „Die drei ???“ hören lassen. Auch wenn ich mir den Kultstatus nicht ganz erklären kann, fiel der Beginn in eine sonnenbeschienene Stunde des Hörspiels: Die Folgen spielten in Amerika. Das war damals ein weit entferntes Land, man konnte alles behaupten. Die Cover waren sehr einprägsam und stylish, nicht unbedingt wie bei Kinderhörspielen, daher konnten auch Erwachsene das kaufen, ohne rot zu werden. Inzwischen ist das ein Familien-Produkt, bei den Live-Auftritten versammeln sich die Generationen, jeder hat seine eigene Assoziation.

Die Geschichten bedienen Heldenfantasien von Heranwachsenden; zugleich kriegen Erwachsene erzählt, dass die Dinge in einer vermeintlich komplizierten Welt mit Tatendrang und Aufrichtigkeit ganz einfach zu regeln sind. Ist das der Trick?

Wir stehen in der Tradition erfolgreicher Kinderbücher, die den Erwachsenen zeigen: Ihr wisst nicht alles, ihr könnt nicht alles. Zudem sind Justus, Peter und Bob sozusagen Teile eines gesplitteten Menschen. Jeder steht für verschiedene Eigenschaften: Justus ist das Gehirn, Peter eher die Emotion, Bob erdet alles.

Haben sich die Hauptfiguren und ihre Geschichten über die Jahrzehnte verändert, vielleicht auch verändern müssen – um diejenigen zu bleiben, die sie sind?

Veränderungen sind nötig, um dem Zeitgeist gerecht zu werden – vor allem bei technischen Neuerungen. Aber alles, was diesen Kosmos zu sehr aus der Balance bringt – Freundinnen etwa – wird vom Publikum nicht akzeptiert und hat die Geschichten auch nicht befruchtet. […] Und je nostalgischer die Geschichten sind, desto besser funktionieren sie meines Erachtens. Auf keinen Fall wollen wir sprachlich hipp sein, wir verwenden keine extremen Schimpfwörter. Morde passieren eigentlich nie. Es ist dann vielleicht von Toten aus der Vergangenheit die Rede, aber es ist, glaube ich, noch nie richtig Blut geflossen.

Wie ticken Serienfiguren, damit sie für mindestens eine Generation das Potenzial zu Kindheitshelden haben?

Sie müssen authentisch sein. Meine Helden haben eine Haltung und enttäuschen mich darin nicht. Sie verkörpern ein Ideal, aber eines mit Schwächen. Glatte Helden sind uninteressant. Eine Identifikation muss schon möglich sein. Ein Held ist im Grunde jemand, der uns in einer idealen Form zeigt. Und „Die drei ???“ zeigen eine ideale Form der Freundschaft.

480 Wörter

Quelle: Stefan Fischer, Jens Wawrczeck, Männerliebe, SZ.de *vom 23. 09. 2015, http://www.sueddeutsche.de/reise/synchronsprecher-maennerliebe-1.2657218.*

Anmerkung

14 amerikanischer Originaltitel: *The Three Investigators*

TEXTAUFGABE

Von den zwei Aufgaben ist eine auszuwählen und zu bearbeiten.

Aufgabe I: Aufgabenstellung

1 Sum up the reasons why writers turn to crime fiction according to Elizabeth George. (30 %)

2 Analyse the stylistic means the author uses and the effect they have on the reader. (30 %)

3 You are invited to take part in an international summer school project organized by the British Council, entitled "Why not crime? Opening up the curriculum in schools." Your task is to write an essay discussing whether crime fiction should be dealt with in school. Write this essay, referring to Elizabeth George's text and materials studied in class. (40 %)

Text I **Elizabeth George, "Introduction to *Crime from the Mind of a Woman*" (2002)**

Whether the story is a murder mystery, a tale of suspense, a psychological study of the characters affected by a devastating event, the retelling of a famous criminal act, a courtroom drama, an exposé, a police procedural, or a truthful account of an actual offense, the question remains the same. Why crime? Whether the characters involved are FBI agents, policemen and women, forensic scientists, journalists, military personnel, the man or woman on the street, private detectives, or the little old lady who lives next door, the question remains the same. Why crime? […] Why exists this fascination with crime and why, above all, exists this fascination with crime on the part of female writers?

I think there are several answers to these questions.

Crime writing is practically as old as writing itself and is consequently very much part of our literary tradition. The earliest crime stories come to us from the Bible: in a jealous rage, Cain kills Abel; in a jealous conspiracy, Joseph's brothers sell him into slavery in Egypt and fake his death for their devastated father […].

Crime is mankind on the edge, *in extremis*, but more than that, crime is mankind stepping outside of the norm. For every Cain, there are a billion brothers who have coexisted throughout the centuries. […] But this is what makes crime so interesting. It isn't what people normally do.

It would be nice to believe that cars slow down on the freeway when there is an accident because of the drivers' heightened sense of caution: everyone sees the flashing lights up ahead, the smoke, the flares, the ambulances, the fire trucks, and hits the brakes so as not to end up in the same condition as the unfortunates currently being extricated from mangled metal. But this is not generally why people slow down. They slow down to gawk, their curiosity piqued. Why? Because an accident on the freeway is an anomaly, and anomalies interest us. They always interest us: have done from the beginning of time and will do till the end of it. […]

For the writer who wishes to explore characters, there is nothing so catastrophically catalytic as the intrusion of a crime into an otherwise peaceful landscape. A crime places everyone into a crucible: […] the investigators, the perpetrator, and the victims. Within this crucible of life's most monstrous acts the mettle of the characters is tested. It is when characters confront the most serious challenges to their beliefs, their peace, their sanity, and their way of life that their pathology is triggered. And it is the pathology of the individual character clashing with the pathology of all the other characters that is the stuff of drama and catharsis. […]

What a crime does in a piece of literature is two-fold. First, it serves as a throughline for the story to follow: the crime must be investigated and solved within the twists and turns of the plot. But secondly and perhaps more importantly, the crime also acts as a skeleton for the body of the tale that the writer wishes to tell. On this skeleton, the writer can hang as much or as little as she likes. She can keep the skeleton down to the bones alone and tell a story that moves smoothly, concisely, and without deviation or decoration to its revelation and conclusion. Or she can hang upon the skeleton the muscles, tissues, veins, organs, and blood of such diverse elements of story-telling as theme, exploration of character, life and literary symbols, subplots, etc., as well as the specific crime-oriented story elements of clues, red herrings, suspense, and a list of time-honoured motifs peculiar to mysteries: the hermetically sealed death chamber (or locked room), the most obvious place, the trail of false clues left by the real killer, the fixed idea, and on and on. […]

Why, then, would a writer ever consider dabbling in anything else? There is no reason that I can see. For as long as a writer adheres to the notion that the only rule is there are no rules, the sky's the limit within this field. *679 words*

From: Elizabeth George. "Introduction." Crime from the Mind of a Woman: 26 Compelling Crime Stories from some of the 20th Century's Best Women Writers. *London: Hodder and Stoughton, 2002. 1–4.*

Annotations

3 police procedural: a subgenre of detective fiction
15 *in extremis:* to the highest degree
24 to gawk: to stare stupidly
28 catalytic: triggering a change
29 crucible: *here:* a situation in which people are tested
30 mettle of the character: a character's ability to cope with difficult situations
32 pathology: *G.: krankhaftes Verhalten*
34 catharsis: *(a literary term)* the creation of strong feelings as a way of providing relief
35 throughline: a connecting theme or plot in a movie, play, book, etc.
48 to dabble in sth: to do sth, but not very seriously

Aufgabe II: Aufgabenstellung

1 Summarize the text. (30 %)

2 Analyze how Mr. Yacobowski's behavior affects Pecola's self-esteem. (30 %)

3 Your school is taking part in a European project on "The Power of Imagery in Literature." You have decided to focus on the image of the "dandelion" used by Toni Morrison in *The Bluest Eye*. For the project's online journal you submit an article in which you assess whether the image of the dandelion is an appropriate literary symbol for Pecola as well as for other African-American characters in literature.
Write this article in which you refer to Toni Morrison's text and to materials studied in class. (40 %)

Text II Excerpt from Toni Morrison, *The Bluest Eye* (1970)

The protagonist of the following excerpt is Pecola, a young African-American girl living in the American Midwest in the late 1930s. The excerpt starts when Pecola is on her way to a small grocery store.

There is plenty of time to consider what to buy. Now, however, she moves down an avenue gently buffeted by the familiar and therefore loved images. The dandelions at the base of the telephone pole. Why, she wonders, do people call them weeds? She thought they were pretty. But grown-ups say, "Miss Dunion keeps her yard so nice. Not a dandelion anywhere." Hunky women in black babushkas go into the fields with baskets to pull them up. But they do not want the yellow heads – only the jagged leaves. They make dandelion soup. Dandelion wine. Nobody loves the head of a dandelion. Maybe because they are so many, strong […].

She climbs four wooden steps to the door of Yacobowski's Fresh Veg. Meat and Sundries Store. A bell tinkles as she opens it. Standing before the counter, she looks at the array of candies. All Mary Janes, she decides. Three for a penny. The resistant sweetness that breaks open at last to deliver peanut butter – the oil and salt which complement the sweet pull of caramel. A peal of anticipation unsettles her stomach.

She pulls off her shoe and takes out the three pennies. The gray head of Mr. Yacobowski looms up over the counter. He urges his eyes out of his thoughts to encounter her. Blue eyes. Blear-dropped. […] At some fixed point in time and space he senses that he need not waste the effort of a glance. He does not see her, because for him there is nothing to see. How can a fifty-two-year-old white immigrant storekeeper with the taste of potatoes and beer in his mouth, his mind honed on the doe-eyed Virgin Mary, his sensibilities blunted by a permanent awareness of loss, *see* a little black girl? Nothing in his life even suggested that the feat was possible, not to say desirable or necessary.

"Yeah?"

She looks up at him and sees the vacuum where curiosity ought to lodge. And something more. The total absence of human recognition – the glazed separateness. She does not know what keeps his glance suspended. Perhaps because he is grown, or a man, and she a little girl. But she has seen interest, disgust, even anger in grown male eyes. Yet this vacuum is not new to her. It has an edge; somewhere in the bottom lid is the distaste. She has seen it lurking in the eyes of all white people. So. The distaste must be for her, her blackness. All things in her are flux and anticipation. But her blackness is static and dread. And it is the blackness that accounts for, that creates, the vacuum edged with distaste in white eyes.

She points her finger at the Mary Janes – a little black shaft of finger, its tip pressed on the display window. The quietly inoffensive assertion of a black child's attempt to communicate with a white adult.

"Them." The word is more sigh than sense.

"What? These? These?" Phlegm and impatience mingle in his voice.

She shakes her head, her fingertip fixed on the spot which, in her view, at any rate, identifies the Mary Janes. […]

"Christ. Kantcha talk?"

His fingers brush the Mary Janes.

She nods.

"Well, why'nt you say so? One? How many?"

Pecola unfolds her fist, showing the three pennies. He scoots three Mary Janes toward her – three yellow rectangles in each packet. She holds the money toward him. He hesitates, not wanting to touch her hand. She does not know how to move the finger of her right hand from the display counter or how to get the coins out of her left hand. Finally he reaches over and takes the pennies from her hand. His nails graze her damp palm.

Outside, Pecola feels the inexplicable shame ebb.

Dandelions. A dart of affection leaps out from her to them. But they do not look at her and do not send love back. She thinks, "They *are* ugly. They *are* weeds."

Preoccupied with that revelation, she trips on the sidewalk crack. Anger stirs and wakes in her; it opens its mouth, and like a hot-mouthed puppy, laps up the dredges of her shame.

Anger is better. There is a sense of being in anger. *698 words*

From: Toni Morrison. The Bluest Eye. *1970; London: Picador, 1990. 35–37.*

Annotations

2 buffeted: *G.: beschwingt*
2 dandelion: *G.: Löwenzahn, Pusteblume*
5 hunky: a derogatory term for unskilled workers from Eastern Europe
5 babushka: traditional Russian clothing
11 Mary Jane: a kind of candy
13 peal: *here:* a sudden strong feeling
16 blear dropped. half closed and tired
19 honed on the doe-eyed Virgin Mary: always thinking of the image of the (white) Virgin Mary with her mild eyes
20 blunted: becoming less sensitive
21 feat: action which requires strength, effort
52 dredge: *here:* trace, mark

Lösungsvorschlag

HÖRVERSTEHEN

Transkript 1 Morning News

Hinweis: Aus lizenzrechtlichen Gründen ist die ungekürzte Original-Passage der NPR-Sendung abgedruckt. Die in der Abituraufgabe nicht berücksichtigten Passagen sind durch eine kleinere Schriftgröße kenntlich gemacht und für die Bearbeitung der Aufgaben nicht relevant.

Speaker 1: Good morning. I'm Steve Inskeep with the story of an overachiever. Moshe Kai Cavalin of California says he's nothing special, which is sort of true. Many people have published two books as he did, except he's done it by age 17. He earned a bachelor's degree from UCLA and is seeking a master's in cybersecurity. He's also working for NASA in his spare time. Not only that, California's legal driving age is 18, meaning that next year he can even drive by himself. It's MORNING EDITION.

Speaker 2: Good morning. I'm Steve Inskeep. It's like the old movie, "The Birds," except that instead of many attacking birds, there's one. An owl is attacking runners on a trail in Bethesda, Maryland. The trail is near Washington, favored by super-fit residents in the nation's capital. At least three were attacked and scratched by the owl. Rather than hunt the attacker, officials have posted a warning sign. Officials explain owls are territorial. And who's to say the area does not belong to the bird? You are listening to MORNING EDITION.

Speaker 3: Good morning, I'm Renee Montagne. And Big Ben is getting old. And at 156 years old, London's famous clock is slowing down, chiming a whole six seconds behind schedule. Fixing water erosion and cracks could silence its chimes for three years. Still, Big Ben's unauthorized Twitter account is keeping time, typing out B-O-N-Gs on the hour – bong, bong, bong, bong, bong, bong. It's MORNING EDITION.

Speaker 4: Good morning. I'm Steve Inskeep with a benefit of the information age – Melissa Gonzales can track her stolen car. Ever since somebody took the Colorado woman's SUV, she's been receiving clues to its location in the mail. She tells KMGH-TV she received a parking ticket, then a highway toll charge, and she received a photo radar ticket. We do not know the names of the four people photographed in the car. We do know they were driving 85 in a 45-mile-an-hour zone. It's MORNING EDITION.

From: © 2015 National Public Radio, Inc. NPR News report "Tickets, Toll Charges Sting For Stolen Car Owner" was originally broadcast on NPR's Morning Edition on October 21, 2015, and is used with the permission of NPR. Any unauthorized duplication is strictly prohibited.

Speaker 5: Good morning, I'm Renee Montagne. Voter turnout is a concern all over the country. But in one city, trudging to the polls for a mayoral election just got more rewarding. The online publication *Philadelphia Citizen* is sponsoring a kind of lottery, offering a $ 10,000 prize to one lucky voter. A polling place will be chosen at random and the prize money given to a random voter. As one organizer told the *Philadelphia Inquirer*, "desperate times require desperate measures". It's MORNING EDITION.

From: © 2015 National Public Radio, Inc. NPR News report "Philadelphia Publication To Give $10,000 To A Random Mayoral Race Voter" was originally broadcast on NPR's Morning Edition on October 23, 2015, and is used with the permission of NPR. Any unauthorized duplication is strictly prohibited.

Speaker 6: Good morning. I'm Steve Inskeep. This technique comes right out of a James Bond movie, though it no doubt happened by accident. A truck in Missouri spilled boxes of nails on the highway – 200 boxes – each box containing 2,000 nails. KOMU-TV reports that traffic on I-70 was stopped during the cleanup, and nobody caught the truck, of course, because who could pursue it after it dropped 400,000 nails? You're listening to MORNING EDITION.

From: © 2015 National Public Radio, Inc. NPR News report "Thousands Of Nails Stop Traffic On Missouri Highway" was originally broadcast on NPR's Morning Edition on October 27, 2015, and is used with the permission of NPR. Any unauthorized duplication is strictly prohibited.

TIPP

These text passages will help you find the correct answer:

1 "the story of an overachiever." (l. 1); "Many people have published two books as he did, except he's done it by age 17. He earned a bachelor's degree from UCLA and is seeking a master's in cyber security. He's also working for NASA in his spare time." (ll. 2–5)

2 "An owl is attacking runners on a trail in Bethesda, Maryland." (ll. 9/10); "Officials explain owls are territorial." (ll. 12/13)

3 "Big Ben is getting old. And at 156 years old, London's famous clock is slowing down, chiming a whole six seconds behind schedule. Fixing water erosion and cracks could silence its chimes for three years." (ll. 15–17)

4 "Melissa Gonzales can track her stolen car. Ever since somebody took the Colorado woman's SUV, she's been receiving clues to its location in the mail" (ll. 20–22); "she received a parking ticket, then a highway toll charge, and she received a photo radar ticket." (ll. 22–24)

5 "in one city, trudging to the polls for a mayoral election just got more rewarding." (ll. 27/28); "a kind of lottery, offering a $ 10,000 prize to one lucky voter. A polling place will be chosen at random and the prize money given to a random voter." (ll. 28–30)

6 "it no doubt happened by accident. A truck in Missouri spilled boxes of nails on the highway" (ll. 33/34); "traffic on I-70 was stopped during the cleanup" (l. 35)

Speaker	1	2	3	4	5	6
Headline	E	D	A	G	B	F

Transkript 2 Cereal Killer Café

Interviewer: Yesterday several hundred demonstrators held a protest, which turned into a riot against gentrification and middle-class hipsters moving into the neighbourhood. The world's man at the BBC in London is Leo Hornak. He filled me in on the protest.

Leo Hornak: Well, this group of self-described anarchists – several hundred of them marched through the streets of, err, Whitechapel, which is one of the oldest parts of the East End, traditionally a very poor area, and they targeted some of the classic symbols of gentrification. There were attempts to smash the windows of estate agents, rents going up, and also as you said this "Cereal killer café", which is a bit of a sort of symbol of what some people see as the hipsterfication of the East End and of London.

Interviewer: Yeah, has that café taken on any notoriety just because of what it does and what it serves?

Hornak: Well, I, I mean, I think that a lot of people maybe feel a little bit sorry for the people running this café. It's a small independent business. It does sell, err, novelty, err *(laughs),* breakfast cereals at a very, pretty high price. I think the going rate for some Coco Pops is about five and a half dollars, which obviously is just the Coco Pops plus some cold milk. And the reason this has attracted so much attention is that it's serving a crowd of young, quite affluent middle-class people [who] just maybe recently left university and this is a real area where they're attracted to and where they hang out – where there's clubs, bars and novelty kind of shops like this. Just looking at "Class War" – that's the group who organised this – this protest. Looking at their manifesto, they said, "We don't want luxury flats that no one can afford. We want genuinely affordable housing. We don't want pop-up gin bars and brioche buns. We want community."

Interviewer: So, what's been the response to demands like that?

Hornak: Well, it's really interesting, Marco, because it's divided people. I mean I live not that far from Whitechapel where this happened – you might say maybe I'm part of the problem – and it is an area which is traditionally the first place where new communities and immigrants arrive in London for hundreds of years. In the 19th century, at the time of Jack the Ripper, it was when Jewish immigrants from Eastern Europe arrived in London. And then, later on, it became the area where South Asian communities arrived and currently it's a mainly Bengali community. Now when you looked at the protestors who were throwing paint at the "Cereal Café" yesterday, most of them were themselves white and possibly middle class. They certainly weren't the community, the South-Asian community that is being forced out and most affected by gentrification in this area. It was only a few years ago that we had the London riots, which were much more widespread and maybe less overtly political. But it was the same sense that a certain sub-section of the poorest in London were being forgotten as a different section raced ahead.

From: Leo Hornak, Anti-hipster protest in London targets breakfast cereal cafe, 28 September 2015, http://www.pri.org/stories/2015-09-28/anti-hipster-protest-london-targets-breakfast-cereal-café (accessed: 10 February 2016).

TIPP

These text passages will help you find the correct answer:

1 "this group of self-described anarchists – several hundred of them marched through the streets of, err, Whitechapel [...] and they targeted some of the classic symbols of gentrification. There were attempts to smash the windows" (ll. 5–8)

2 "it's serving a crowd of young, quite affluent middle-class people" (l. 19)

3 "Looking at their manifesto, they said, 'We don't want luxury flats that no one can afford. We want genuinely affordable housing.'" (ll. 22–24)

4 "it is an area which is traditionally the first place where new communities and immigrants arrive in London for hundreds of years." (ll. 29/30)

5 "Now when you looked at the protestors who were throwing paint at the 'Cereal Café' yesterday, most of them were themselves white and possibly middle class. They certainly weren't the community, the South-Asian community that is being forced out and most affected by gentrification in this area." (ll. 33–37)

6 "a protest, which turned into a riot against gentrification and middle-class hipsters moving into the neighbourhood" (ll. 1–3); "rents going up" (l. 9); "this 'Cereal killer café', which is a bit of a sort of symbol of what some people see as the hipsterfication of the East End and of London." (ll. 9–11); "traditionally a very poor area" (l. 7); "it's serving a crowd of young, quite affluent middle-class people [...] this is a real area where they're attracted to and where they hang out – where there's clubs, bars and novelty kind of shops like this." (ll. 19–21)

1 When Leo Hornak talks about "self-described anarchists", he is referring to people who

c ☑ took part in violent demonstrations.

2 The Cereal Killer Café featured in the radio report

c ☑ attracts mostly people with money.

3 "Class War" wants

a ☑ low-cost flats.

4 Whitechapel, London

c ☑ used to be the location for newcomers.

5 The demonstrators mentioned in the programme

a ☑ are relatively well off.

6 The main focus of this programme is on

b ☑ urban change in London.

Transkript 3 Boredom

Sandi Mann: Boredom is excellent for many things, but one thing in particular that it's good for is to enable your creativity and I've done some research about all this actually that was published in 2014. We got people really bored. I got them to copy out phone numbers from a telephone book, which was not just boring and repetitive, but it's meaningless.

Interviewer: Oh, so they don't like that it's pointless?

Mann: Pointless and I think there's something about something not having meaning that makes us more bored. You know we like to have meaning in our lives. So, it was a pointless, meaningless task. They got really bored and then we gave them a test of creativity. We wanted to see how creative they were. So we gave them two polystyrene cups and said, "How many things can you think of – how many uses can you think of for these two cups?" The people who had the boring task to do actually came up with more – more things to do with these cups and they were more creative in the ideas they came up with than the people who weren't bored. And we thought that the reason for that is because when you're bored, your mind wanders, and when your mind wanders, you daydream, and when you daydream, you can come up with all sorts of fantastical ideas. Your mind can go on to flights of fancy, you can think laterally, because you're not constrained by your sub-conscious mind. So, what's good about boredom, it allows that creativity. That's the main thing, I think, for me.

Interviewer: So, boredom isn't necessarily the same as doing nothing. It's whether you wanted something to do and you haven't got something to do.

Mann: Boredom is a negative thing. It's a search for neural stimulation. So, once you've satisfied that search, then you are no longer bored, even though you may still not be doing anything. But your mind is active. So, if you're in a boring situation and you can't escape it and you're not allowed to have your mind wandering, then it's a very frustrating, negative feeling and it feels like boredom.

Interviewer: Sometimes people will count things, won't they?

Mann: Yes, I … oh my gosh, yeah I …

Interviewer: … and do anything to sort of change their mindset?

Mann: I had a paper that I published called "Counting window panes" and that was the strategy that a teacher used to cope in boring meetings. So, they counted the window panes. So yeah, when you have a strategy that is satisfying, then the experience becomes pleasant if you like – a kind of relaxation instead – and therefore technically would no longer be classified as boredom, but perhaps downtime instead.

Interviewer: At other times people are so bored that they vandalise things or do graffiti or do other anti-social things, because they're so bored and there's nothing to do. So how do you balance it?

Mann: Yes, so that's the downside. If you have too much boredom and especially chronic boredom with a lack of meaning. So, for those people they need to find meaning in their lives and that is very important because that's one of the problems of negative boredom, when you start doing negative things to cope with it. And this is the other thing about boredom. It's how you cope with it. There are negative ways and there are positive ways and we tend to do the negative things, like the anti-social behaviour, like eating, overeating. For example, I've got a piece of research coming out called "Bored people don't eat nuts" and what I've shown with this research is that if you get people bored and you give them a variety of snacks to eat, they won't go for the healthy stuff. They'll choose, they'll eat more of the unhealthy stuff, the fatty, sugary stuff. And the reason for that is that when we are bored we are seeking stimulation.

Interviewer: Oh, and everyone has done that – going to open the fridge cos you're just a bit bored.

Mann: It's that and it's also that we actually get a dopamine hit from sugary and fatty foods. Dopamine is the reward chemical – so it feels good.

Interviewer: And the psychological literature seems to divide boredom into two kinds.

Mann: There's a kind of negative and a positive side. I think there's this kind of misconception between boredom and relaxation, because I have a lot of people that say to me, "Well, I like doing nothing, you know, it's relaxing." That's not boredom. The thing about boredom is that it's a negative thing in that you are seeking stimulation. So, if you're in a situation where you're happy to have nothing to do and relaxing – that's the kind of positive boredom that I guess we're looking for, where we can just enjoy letting our minds go freely where they want to go.

From: Sandi Mann, Claudia Hammond, Why boredom could be good for you,
BBC *11 May 2016, http://www.bbc.co.uk/programmes/p03tsr5n (accessed: 29 November 2016).*

TIPP

These text passages will help you find the correct answer:

1 "Boredom is excellent for many things, but one thing in particular [...] is to enable your creativity" (ll. 1/2); "So, what's good about boredom, it allows that creativity." (l. 19)

2 "We got people really bored. I got them to copy out phone numbers from a telephone book" (ll. 3/4)

3 "not just boring and repetitive, but it's meaningless." (ll. 4/5); "they don't like that it's pointless?" (l. 6); "Pointless and I think there's something about something not having meaning that makes us more bored. You know we like to have meaning in our lives. So, it was a pointless, meaningless task." (ll. 7–9)

4 "They got really bored and then we gave them a test of creativity. [...] So we gave them two polystyrene cups and said, 'How many things can you think of – how many uses can you think of for these two cups?'" (ll. 9–12)

5 "The people who had the boring task to do actually came up with more – more things to do with these cups and they were more creative." (ll. 12–14)

6 "when you're bored, your mind wanders, and when your mind wanders, you daydream, and when you daydream, you can come up with all sorts of fantastical ideas. Your mind can go on to flights of fancy, you can think laterally, because you're not constrained by your sub-conscious mind." (ll. 15–18)

7 "So, if you're in a boring situation and you can't escape it and you're not allowed to have your mind wandering, then it's a very frustrating, negative feeling and it feels like boredom." (ll. 25–27)

8 "I had a paper that I published called 'Counting window panes' and that was the strategy that a teacher used to cope in boring meetings." (ll. 31/32)

9 "people are so bored that they vandalise things or do graffiti or do other anti-social things" (ll. 36/37); "that's the downside. If you have too much boredom and especially chronic boredom with a lack of meaning. [...] one of the problems of negative boredom, when you start doing negative things to cope with it. [...] There are negative ways and there are positive ways and we tend to do the negative things, like the anti-social behaviour." (ll. 39–45)

10 "we tend to do the negative things, like [...] overeating. For example, I've got a piece of research coming out called 'Bored people don't eat nuts' [...] if you get people bored and you give them a variety of snacks to eat, they won't go for the healthy stuff. They'll choose, they'll eat more of the unhealthy stuff, the fatty, sugary stuff." (ll. 44–49)

11 "a kind of negative and a positive side. [...] there's this kind of misconception between boredom and relaxation, because I have a lot of people that say to me, 'Well, I like doing nothing, you know, it's relaxing.' That's not boredom." (ll. 56–58)

12 "you're happy to have nothing to do and relaxing – that's the kind of positive boredom that I guess we're looking for, where we can just enjoy letting our minds go freely where they want to go." (ll. 60–62)

1	Why might boredom be positive?	it makes creativity possible
2	What was the first thing people had to do in an experiment?	copy phone numbers from a telephone book
3	What was special about this activity?	it had no meaning / was meaningless / was pointless
4	What did people have to do in the second task?	complete a creativity test / think of as many different uses for two polystyrene cups as possible / come up with things to do with two polystyrene cups
5	What was the result of this experiment?	bored people had more ideas and were more creative
6	What happens when you daydream?	your mind wanders / you can have fantastical ideas / flights of fancy are possible / lateral thinking is possible / there are no constraints by your subconscious
7	When does boredom become a particularly unpleasant experience?	when you cannot escape a boring situation / when it is not possible to let your mind wander
8	What did a teacher do in meetings to overcome boredom?	he counted window panes
9	How does the psychologist explain behaviour like vandalizing?	result of too much boredom / result of chronic boredom / result of people lacking meaning in their lives / people do negative things to cope with negative boredom
10	Which eating habits of bored people are mentioned? Name two.	*Name two of the following:* bored people tend to overeat / bored people do not eat healthy food (like nuts) / bored people eat unhealthy/fatty/sugary food
11	What is boredom often confused with?	relaxation
12	What does "positive boredom" imply?	you are happy about having nothing to do / you are relaxing / you can enjoy letting your mind run free

SPRACHMITTLUNG

TIPP

In this task you are required to write an article for the website of a project about popular fiction series. Do not forget to include a heading, an introduction, a well-structured and coherent main body as well as a conclusion. As your article mainly addresses students at an American high school, some colloquial expressions are possible. However, the general style or register should be rather formal, respectively neutral. Your text should contain the following aspects:

- Reihe hat ihren Ursprung in den USA, wurde dort allerdings abgesetzt
- erfreut sich großer Beliebtheit in Deutschland seit 1968
- generell ein Kinderbuch, aber auch für Erwachsene ansprechend
- Hauptfiguren: drei junge Hobbydetektive
- Handlungsort: imaginärer Ort in Kalifornien
- Gründe für den Erfolg:
  - ansprechend für verschiedene Generationen
  - authentische Helden verkörpern Ideale, ohne dabei perfekt zu sein
  - nostalgische Darstellung einer geordneten Welt
  - unverwechselbares Design der Cover
  - vielseitige Verfügbarkeit (Bücher, Hörspiele, Live-Shows)

***The Three ???*: How an American Detective Series for Children has been Capturing Germans of all Generations for more than 50 years**

Having started in 1968, the children's detective series *The Three Investigators*, which in German reads *The Three ???*, became an immediate success, and while the American original petered out in 1994, its German counterpart has been selling record numbers of books and CDs and has been filling venues all across Germany with live performances of the stories. So what makes the adventures of three young amateur detectives in an imaginary place in California so popular?

The formula for success could be narrowed down to the series offering exciting and slightly scary detective stories with a feel-good factor which are written for children but are still popular with the older generations. The three young heroes serve as an authentic embodiment of basic human characteristics, with one of the boys being the intellectual, the second his emotional counterpart and the third down-to-earth and pragmatic. While they present an ideal of teamwork and friendship, they retain individual weaknesses and are therefore perfect for identification. Furthermore, the well-ordered, somewhat nostalgic setting, to which only necessary technological innovations, but no swear words or excessively violent scenes have been added throughout the years, offers a simple and welcome escape from an otherwise complex and chaotic world.

The distinctive cover design and the fact that the stories are available as books, radio plays and live shows enabling different generations to listen to or watch the stories together adds to *The Three Investigators'* success. No wonder that in Germany the love of the series has been passed on from one generation to the next.

TEXTAUFGABE

Text I **Elizabeth George, "Introduction to *Crime from the Mind of a Woman*" (2002)**

1 **TIPP**

The command term *(dt. Operator)* "sum up" generally requires you to state the main points of a text in your own words. In this task, the summary's focus is on the reasons Elizabeth George gives for authors deciding to write crime fiction. Only write down what is essential. Your text should be well-structured and significantly shorter than the original. Do not copy from the excerpt and refrain from commenting on the text.

Your text should include the following reasons why writers turn to crime fiction:

- Crime fiction has been an integral component of our literary tradition for basically as long as writing itself exists.
- People have an inherent interest in any occurrence that is out of the ordinary.
- A crime gets characters into situations full of difficulties, drama and emotions, and thus serves as a perfect means to explore character traits.
- A crime serves as the story's structure, which can be kept simple or made more complex by the writer.

In the introduction to her crime stories collection *Crime from the Mind of a Woman*, which was published in 2002, Elizabeth George names several reasons why writers, and particularly female writers, find appeal in writing crime fiction.

According to George, many people are fascinated by crime stories due to the fact that crime is an anomaly, something outside the norm. What is more, this interest in something that is not part of our everyday life is age-old. Thus, crime writing plays an essential part in our literary tradition and there have practically always been crime stories.

George also states that placing characters in a situation where they are confronted with a crime – whether it be as victims, perpetrators or investigators – allows the author to explore facets of these characters that were previously unforeseen and unavailable for examination. The crime confronts them with a challenge that tests their ability to cope with difficult situations. This in turn results in drama and catharsis, which is a way to make the story more interesting to the reader.

Last but not least, a crime serves as a way to connect all the elements of the story. When it happens, its investigation and solution must take place within the duration of the book's plot. Thus, it gives the story a basic structure that can be developed according to the author's wishes, which means that he/she can decide whether to keep the tale more simple and straightforward or whether to embellish it with various elements of storytelling.

2 **TIPP**

In this task, the command term "analyse" requires you to take a closer look at the stylistic means used by the author and explain the resulting effects on the reader. It is essential that you work closely with the text at hand and support your points by giving evidence. Be as specific as possible in explaining what effect the different stylistic devices actually have on you as a reader.
Your analysis could include the following findings:

- The author uses rhetorical questions, which catch the readers' interest and lead to their feeling involved in the argumentation.
- She repeats the key question ("Why crime?") to stress her main concern.
- She uses further repetitions to allow the readers to follow easily.
- She makes use of enumerations and examples to illustrate her arguments.
- She applies figurative language, especially a metaphor of a skeleton, to make the readers visualise what she is trying to say.
- She uses expressive words to create emotion.

In explaining why writers turn to crime fiction, Elizabeth George uses several stylistic devices in order to strengthen her arguments.
Her use of multiple rhetorical questions containing the interrogative particle "why" (cf. ll. 4, 7–9, 24, 48) serves as a means to captivate and interest the readers in what she has to say. Rhetorical questions give the readers the impression that these are actually their own questions, which motivates them to carry on reading, as they want to find the answers to them. This is why rhetorical questions can mainly be found in the first paragraph. What is especially remarkable here is the fact that George even repeats the question "Why crime?" (ll. 4, 7) twice. She thus points out that this is the key question she wants to give answers to in what follows.
On top of that, George uses further examples of repetition as a way to connect the readers' thoughts and make it easier for them to follow. These examples include the repetition of the phrase "Crime is mankind" (l. 15) as well as repeating the words "slow down", "anomaly" and "interest" in successive sentences (cf. ll. 23–25).
Furthermore, there are many enumerations to be found throughout the text (cf. ll. 1–4, 4–7, 29, 31/32, 41–47). Instead of simply stating that several kinds of crime stories exist, that a number of different characters can be involved in the investigation, that everyone in a crime story is confronted with a challenge, or that the tale can be amplified by several elements of storytelling, Elizabeth George always lists various examples. By doing so, she illustrates her points and allows the readers to get a better idea of what she means.
To strengthen her arguments as to why crime fiction is so appealing, George also uses an abundance of figurative language. Phrases like "the intrusion of a crime into an otherwise peaceful landscape" (l. 28) – when explaining why a crime allows authors to explore their characters in detail – or "the unfortunates currently being extricated from mangled metal" (ll. 22/23) – when comparing the attractive power of a crime as

something out of the ordinary to that of a car accident on the freeway – increase the use of the readers' imagination.
Another means that is intended to create pictures in the readers' minds is used by George in describing "[w]hat a crime does in a piece of literature" (l. 35): the metaphor of the skeleton (cf. ll. 37–47). In a biological sense, the skeleton is what gives a body its structural integrity. In crime literature, this means that the crime itself gives the author a structure for the story he/she wants to tell. The writer then has two options regarding what to do with the skeleton. Either he/she uses only the bones and tells a story that is straightforward and without embellishment, or the skeleton is covered with muscles and other body parts – which represent different elements of storytelling, stylistic devices and motifs – to achieve a more complex story with several possibilities for interpretation. The metaphor of the skeleton enables the readers to visualise this concept and obtain a better understanding of what Elizabeth George is trying to say.
Finally, the author uses several expressive words, for example "devastated" (l. 14) or "gawk" (l. 24), which fuel the text's emotional effect on the readers.
To draw a conclusion, Elizabeth George's intention is to convince her readers of what she thinks are the reasons for writers turning to crime fiction. To reach this goal, she makes use of several stylistic devices which have the effect of capturing the readers' attention, creating emotions, illustrating points or emphasising arguments.

3 **TIPP**

This exercise is embedded in a situational context to which you should refer in some way. It requires you to write an essay in the course of your participation in an international summer school project that deals with crime fiction in schools. Your essay needs an introduction, a main part and a conclusion as well as a heading. As you have to discuss whether crime fiction should be dealt with in school or not, you are supposed to adduce arguments for and against the matter in question before you come to a logical conclusion that mirrors your personal opinion. Besides referring to Elizabeth George's text, you are also expected to mention materials studied in class. This could include the two short stories "A Scandal in Bohemia" and "The Tell-Tale Heart" as well as the television series *Sherlock*.
The following aspects could be mentioned in your essay:
– Possible arguments for incorporating crime fiction into the curriculum:
  - Crime stories are usually dramatic and exciting and therefore quite appealing to pupils.
  - Crime fiction is more accessible to younger readers, especially compared to classical literature, which often contains difficult language or unfamiliar topics.
  - Crime stories are representative of different literary periods.

- Possible arguments against incorporating crime fiction into the curriculum:
  - Some crime stories are not appropriate for pupils as they contain quite a large amount of violence.
  - Most curricula are already packed and adding crime fiction would mean even less time to read classical literature and deal with a story in detail.

Crime fiction in schools?

There is little to no debate as to whether plays like Shakespeare's *Romeo and Juliet* or classic novels such as Harper Lee's *To Kill a Mockingbird* should be an integral part of a school's literary curriculum. However, what about pieces such as the short stories "A Scandal in Bohemia" by A. C. Doyle or "The Tell-Tale Heart" by E. A. Poe? Should such crime stories also be dealt with in school? Opinions are deeply divided on this issue.

First of all, let me briefly explain how Elizabeth George, herself a writer of crime novels, summarises the advantages of crime stories. She states that a crime brings out the most in all characters involved, as they are tested in difficult situations, and attracts the attention of the reader because of our inherent curiosity about anything that is not ordinary. There is drama and action, and the plots are usually full of suspense. This is probably the most obvious reason why pupils generally tend to find crime stories interesting. On top of that, I could imagine that works of classical literature are not that accessible to many of them, as they often have problems with understanding the language or because the topics are foreign to them. Crime fiction, by contrast, is usually more approachable to young readers. Furthermore, crime stories are simply part of our literary tradition and thus should not be neglected.

For all these reasons, one could argue that crime fiction should be incorporated into the curriculum. Yet to what extent are these positive findings true in the case of concrete examples? Is the view of Elizabeth George correct when it comes to the two stories mentioned above?

Regarding "The Tell-Tale Heart", it must be said that this story would certainly complement every curriculum very well. It features quite a challenging symbol (the "vulture eye"), whose meaning one could speculate on for ages. What is more, the narrative perspective leaves the reader in the dark as to what exactly happens. Was the murder just a figment of the narrator's imagination, who shows clear signs of being mentally handicapped? Or if we happen to believe the narrator, what were the reasons for the crime? There is an air of mystery surrounding the story, and it serves as a prime example of how an alleged crime brings out extremes in a character. All in all, the story is fascinating, quite short and leaves a great deal of room for interpretation – good reasons for reading it in class.

Considering "A Scandal in Bohemia", however, it is doubtful whether this story meets the criteria mentioned by George. First of all, although the story does feature some dramatic twists and turns and therefore catches the reader by surprise from time to time, the plot is still comparatively simple. Besides, the reader is spoon-fed with information by a demigod-like protagonist, which leads to the fact that the "crime" could never scare or mesmerise the reader. As a consequence, there is the risk of this short story not being appealing to many pupils. However, it could perhaps be an option to include watching the BBC adaptation of the story, *A Scandal in Belgravia*. This film is part of the popular *Sherlock* series and therefore attracts a younger audience. In this case, reading "A Scandal in Bohemia" would be at least justifiable for comparative purposes.

As the examples show, George's positive appraisal does not apply equally to all crime stories.

Apart from that, I think there are also some more general reasons why crime fiction should not be added to the curriculum.

One argument against reading crime stories in the classroom is that they might overwhelm young, impressionable minds, as they sometimes contain quite a large amount of violence. For younger children especially, it may simply not be suitable to meet "mankind on the edge" (l. 15).

Furthermore, according to Elizabeth George, "a courtroom drama" (ll. 2/3) and other "tale[s] of suspense" (l. 1) also qualify as a crime story. It logically follows that *To Kill a Mockingbird* and *Romeo and Juliet* could also be considered crime stories in a broad sense. Both feature a crime (the forbidden marriage in *Romeo and Juliet* and the false accusations against Tom Robinson in *To Kill a Mockingbird*) and in both cases, this brings out the most in the characters – which, to quote George, "is the stuff of drama and catharsis" (l. 34). Just think of Romeo's final speech ("oh happy dagger") or the development of Jem Finch as a result of the unfair trial. In a nutshell: Why should the curricula in schools, which are usually too packed already, be charged with yet another literary genre when crime also features in the classics?

To sum up, I personally think there are some crime stories that are indeed suitable for being dealt with by pupils, whereas there are others that I would not want to read in class. In my view, the issue should not be whether or not to incorporate crime stories into the curriculum at all, but rather which ones to incorporate. In this regard, age is one of the factors that should not be ignored, as many crime stories tend to be more appropriate for older pupils. All in all, if the choice of stories is carefully considered, dealing with crime fiction in class can make sense. Nevertheless, the question remains whether it is absolutely necessary to make modifications to the curriculum as there is a sufficient amount of crime in classics anyway.

Text II Excerpt from Toni Morrison, *The Bluest Eye* (1970)

1 **TIPP**

The command term *(dt. Operator)* "summarize" asks you to state the main points of a text. For this task therefore, you need to find all the important aspects concerning Pecola's experience as depicted in the excerpt at hand: before, during and after buying candy. Only write down what is essential. Your text should be well-structured and significantly shorter than the original. Paraphrase the main points in your own words rather than copying from the excerpt. Furthermore, refrain from commenting on the text.
Your text could include the following aspects:

- Pecola, a young African-American girl, is on her way to the grocery store.
- Inside the store, the white shop owner treats her in a very unfriendly manner:
  - he does not really acknowledge her
  - he talks to her in a rude way
  - he tries to avoid touching her hand
- When Pecola leaves the store, she is embarrassed and sad.
- Outside, however, these feelings turn into anger.

The excerpt from the novel *The Bluest Eye*, which was written by Toni Morrison and published in 1970, deals with what the protagonist Pecola, a young African-American girl who lives in the American Midwest during the 1930s, experiences while going to the grocery store to buy candy.

While Pecola is still on her way to the store, she notices some dandelions at the bottom of a telephone pole. Whereas she herself thinks they are beautiful, she knows that other people call them weeds and that they often get rid of them. She remembers that people always care about the leaves but disregard the yellow heads, and wonders whether this might be because there are so many of them.

As soon as she arrives at the store, the young girl chooses which candies she wants, pulls her money out of her shoe – which is where she carries it around – and is ready to buy them. In the following, however, she is confronted with the unfriendly behaviour of the white shop owner, Mr. Yacobowski, which is expressed in his vacant, disapproving look, rude remarks and the attempt to avoid physical contact with her. Pecola, who is already familiar with reactions like this, attributes the man's behaviour to her skin colour.

When stepping out of the store, she feels ashamed and sad. Then, her eyes meet the dandelions once more. This time, though, she cannot see the beauty in them anymore and anger increasingly replaces the shame inside her.

2 **TIPP**

The command term "analyze" requires you to describe particular aspects or characteristics of a text in detail and support your points by giving evidence from the text. So, in this task, you are supposed to describe the white shop owner's behaviour towards Pecola, refer to significant text passages and explain how this behaviour changes the girl's self-esteem. Your text should be well-structured and contain an introduction as well as a conclusion.
The following findings could be mentioned in your text:
- shop owner's behaviour:
  - he does not really recognise Pecola, but just gives her an empty look
  - he is unfriendly and confronts her very rudely
  - he does not want to touch her hand while exchanging candy and money
- influence on Pecola:
  - her self-esteem is lowered
  - she feels less of a person

Self-esteem plays an important role in our lives, as it is often reflected in our behaviour. Apart from ourselves one of the biggest influences on our self-esteem are the people in our environment. To let people have an impact, we do not necessarily have to know them personally or be close to them – it is sufficient to simply bump into them on the street or meet them at a store, for example, just like Pecola meets Mr. Yacobowski in the novel *The Bluest Eye*.
In order to be able to see how Pecola's self-esteem changes, it is important to compare her behaviour at the beginning of the story with that at the end.
At the beginning of the story, the young girl comes across as a confident person who enjoys her life and sees the good in everything – a fact which is conveyed with the help of the dandelions. While everyone she knows detests them and calls them weeds, Pecola sees their beauty and does not care about what others think (cf. ll. 3–8). After leaving the store at the end of the story, however, she is disgusted by them and calls them ugly like everybody else (cf. ll. 49/50). This clearly shows that her attitude towards life has changed. While she was full of love for life and did not let the opinions of others influence her own at the beginning, she has adopted their negative view by the end. She feels worthless and inferior, and her "inexplicable shame" (l. 48) even turns into anger.
Thus, what Pecola experienced inside the store must have affected her behaviour and lowered her self-esteem. Since the shop owner Mr. Yacobowski is the only person she met there, it is glaringly obvious that it was he who played a significant role. However, what exactly did he do to cause such a drastic change?
The first interaction between the two characters that is noteworthy is the look Mr. Yacobowski gives the young girl after she enters the store. His gaze is portrayed as being pejorative and uninterested, as he looks at her but "does not see her, because for him there is nothing to see" (ll. 17/18). Additionally, Pecola describes this empty look as a "vacuum edged with distaste" (l. 31) – instead of showing interest in her as a person

and customer, he does not even seem to recognise her as a human being. Although Pecola has experienced being treated like this before (cf. ll. 27/28), it still affects her: she feels as if the white man – like all white people – is disgusted by her due to her skin colour and race (cf. ll. 28–31). Whereas she knows that the colour of her skin does not define who she is as a person, the shop owner's dehumanising behaviour still makes her feel out of place and insecure, which leads to a lowering of her self-esteem. In the interaction that follows, Pecola seems to be walking on eggshells, trying hard not to offend Mr. Yacobowski (cf. ll. 32–34). Feeling intimidated, she only points a finger at the candy she wants to buy. The shop owner, however, cannot identify which candy she is pointing to and confronts her in a very rude and condescending manner (cf. ll. 36, 39, 42), which amplifies the girl's insecurity even more.
When Mr. Yacobowski tries to avoid touching the girl's hand as best he can while giving her the candy and taking her money (cf. ll. 43–47), Pecola's self-esteem is finally deflated. Hence, she simply cannot help but feel ashamed when she leaves the store. Soon, however, this shame changes into anger (cf. ll. 48, 51–53).
To draw a conclusion, all these incidents show how Mr. Yacobowski's behaviour gradually leads to Pecola leaving the shop as a different person from when she entered it.

3 **TIPP**

This assignment is embedded in a situational context you should refer to in some way. It requires you to write an article for the online journal of a European school project. Your article needs an introduction, a main part and a persuasive conclusion as well as a headline. Furthermore, subheadings might be good to make the structure of the text more obvious to the reader. As you have to assess whether the image of the dandelion is an appropriate literary symbol for African-American protagonists in literature, you should explain the symbol's meaning first. Then, arguments for and against the matter in question are needed. Besides referring to the excerpt from Toni Morrison's novel *The Bluest Eye*, you are also expected to adduce examples from materials studied in class. This could include Harper Lee's novel *To Kill a Mockingbird*.

- Meaning of the symbol:
  - Many people have a stereotypical opinion of dandelions and reject them as weeds. → Many white people consider black people to be inferior and worthless.
  - First, Pecola thinks dandelions are pretty and strong, but then she, too, regards them as ugly weeds. → First, the girl has a positive view of herself and other African-American people, but then her opinion is negatively influenced by the discriminatory experience with the white shop owner.
- Possible arguments for the appropriateness of the symbol:
  - The white shop owner is impolite and condescending towards Pecola because, in his view, she does not deserve his attention.
  - The man's behaviour makes Pecola herself feel unwelcome and inferior.

- Black people are often discriminated against by the white majority (e. g. in *To Kill a Mockingbird*: Tom Robinson's discriminatory treatment and unfair trial, the fact that black people are regarded as only good for hard work in the fields).

– Possible arguments against the appropriateness of the symbol:
  - The symbol is too subjective (it expresses Pecola's specific point of view rather than a general perception).
  - Related to the first argument, the symbol is also too negative (e. g. in *To Kill a Mockingbird*: The Finches' unprejudiced attitude towards black people and their caring treatment of Calpurnia as an equal).

Flower Power – The power of dandelions

As part of the project on "The Power of Imagery in Literature", it is our main goal to first identify images used in different works of literature and then assess how well these images convey the intended meaning.

In her novel *The Bluest Eye*, Toni Morrison uses the dandelion as a literary symbol for the protagonist Pecola, a young African-American girl who lives in the American Midwest during the late 1930s, and for black people in general. However, is the dandelion really an appropriate image within Morrison's story? Could other African-American characters in literature also be symbolised by a dandelion? To answer this second question, Harper Lee's novel *To Kill a Mockingbird* will be taken as a reference.

A dandelion – what does that mean?

In *The Bluest Eye,* it is argued that many people have a rather stereotypical opinion of dandelions, regard them as weeds and want to get rid of them. Furthermore, if dandelions are plucked with the purpose of being used to make soup or wine, people are not interested in their yellow heads but only their leaves. If we assume that the plants stand for African Americans, this image symbolises the fact that many white people regard black people as inferior and worthless. Pecola initially considers dandelions to be beautiful and strong but later finds them ugly and useless. This illustrates that, at first, the black girl is a confident and happy person who views herself and other African-American people as being pretty, but is then influenced by the white shop owner's discriminatory behaviour while buying candy. She suffers from low self-esteem and accepts her fate of being seen as worthless, inferior and ugly by the white majority – although this makes her angry.

Are dandelions an appropriate choice?

In some respects, the image of the dandelion is an appropriate literary symbol for both Pecola and other black characters. Both in *The Bluest Eye* and *To Kill a Mockingbird*, for instance, there are African-American people who suffer discrimination due to their race. Many white people regard them as "weeds" because of the colour of their skin. In *The Bluest Eye*, the white shop owner considers the black girl to be unworthy of receiving his attention or polite treatment, so that eventually Pecola herself feels inferior and rejected. Similarly, in *To Kill a Mockingbird*, Tom Robinson is discriminated against by the white community of Maycomb and receives an unfair trial. The white jury convicts him, which, in view of the fact that his lawyer Atticus refutes all evidence speaking against Tom Robinson, is clearly wrong and is highly likely to stem from the fact that he is black. Furthermore, in Pecola's description of the dandelions it is also said that people are usually only interested in their leaves and not their heads. In this regard, the image is again quite fitting for the situation depicted in *To Kill a Mockingbird,* where Maycomb's white society only shows interest in the bodies of the black people – as they work for them in the fields.

All in all, *The Bluest Eye* and *To Kill a Mockingbird* are two examples of stories in which many black people are marginalised by the white majority – just as dandelions are not wanted by many people.

To what extent are dandelions an inappropriate choice?

Nevertheless, dandelions are not necessarily an appropriate symbol for all African-American characters in literature. In *To Kill a Mockingbird,* this becomes very clear when comparing the attitude of the Finch family with those of the rest of Maycomb society. The Finches are not racist and get along very well with the black people around them. They have nothing to criticise about the black people, meaning that they do not regard them as "weeds" but rather as beautiful and equal, not to mention that they love their black housekeeper Calpurnia as if she was a family member. In contrast to Pecola in *The Bluest Eye*, Calpurnia does not get the feeling of being unwanted. Consequently, the image depicted in *The Bluest Eye* is quite subjective. It mirrors the way Pecola perceives the situation. However, as the symbol is rather negative, it is not appropriate as a general image for all African-American characters.

We can therefore conclude that the dandelion, as used by Toni Morrison in her novel *The Bluest Eye*, is a very appropriate literary symbol in this specific story and could also be transferred to some other African-American characters in literature. Nevertheless, it is not an image which can be used universally.

HÖRVERSTEHEN

You will hear each recording twice. After each listening you will have time to complete your answers.

Task 1: Young People and Their Education (5 BE)

You will hear five young people talking about their education. While listening, match the speakers 1 to 5 with the headings A to G. There are two more headings than you need.

Headings

A Choice of institution and consequences for family
B Choice of institution and student's peers
C Family expectations and career choice
D Family traditions and choice of institution
E Family traditions and reality of teaching
F School requirements and chances of good placement
G School requirements and student's dissatisfaction

Speaker	1	2	3	4	5
Heading					

Task 2: Buckingham Palace (6 BE)

You will hear a news report about Buckingham Palace. While listening, tick (✓) the correct answer (a, b, c, or d). There is only one correct answer.

1 The refurbishment of Buckingham Palace requires

a ☐ risky but important repair work.
b ☐ the Queen to spend less money.
c ☐ the agreement of Britain's legislation.
d ☐ a large sum of money from private donations.

2 The palace is in a bad state because

a ☐ not much has been done for decades.
b ☐ there are too many visitors every year.
c ☐ heavy rainfalls have damaged the roof.
d ☐ mistakes were made during the construction.

3 The refurbishment work will be paid for by

a ☐ selling specially-designed souvenirs.
b ☐ putting up the entrance fee for visitors.
c ☐ collecting money through sponsored events.
d ☐ raising the monarch's income from the state.

4 Graham Smith points out that

a ☐ the British monarchy should be abolished.
b ☐ the majority of people opposes the project.
c ☐ the Royals already get an annual monetary rise.
d ☐ everyone is affected by reductions in state spending.

5 Duncan Wilson states that

a ☐ the British monarchy needs to be preserved.
b ☐ spending public money on the project is justified.
c ☐ the disapproving Members of Parliament have a point.
d ☐ many tourist sights in Great Britain are in need of repair.

6 At the end the tone of the news report is

a ☐ critical.
b ☐ neutral.
c ☐ humorous.
d ☐ enthusiastic.

Task 3: Huckleberry Finn (14 BE)

You will hear a radio feature about Mark Twain's novel *The Adventures of Huckleberry Finn.* While listening, answer the questions. You need not write complete sentences. Unless otherwise specified, one aspect is enough.

1	What did Ernest Hemingway say about Mark Twain's novel? *(Name **one** aspect.)*	
2	What is / was the novel criticized for? a) today b) when it first came out	 a) b)
3	What did Tom Reigstad and Mark Twain have in common?	
4	How did the Buffalo library get a part of Twain's manuscript?	
5	What did the *Buffalo Young Men's Association* do?	
6	What did Gluck do to get a part of Twain's manuscript?	
7	What happened shortly before Gluck died?	
8	Why wasn't the other part of the manuscript discovered earlier?	
9	What did Pam's sister wrongly assume?	
10	What did Reigstad want to find out after hearing about the discovery?	
11	What did some book dealers plan to do with the manuscript? *(Note down the **two** steps.)*	a) b)
12	How does the Buffalo library make sure that the manuscript is protected?	

SPRACHMITTLUNG

Aufgabenstellung

Your school is organizing an exchange with a high school in the USA. To help the American students prepare for their stay in Germany, your school is creating a website with information on different aspects of German customs and culture.
Using the information in the text, write an article for this website on the Germans' consumption of drinking water both in general and in restaurants.

Text

Michael Frank, „Leitungswasser hat in der deutschen Tischkultur keinen Stellenwert" (2016)

Ein Festmahl, ein Zechgelage ist eigentlich nur so gut, wie gut und reichlich seine wichtigste Ingredienz fließt, nämlich frisches, klares Wasser. Es stillt den Durst, es begleitet und umspielt Speisen und Getränke, es erschließt oft erst den genüsslichen Gehalt des Weiteren, denn ein feiner Tropfen gegen den Durst getrunken, das wäre erstens kein Genuss und zweitens groteske Verschwendung. Überdies schmeckt frisches, klares Wasser wunderbar.

In der deutschen Tischkultur hat es diesen Stellenwert nicht. Es ist kaum zwei Generationen her, dass man sich im privaten Rahmen wirklich Gedanken über Qualität und Geschmack von Wasser macht. Dass sich etwa Brauer für ihr Bier um die Qualität dieses Grundstoffes sorgen müssen, das kannte man. Einige wussten sogar noch, dass der Geschmack von Nudeln nicht zuletzt von der Beschaffenheit des Teigwassers abhängig ist. Aber Wasser als Geschmackserlebnis, das ist neu. Vielfach wird mit Wasser immer noch achtlos umgegangen, allenfalls zwischen „mit und ohne Kohlensäure" unterschieden und dabei Leitungswasser nachgerade verachtet. Die Zunft des Wassersommeliers ist noch exotisch, sie hat mit Missionstätigkeit zu tun.

Rigidere Alkoholbestimmungen im Verkehr und eine Rückbesinnung auf alles, was gesund und „pur" ist, haben dem Wasser im Alltagsgebrauch dennoch eine ganz neue Rolle beschert. 1970 trank jeder Bundesbürger pro Kopf und Jahr statistisch etwa 14,5 Liter Mineralwasser, heute sind es 175 Liter. Haben die Leute vorher Leitungswasser getrunken? Eher nicht, sonst hatte sich die Vorliebe doch halten müssen, indem man auch in Restaurant, Gasthaus oder Imbiss leichthin Leitungswasser bekäme. Seinetwegen muss man es in mancher Gaststube beinahe auf einen Streit ankommen lassen.

Bestellt man zum Essen ein Glas Wasser, macht man sich sofort verdächtig, ein ekelhafter Geizhals zu sein. Der Wirt nimmt an, man wolle das Glas Leitungswasser gratis. Denn Mineralwasser aus der Flasche – oder heute Tafelwasser aus dem Zapfhahn – ist die Ware, die einem Gastronomen in Deutschland die mit Abstand höchste Gewinnmarge bringt. Der Generalfehler der Leitungswasserdebatte ist aber, dass sie meist unter der Rubrik Sparsamkeit abgehandelt wird, also als Frage des Geldes. Dass der Geschmack, aber auch Umweltbewusstsein das Hauptmotiv hartnäckiger Nachfrage nach Leitungswasser sein kann, glaubt fast niemand.

Leitungswasser war bis vor relativ kurzer Zeit tatsächlich so eine Sache. Der auch in kulinarischen Dingen äußerst engagierte Historiker Hans Ottomeyer, lange Chef des Deutschen Historischen Museums in Berlin, erinnert daran, dass Leitungswasser noch bis in die Achtziger meist „fast bis zur Ungenießbarkeit" mit Chlor versetzt war. [...]

Selters, Urmarke des deutschen Mineralwassers, war lange Zeit ein gesuchtes Luxusgut, weil gesundheitlich absolut unbedenklich und damit die Ausnahme. Einst durften etwa in München Färber, Gerber und Kürschner an Brautagen nicht arbeiten. Da man aus den Zuflüssen der Isar schöpfte, wollte man keine giftigen Säuren und Laugen aus deren Abwasser im Bier haben. Im 19. Jahrhundert erkannte man städtische Gewässer als Brutstätten der Cholera und anderer teuflischer Gefahren. „Wasser macht Läuse im Bauch", haben noch die Großeltern nur halb im Scherz gewarnt. Das sitzt tief.

In vielen Nachbarländern ist es schon lange Brauch, dass für den Gast als Erstes eine Karaffe Wasser auf den Tisch kommt. Dies wohlgemerkt in Gegenden, deren Wasserqualität weit unter der deutschen liegt. In Frankreich, berichtet der Wassersommelier Armin Schönenberger, hat schon seit den Sechzigerjahren jeder Gast das gesetzliche Anrecht auf einen Krug Gratiswasser. [...]

Wenn Höchstpreislokale Mineralwassersorten von bis zu 100 Euro die Flasche anbieten, hat das mehr mit Verpackungsfirlefanz zu tun als mit Qualität. Auch mit Wasser wird geprotzt heutzutage. Und da kommen ernsthaft Menschen und insistieren auf Wasser aus der Leitung?

Armin Schönenberger, der Wassersommelier, sieht das so: „Wasser ist ein Menschenrecht. Jeder Gast kann meiner Meinung nach überall Leitungswasser verlangen. Der Wirt kann das nicht verweigern, aber er hat nun mal das Hausrecht. Er kann bestimmen, zu welchem Preis er diese Leistung gewährt." Alles, was ein Wirt seinen Gästen bietet, soll seinen Preis haben. Auch Leitungswasser muss serviert werden und braucht ein ansprechendes Glas. Es auszuschenken ist Leistung. Leitungswasser darf im Lokal also etwas kosten.

640 Wörter

Quelle: Michael Frank, „Leitungswasser hat in der deutschen Tischkultur keinen Stellenwert", in: Süddeutsche Zeitung, *30. 12. 2016*

Anmerkungen

15 Sommelier: Experte, der Restaurantgäste bei der Auswahl von Wein berät
50 Firlefanz: Überflüssiges oder wertloses Zeug

Lösungsvorschlag

HÖRVERSTEHEN

Transkript 1 Young People and Their Education

Speaker 1: My parents immigrated to the US from India to pursue a better life than their parents and to give me a better life than them, specifically sending me to an elite private school with a pricey tuition. This was so important that they accepted the yearly five-figure payment even if it wasn't always easy. I can't remember the last time we've gone on a vacation as a family.

From: Nila Venkat: My pricey education, https://yr.media/news/my-pricey-education/, © Youth Radio

Speaker 2: I went to a big, public high school. It wasn't the best learning environment for me. I was stressed out by all the homework, work sheets and tests. Rather than encouraging me to think for myself, my grades seemed to be determined by how well I could memorise facts and dates. I felt like a robot.

From: Marie Sosa: What I didn't learn in high school, https://yr.media/news/what-i-didnt-learn-in-high-school/ © Youth Radio

Speaker 3: I come from a family of high achievers. Both my parents attended Ivy League universities but for college I chose a different path. For much of high school, I put everything into school work. I didn't think too much about girls, looks or popularity. My outlook changed when my sister chose a small liberal arts college over an Ivy. I was shocked but over time I saw how happy she was at her school. It made me reconsider how I viewed college, how my choice didn't have to be based on rankings or legacy.

From: Benjamin Rossi: Turning away from the IVY League, https://yr.media/news/turning-away-from-the-ivy-league-2/, © Youth Radio

Speaker 4: For three years I attended a private middle school. Our books were always new, the food always organic and my teachers had one-on-one check-ins with us every week. But something was missing. I would talk with my friends at lunch, all of them white and middle class like me, and note how we all had the same opinions and things to say. By eighth grade it was getting really old. Throughout middle school people talked about public schools the same way you'd talk about city sewers but I was fascinated. I wanted to meet people who were different than me, and have friends who I could actually learn from.

From: Natalie Bettendorf: The benefits of a public education, https://yr.media/news/the-benefits-of-a-public-education/, © Youth Radio

Speaker 5: My 18-year-old sister is studying for medical school. My 14-year-old brother already designs programs with my dad, a software engineer. My aunt a doctor, my uncle an engineer. And me? I'm interested in public affairs. My mom regularly asks me in the car, "Do you know what you want to be when you grow up?" I used to answer, "a lawyer, a journalist, a politician" but we got into arguments so often that now I just tell her I don't really know yet. I know my parents want the best for me and I keep their suggestions in mind. In Indian culture, careers in STEM are seen as good, high-paying jobs. The rest? Not so much. The thought of their son in a liberal arts profession is a difficult pill for them to swallow.

From: Arnav Gupta: Going against my family's career goals, https://yr.media/news/going-against-my-familys-career-goals/, © Youth Radio

TIPP

These text passages will help you find the correct answer:

1 "sending me to an elite private school with a pricey tuition. […] they accepted the yearly five-figure payment even if it wasn't always easy. I can't remember the last time we've gone on a vacation as a family." (ll. 2–5)

2 "I was stressed out by all the homework, work sheets and tests. […] I felt like a robot." (ll. 7–9)

3 "I come from a family of high achievers. Both my parents attended Ivy League universities but for college I chose a different path. […] my choice didn't have to be based on rankings or legacy." (ll. 10–16)

4 "For three years I attended a private middle school. […] I would talk with my friends at lunch, all of them white and middle class like me […]. Throughout middle school people talked about public schools the same way you'd talk about city sewers but I was fascinated. I wanted to meet people who were different than me" (ll. 17–23)

5 "I know my parents want the best for me and I keep their suggestions in mind. […] The thought of their son in a liberal arts profession is a difficult pill for them to swallow." (ll. 30–33)

Speaker	1	2	3	4	5
Heading	A	G	D	B	C

Transkript 2 Buckingham Palace

Reporter: Here in Britain it's been announced that Queen Elizabeth's official London residence, Buckingham Palace, is to have refurbishment, which will cost around $ 450 million. The work, which will go before Parliament for approval, will involve the replacement of the palace's wiring, heating and plumbing. Officials say the repairs are needed to avoid catastrophic problems but critics of the royal family have questioned whether the spending can be justified during a time of austerity. Here's our royal correspondent, Sarah Campbell.

Sarah Campbell: The official London residence of the Queen, a building which palace officials describe today as part of the nation's DNA is now in a dangerous state of disrepair. It contains more than 100 miles of electric cabling and 20 miles of heating pipes, along with six and a half thousand plug sockets and 5,000 light fittings. Little has been replaced since the 1950s, leaving the palace at risk of fire or flood damage on a catastrophic scale according to an independent assessment. The plan is to spread the refurbishments over 10 years. The tax payer will fund the work through a 66 % increase in the annual treasury payments to the Queen, known as the Sovereign Grant. Graham Smith is from the anti-monarchy group, Republic.

Graham Smith: I think it's pretty appalling that the palace have gone yet again to the taxpayer to ask for more money. Everybody else is suffering huge cuts: public services, you know, welfare, benefits and so on. Thirty-eight per cent increase on royal funding over the last five years and yet they're demanding even more.

Sarah Campbell: Some MPs have also questioned the amount of public money to be used, however Duncan Wilson from Heritage England, which will be involved in approving the works, says the palace is a special case.

Duncan Wilson: If any building deserves the title 'iconic', and representing the UK to the world outside, it must be Buckingham Palace, so surely we need to protect it for future generations and do that properly.

Sarah Campbell: The Queen is completely supportive of the plan, say palace officials, and although she won't have to move out when the builders move in, she is prepared to move rooms to accommodate them. With 775 to choose from, Her Majesty should be able to avoid the noise.

TIPP

These text passages will help you find the correct answer:

1 "The work, which will go before Parliament for approval, […]" (l. 3)
2 "Little has been replaced since the 1950s, leaving the palace at risk of fire or flood damage on a catastrophic scale according to an independent assessment." (ll. 11–13)
3 "The tax payer will fund the work through a 66 % increase in the annual treasury payments to the Queen, known as the Sovereign Grant." (ll. 14–16)
4 "Everybody else is suffering huge cuts: public services, you know, welfare, benefits and so on." (ll. 18/19)
5 "If any building deserves the title 'iconic' […], it must be Buckingham Palace, so surely we need to protect it for future generations and do that properly." (ll. 24–26)
6 "With 775 to choose from, Her Majesty should be able to avoid the noise." (ll. 29/30)

1 The refurbishment of Buckingham Palace requires

c [✓] the agreement of Britain's legislation.

2 The palace is in a bad state because

a [✓] not much has been done for decades.

3 The refurbishment work will be paid for by

d [✓] raising the monarch's income from the state.

4 Graham Smith points out that

d [✓] everyone is affected by reductions in state spending.

5 Duncan Wilson states that

b [✓] spending public money on the project is justified.

6 At the end the tone of the news report is

c [✓] humorous.

Transkript 3 Huckleberry Finn

Rachel Gillman: […] *The Adventures of Huckleberry Finn* tells the story of the young white Huck Finn and his black friend Jim and the things they got up to on the Mississippi River.

Tom Reigstad: The American novelist Ernest Hemingway proclaimed that it's the best American novel ever written, that nothing will ever be written like it and that all American literature came from that book. The novel, while mildly controversial when it was first published, has become increasingly controversial.

Rachel Gillman: Controversial because the racial stereotypes and language used in the book seem shocking to a modern audience. But at the time it was published, it was seen as vulgar and challenging to social norms. Tom Reigstad is a professor of English at Buffalo University. […]

Tom Reigstad: My first job out of college was at the *Buffalo Courier-Express,* a thriving Buffalo newspaper, a daily newspaper that Twain had worked for years earlier and I started reading some of Twain's original writings […] and in 1979, I wrote a feature story where I researched the handwritten manuscript of *Adventures of Huckleberry Finn* that was housed in the Buffalo Library. The only known part of that handwritten manuscript to that date was the second half of the novel. […]

Rachel Gillman: Tom found out that the manuscript had been donated to the library in the late 19th century by a Buffalo lawyer called James Gluck. His granddaughter is Pam Lindholm. […]

Pam Lindholm: My grandfather'd started or he was one of the people that'd started *The Buffalo Young Men's Association* and that's what they did: they collected signatures and poems and whatnot and he thought it would be good to collect manuscripts and

I'm sure a few others did too but he was one of the first that thought that that was a good idea. […]

Rachel Gillman: Pam's grandfather had written to Mark Twain and asked the author if he would mind sending any original manuscripts of his books that he had kept.

Pam Lindholm: Mark Twain sent him the manuscript. He said, "I can only find half of it. I can only find the second half but I'll send it to you." So he did. Well, a couple of years later Mark Twain wrote my grandfather and said, "I've found the second half and I'll send it along." […]

Rachel Gillman: But the two parts of the manuscript didn't get reunited. Shortly after receiving the other half from Twain, James Gluck died. The manuscript was left in a trunk and it was passed down through the generations of the Gluck family. Nobody rifled through the papers inside the trunk and nothing more was heard about the missing pages, until Pam Lindholm received a phone call from her sister, a librarian, in February 1990.

Pam Lindholm: So, she called and she said, "Guess what I found?" And I said, "Heavens, what?" And she said, "I found the original handwritten manuscript of *Huck Finn.*" And at that time, she thought it was the whole thing because it was very fat. […]

Rachel Gillman: The sisters decided to call the auction house Sotheby's. […] News began to leak out about the remarkable discovery. […]

Tom Reigstad: […] The news went viral. The next day, there was a big story in *The New York Times.* The news went international because it was such a, you know, stunning find.

Rachel Gillman: And how did you feel at that moment?

Tom Reigstad: I just, you know, was shocked and amazed. It was such terrific news and I couldn't wait to take a look at the manuscript and see what changes Twain had made, the way he would, you know, cross things out, and add words. It's just as if you're looking over Twain's shoulder when he's in the midst of the composing process. […]

Rachel Gillman: […] Gluck's family, the Buffalo Public Library and The Mark Twain Project, an archive of some of Twain's works, fought a legal battle over the manuscript. […]

Tom Reigstad: Publicly, Sotheby's planned to auction off the newly discovered portion of *The Adventures of Huckleberry Finn* manuscript for between $ 500 and $ 750,000. Secretly, there was some movement by a consortium of rare book dealers across the country, who got wind of this and they had agreed with Sotheby's to purchase the manuscript for a million and a half dollars and then divide it up. […] Thankfully, that didn't happen.

Rachel Gillman: Pam and her sister settled for a much smaller amount of money to ensure it went to the Buffalo Public Library. The complete century-old manuscript is safely housed there to this day in a temperature-controlled vault where thousands of tourists come to visit it. […]

https://www.bbc.co.uk/sounds/play/p04svth5

TIPP

These text passages will help you find the correct answer:

1 "The American novelist Ernest Hemingway proclaimed that it's the best American novel ever written, that nothing will ever be written like it and that all American literature came from that book." (ll. 4–6)

2 "Controversial because the racial stereotypes and language used in the book seem shocking to a modern audience. But at the time it was published, it was seen as vulgar and challenging to social norms." (ll. 8–10)

3 "My first job out of college was at the *Buffalo Courier-Express,* a thriving Buffalo newspaper, a daily newspaper that Twain had worked for years earlier" (ll. 12/13)

4 "Tom found out that the manuscript had been donated to the library in the late 19th century by a Buffalo lawyer called James Gluck." (ll. 18/19)

5 "My grandfather'd started or he was one of the people that'd started *The Buffalo Young Men's Association* and that's what they did: they collected signatures and poems and whatnot and he thought it would be good to collect manuscripts" (ll. 21–23)

6 "Pam's grandfather had written to Mark Twain and asked the author if he would mind sending any original manuscripts of his books that he had kept." (ll. 26/27)

7 "Shortly after receiving the other half from Twain, James Gluck died." (ll. 32/33)

8 "The manuscript was left in a trunk and it was passed down through the generations of the Gluck family. Nobody rifled through the papers inside the trunk" (ll. 33–35)

9 "she said, 'I found the original handwritten manuscript of *Huck Finn.*' And at that time, she thought it was the whole thing because it was very fat." (ll. 39/40)

10 "I couldn't wait to take a look at the manuscript and see what changes Twain had made, the way he would, you know, cross things out, and add words. It's just as if you're looking over Twain's shoulder when he's in the midst of the composing process." (ll. 49–52)

11 "Secretly, there was some movement by a consortium of rare book dealers across the country, who got wind of this and they had agreed with Sotheby's to purchase the manuscript for a million and a half dollars and then divide it up." (ll. 58–60)

12 "The complete century-old manuscript is safely housed there to this day in a temperature-controlled vault" (ll. 63/64)

1	What did Ernest Hemingway say about Mark Twain's novel? *(Name **one** aspect.)*	(it's the) best American novel (ever written) / nothing will ever be written like it / all American literature came from it
2	What is/was the novel criticized for? a) today b) when it first came out	 a) racial stereotypes/language / racism b) vulgar / challenging to social norms
3	What did Tom Reigstad and Mark Twain have in common?	(they) worked for the same (daily) newspaper / (they both) worked in Buffalo
4	How did the Buffalo library get a part of Twain's manuscript?	(it) was donated (to the library) / (James) Gluck donated it
5	What did the *Buffalo Young Men's Association* do?	(they) collected signatures/poems/ manuscripts
6	What did Gluck do to get a part of Twain's manuscript?	(he) wrote to the author (and asked for manuscripts)
7	What happened shortly before Gluck died?	Twain sent Gluck the other half of the manuscript / (he) got the other half of the manuscript from Twain
8	Why wasn't the other part of the manuscript discovered earlier?	(it) was left in a trunk / nobody looked through the papers
9	What did Pam's sister wrongly assume?	(that) she had found the whole manuscript
10	What did Reigstad want to find out after hearing about the discovery?	what changes Twain had made / which words Twain had crossed out/added / (about) Twain's composing process
11	What did some book dealers plan to do with the manuscript? *(Note down the **two** steps.)*	a) purchase the manuscript (for a million and a half dollars) b) divide it up
12	How does the Buffalo library make sure that the manuscript is protected?	(it is) housed in a temperature-controlled vault/room

SPRACHMITTLUNG

TIPP

Your task is to create an article for a website with information for high school students. Usually, this allows for quite colloquial language, but given the topic of the article you have to deal with, a mainly neutral language register is required. Don't forget the heading which does not have to be the same as in the German article and round off your text with a short conclusion. Keep in mind your readership, who consist of American high school students. So, you ought to mention differences between Germany and the USA. A possible structure for your text could be:

- Allgemeines zum Wasserkonsum in Deutschland
- Leitungswasser versus (in Flaschen abgefülltes) Mineralwasser
- besondere Regeln in Restaurants

Tap water versus bottled (mineral) water

Coming from a country where customers are served a carafe of free water as a matter of course at any decent restaurant, you may be interested to learn about the Germans' habits concerning drinking water at home and when eating out.

Although it seems that water did not play any significant role in German drinking culture for a long time, its consumption has been rising constantly over the last few decades. Due to a crackdown on drunk driving coupled with a general inclination towards a healthy lifestyle and the realisation that water has its own distinctive taste, people are tending to drink more of it.

A distrust of the quality of tap water, which in the past often tasted of chlorine or was even endangering people's health, still lingers and explains a widespread preference of bottled water over tap water.

In restaurants, being served tap water cannot be taken for granted. Customers ordering it might be eyed with suspicion. It is often thought that they are trying to avoid paying for their drinks. Few will believe that a persistent request for tap water can stem from motives like sustainability or better taste. Obviously, restaurants can charge for tap water as they are offering a service, but that is not nearly as profitable as selling mineral water. At some high-priced restaurants people sometimes even show off by drinking it at 100 euros a bottle.

So, you see, things are different here!

Niedersachsen Englisch ▪ Abiturprüfung 2021
Erhöhtes Anforderungsniveau

HÖRVERSTEHEN

You will hear each recording twice. After each listening you will have time to complete your answers.

Task 1: Street Trees (7 BE)

You will hear a podcast on trees in Detroit.
While listening, answer the questions. You need not write complete sentences. Unless otherwise specified, name one aspect.

1	What are the advantages of street trees according to the presenter? *(Name two.)*	• • • make streets look nicer
2	What did a study say about the effect of planting eleven more trees per block?	
3	What was the paradoxical situation in Detroit between 2011 and 2014?	
4	What was the aim of Christine Carmichael's campaign?	
5	According to Christine Carmichael, what were some people in disadvantaged neighborhoods worried about?	
6	What would change these people's attitude towards street trees?	

Task 2: Border (6 BE)

You will hear a radio report about life on the Mexican-American border with the cities of El Paso on the American side, and Juarez on the Mexican side. While listening, tick (✓) the correct answer (a, b, c, or d). There is only one correct answer.

1 According to the female presenter, how do young locals see the border?

- **a** ☐ as a sad reality
- **b** ☐ as separating families
- **c** ☐ as having little importance
- **d** ☐ as separating different cultures

2 How does Antonio Villasenor-Baca perceive the border?

- **a** ☐ as a protective measure
- **b** ☐ as a necessary measure
- **c** ☐ as an annoying measure
- **d** ☐ as a threatening measure

3 Why are some children from Juarez able to attend an American school?

- **a** ☐ The school is run privately.
- **b** ☐ The American school is in Mexico.
- **c** ☐ They take part in a special program.
- **d** ☐ They have an American and a Mexican passport.

4 What is said about the connection of the two border cities?

- **a** ☐ They are twin cities.
- **b** ☐ They are interdependent.
- **c** ☐ Their police forces cooperate closely.
- **d** ☐ El Paso dominates Juarez financially.

5 Why can Kenia Guerrero cross the border faster?

- **a** ☐ She holds a Green Card.
- **b** ☐ She uses the commercial lane.
- **c** ☐ She only has a small backpack.
- **d** ☐ She has bought a special document.

6 What has made crossing the border more difficult for Kenia?

- **a** ☐ a change in politics
- **b** ☐ rising drug trafficking
- **c** ☐ increased illegal migration
- **d** ☐ the introduction of body scans

Task 3: Ship

(12 BE)

You will hear an interview with Sam King, one of the passengers of the *Empire Windrush*, a ship that took about 500 people from Jamaica to Great Britain in 1948. While listening, fill in the missing information. You need not write complete sentences. Unless otherwise specified, name one aspect.

1	Why the economic situation in Jamaica was so serious in 1948	
2	What Sam King's father wanted his son to do	
3	Why Sam King had spent time away from Jamaica	
4	What Sam King realized when back in Jamaica	
5	What Sam King says about the fare for the passage *(Name **one** aspect.)*	
6	What the journey of the *Windrush* led to	
7	Why some middle-aged passengers found it hard to leave Jamaica	
8	What some travellers did when learning a woman was on board illegally	
9	Why Sam considered the food on board bad *(Name **one** reason.)*	
10	How people spent their time on board *(Name **two** activities.)*	• •
11	What some younger passengers worried about	

SPRACHMITTLUNG

Aufgabenstellung

Your US exchange partner has to give a presentation in class about a German tradition and decides to talk about travelling journeymen, as he/she saw one in your hometown last summer. He/She asks you for some help.
Using the information in the text, write an email in which you present the tradition of travelling journeymen and the situation now.

Text

Andrea Döring, „Mit Stock und Hut auf Wanderschaft gehen" (2018)

Hut, Stock und ein Bündel – der freundliche junge Mann mit den langen Rasta-Locken ist unschwer als Wandergeselle zu erkennen. An einer Raststätte an der A61 in Rheinland-Pfalz fragt er nach einer Mitfahrgelegenheit.

Bis Worms passen die Pläne zusammen, und das kleine Bündel, auch Charlottenburger genannt, hat locker Platz im Kofferraum. Konstantin Schäfer stammt aus Saarlouis und ist Zimmermann. Gerade kommt der 24-Jährige von einer Feier in der Eifel. Jetzt ist er auf dem Weg zu seinem bislang letzten Arbeitgeber im südhessischen Heppenheim. Der soll ihm in seinem Wanderbuch noch ein Zeugnis ausstellen.

Das Wanderbuch, der knotige Stock, auch Stenz genannt, und das Bündel gehören zur Grundausstattung jedes Wandergesellen dazu. Stolz trägt Schäfer den traditionellen schwarzen Hut, einen Ohrring, ein weißes Hemd, darüber eine Weste mit acht Perlmuttknöpfen, ein Jackett und weite Schlaghosen. Seine Kluft ist schwarz. Das weist ihn als Zimmermann aus, denn jedes Gewerk hat seine eigene Farbe.

Wer Meister werden wollte, musste vom Spätmittelalter bis zur beginnenden Industrialisierung auf Wanderschaft gehen. Arbeits- und Lebenserfahrung sollten die jungen Männer sammeln. In ungefähr 35 Handwerken ist das bis heute möglich: Bäcker, Betonbauer, Bootsbauer, Goldschmiede, Köche, Landwirte, Maurer und Schneider gehören etwa dazu.

„Es ist wunderbar, wenn junge Menschen Erfahrungen sammeln. In der Bäckerei habe ich Wandersleute allerdings noch nie gesehen", erzählt Peter Görtz, Inhaber einer großen Bäckerei-Kette in Ludwigshafen und Umgebung. „Ich würde sofort 20 nehmen."

Maternus Burauen von der IG Bau und erster Sekretär der Confôderation Europäischer Gesellenzünfte (CCEG) schätzt, dass derzeit etwa 450 bis 550 Gesellen auf der Walz sind. Eine offizielle Statistik gibt es nicht. Aktuell seien schätzungsweise zehn bis zwanzig Prozent der Wandersleute Frauen. […]

Seit 2014 gehört die Walz in Deutschland zum immateriellen Kulturerbe der UNESCO. Wer sich auf sie begeben will, muss einige Regeln beachten: Er muss in einem Handwerk einen Gesellenbrief erlangt haben, unverheiratet sowie schuldenfrei sein. Die Wanderschaft dauert zwei oder drei Jahre – und einen Tag. In dieser Zeit darf man sich seinem Heimatort bis auf 50 Kilometer nicht nähern. Ursprünglich war dies als Marktkontrolle für die Meister gedacht – ihre Gesellen sollten woanders ihr Glück finden und ihnen keine Konkurrenz machen.

„Ich hatte Fernweh", sagt Schäfer. Seit fast zwei Jahren ist er schon unterwegs. Durch Holland, Belgien, Frankreich, Österreich, die Schweiz und Israel führte ihn bereits sein Weg. „Viele unterschiedliche Arbeitstechniken habe ich kennengelernt, aber wichtiger als die handwerkliche ist die Erfahrung mit Menschen und die Selbsterkenntnis", sagt er.

„Beim Österreichischen Hospiz in Jerusalem habe ich am Eingangsportal Schusslöcher zugespachtelt", berichtet er. Welche Arbeitgeber Schäfer nach seinem Besuch in Heppenheim findet, ist offen. Der Geselle will nach Norwegen. „Die zahlen gut", hofft er. Der Lohn richtet sich nach den ortsüblichen Tarifen. Üblich ist oft auch Kost und Logis.

In Worms am Dom ist die gemeinsame Fahrt zu Ende, es bleibt noch der Weg bis Heppenheim. Dort hat sich Schäfers zwischenzeitlicher Arbeitgeber und früherer Altgeselle Jerome Schmitt bereits mit 25 Jahren selbstständig gemacht. „Ich habe ihn unter meine Fittiche genommen, habe ihm beigebracht, wie das Leben auf der Landstraße funktioniert, wie man Arbeit findet, als ich vor zwei Jahren selber noch unterwegs war", berichtet Schmitt. „Wer auf Wanderschaft geht, hat schon ein gewisses handwerkliches Know-how. Man lernt mehr im Bereich des Menschlichen", erzählt er. „Wichtig ist das vor allem bei problematischen Kunden. Man ist pragmatisch und zielorientiert, wirft nicht so schnell die Flinte ins Korn", sagt er zum Wert der alten Traditionen. „Man gibt sein Wort, man lässt sich festnageln."

Festnageln ist dabei im buchstäblichen Sinne gemeint. „Man wird auch heute noch mit dem Ohrläppchen an einen Balken genagelt. Dann bekommt man Ringe an die Ohren. Ursprünglich waren die dazu da, die Beerdigung zu bezahlen, wenn man unterwegs stirbt", sagt Schmitt. Im Zeitalter von Piercings und Tattoos wirkt das aber gar nicht mehr so archaisch. Und ganz modern erscheint auch die Idee der Walz, an verschiedenen Orten zu leben und zu arbeiten.

638 Wörter

Foto: picture alliance/Andrea Döring/dpa | Andrea Döring
Text: Andrea Döring: Mit Stock und Hut auf Wanderschaft gehen, DPA vom 28. 05. 2018

Anmerkungen

16 Gewerk – Handwerk
28 Walz – Wanderschaft eines Handwerksgesellen

TEXTAUFGABE

Von den zwei Aufgaben ist eine auszuwählen und zu bearbeiten.

Aufgabe I: Aufgabenstellung

1 Sum up the excerpt. (30 %)

2 Examine the atmosphere created in the text. (30 %)

3 You are taking part in an international project entitled "Facing Life's Crossroads," dealing with the choices young people are confronted with. You have to hand in an article for the project website in which you discuss the following statement by the writer Roy T. Bennett: "You are not the victim of the world, but rather the master of your own destiny. It is your choices and decisions that determine your destiny."
Write the article, also referring to the text at hand and materials studied in class, such as the novel *Never Let Me Go* and the story "Two Kinds." (40 %)

Text I Excerpt from Sophie Mackintosh, *Blue Ticket* (2020)

Calla is a 14-year-old teenager living in a dystopian society. She has just reached puberty and therefore has to go to "the lottery," which determines whether she will have children or not.

The lottery station was a lot like the clinic: two storeys of pale brick, a flat roof. When we pulled up, the emissary outside was smoking a cigarette, but he threw it into the road when he saw us. Congratulations, he said to me. He led us inside to where the others waited.

The floorboards were wooden, varnished aggressively. Countless feet had scuffed that floor. It pooled the reflections of all the lights – spotlights from the ceiling, a lamp on the desk where a man in a dark suit sat on an orange plastic chair, watching us, legs crossed. He could have been a doctor, but he wore no white coat, no white plastic gloves. There were four other girls in their own dresses sitting in a row on a wooden bench, flowers both real and fake pinned to chests. They were not the girls from my school. One wore velvet, two wore tulle, and the other wore satin like me. I took a shine to the girl in satin. Same species.

We lined up, waiting to pull our tickets from the machine, the way you would take your number at the butcher's counter. The music popular that year played from speakers on the ceiling. Just gravity enough. Just ceremony enough. Not necessarily such an important thing, after all.

My name was called first. They watched me as I walked the length of the room, towards the machine inside its cloaked box. I put my hand in it. I was apprehensive but ready for my life to be decided. I closed my eyes and thought about my father with the wine bottle to his eye. The machine was silent as it discharged a sliver of hard paper into my hand. It was a deep cobalt. Congratulations, the possible doctor in the dark suit said to me.

The other girls followed, each taking their own ticket from the machine in turn. Almost a full house! he exclaimed at the end, reading a piece of paper spat out from the machine. We huddled and compared tickets. They were all blue, except for one, which was white. The girl with the white ticket was escorted into a separate room by the doctor and another emissary. We watched the three of them walk through an unlit doorway. When the doctor came back he clapped his hands twice. You have been spared, he said with a terrible benevolence. [...]

The bathroom of the lottery house was filled with yellow light, the veins of my thin neck standing out underneath it. I was a plucked chicken with badly applied eye-shadow, but the locket was around my throat now. There was a long, low mirror above the sink, a wicker chair in the corner and two bathroom stalls painted peach. In the mirror I watched the other girls leaning against the wall. Toes flexing. Eyes raised to the ceiling, moving to the door when the girl with the white ticket came in to join us, then back to the ceiling. There was a dying flower arrangement at the corner of the sink, gaps of oasis showing through pink carnations. The music came through in here too, speakers in the ceiling or underneath the sink.

At first I kept looking at the girl who had drawn the white ticket, the other girl in satin, though hers was pale blue and dirty at the hem where it dragged. Her eyes were red. I had the urge to take her arm and run with her somewhere, out to the woodland where I used to smoke with the other girls in my class between lessons, beyond the broken barbed wire of the school perimeter where the teachers could not see us. But I did not touch her; I made myself stop looking.

Inside the cubicle I spent some time reading the names and dates scratched on the door. With the safety pin that held on my fake peony corsage I engraved *Calla, Blue Ticket,* a smiley face and the date underneath. The swell of relief, smooth and natural as a muscle. I would never have children. And I was glad. I had been a child myself, not so long ago. I did not want to put any other puny creature through that. [...]

An emissary handed us each a bottle of water, a compass and a sandwich from the table, wrapped in a napkin. We did not get to pick the filling. The bottle given to the white-ticket girl was larger than ours, I noticed, and she received two sandwiches. It was happening immediately, the diverging of our paths, no time to spare.

Go, the doctor said to us. To the place of your choice. Walk into it. Anywhere but here. Congratulations.

I met my father's gaze. I had a city in mind. He looked back at me and nodded his head.

We walked out together into the cool night. The adults stayed in the light, for coffee and refreshments, to debrief with the doctor. We might see our parents again, we might not. Some of the girls halted at once when we got outside. They didn't know where to go. New and bewildered as the fawns I saw at the edges of the trees, in the dusk. The girl with the white ticket, though, she walked directly into the woods, the lights of our torches bouncing off the satin until she was gone into the dark. We were not so different.

I put the compass in the palm of my hand. North or south, east or west. The flicker of the needle, the splintered light of the moon on its glass casing. I knew I could do this […]. My life was out there, ahead of me. I had to run to it, now that the shape was cast.

967 words

From: Sophie Mackintosh. Blue Ticket. *New York: Doubleday, 2020. 9–12.*

Annotations

2 Calla and her father
20 Earlier in the story, her father holds an empty wine bottle to his eye like a telescope with which he can see into the future.
21 cobalt – *here:* the colour blue
32 Girls and women keep their white or blue ticket in a locket (a small piece of jewellery that opens to show a small picture or object).

Aufgabe II: Aufgabenstellung

1 Outline what makes the Joker an appealing character according to Rob Bricken. (30 %)

2 Compare the Joker and Richard III – in Shakespeare's play and Loncraine's movie – as embodiments of villains. (30 %)

3 Polygon, a website focusing on games and movies, has invited readers to send in articles to be published as part of their online content, commenting on the statement "It is the evil characters that fascinate us most."
Write the article, referring to the text at hand, the play *King Richard III,* and its movie adaptation by Richard Loncraine. (40 %)

Text II **Rob Bricken, "How Joker Became an Unlikely Icon of Anarchy" (2019)**

He's murdered thousands of people. He's tortured, poisoned, and maimed even more. [...] He dresses like a clown. And he's the most popular supervillain in the world.

Actually, DC Comics' Joker is more than that: He's one of the four most recognizable comic book characters in the world, along with Spider-Man, Superman, and Batman. He's a character so well-known that his own self-titled movie – Joker, starring Joaquin Phoenix, opening October 4 – doesn't even need a cameo from his superhero archnemesis to sell tickets.

The Joker's fame makes him the most popular fictional mass murderer in the world. Because the Joker has fans, far beyond his role as Batman's greatest foe and foil.

His hatred of the principles of society often shades him as an anti-establishment figure. Whatever horrible things the character has done, there is a core of the Joker that could appeal to anyone who feels let down by society or disenfranchised. He is the supervillain that inspires anyone who, justly or otherwise, wants to see the world burn. Unfortunately, that inspiration can reach into the real world, too. [...]

Regardless of whatever loose change Two-Face carries around in his pockets, Batman and Joker will always be the two sides of the same coin. They're both obsessed with their missions, but while Batman's goal is to enforce order and to save people, the Joker's desire is to wreak havoc, and his primary tool to achieve that end is murder. Batman believes in the sanctity of life so much he refuses to kill his villains, no matter how dangerous they are.

The Joker will kill for any reason: He's murdered countless policemen to avoid arrest, and when he's caught, he murders his way out of Arkham Asylum to escape. He kills for the fun of it, like when he handed out poisoned cotton candy to Boy Scouts in *The Dark Knight Returns*. [...]

His crimes make the Joker a villain, but that's not what makes the character appealing. Heroes are traditionally represented by light and color, while most villains operate, thematically and literally, in the darkness of night. However, since Batman is a hero who co-opts the dark, the Joker takes on heroic visual signifiers to serve as a contrast. His purple suit and clownish face are designed to draw attention. He announces his murders ahead of time, as in his first comic appearance. In 2011, he escaped Arkham by leaving his own cut-off face stuck on the wall, just to remind people how crazy he is. And whatever heinous acts he does, he does it all with a laugh. Batman is serious and grim, but the Joker is the one having *fun*.

Few comic villains have done more horrible things than the Joker, but there's still a real allure to the character's utter disregard for any conventions of society – especially when it's directed at what seems like a worthy target. He once killed a corrupt Gotham City mayor in Ed Brubaker and Greg Rucka's *Gotham Central* comics, and in Grant Morrison's *Batman R.I.P.*, he was largely responsible for the defeat of the Black Glove criminal organization while Batman was undergoing some mental issues himself. Hell, sometimes the Joker even defeats other villains just because they're in his way, or to be a jerk, or because he got bored. […]

But part of the appeal of this new Joker was his nihilistic take on society. Sure, he was obsessed with Batman, as per usual, but also proving … well, I'll quote him from the film:

> You see, [people's] morals, their code, it's a bad joke. Dropped at the first sign of trouble. They're only as good as the world allows them to be. I'll show you. When the chips are down, these ... these civilized people, they'll eat each other. See, I'm not a monster. I'm just ahead of the curve.

This worldview has also come to be seen as disturbingly sympathetic by those who ignore his body count. In 2015, a theory stating that the Joker was the real hero of *The Dark Knight* got thousands of upvotes and a great deal of media coverage. Googling "the joker is right" brings you hundreds of millions of blogs, vlogs, and this infinitely depressing related search term: "childhood is when you idolize batman, adulthood is when you realize that the joker makes more sense."

The problem here is that the Joker is a lot of things. If you've ever thought "the world seems like it's gone crazy" – I do, at least four times a day – then congratulations, you and I agree with the Joker about something. But there are those disturbed people who feel the Joker is right about everything – how society is dysfunctional and morality a lie, so there's no reason to adhere to either of them. This can be a very attractive idea to someone who feels society has failed them, because it also justifies their revenge. Despite the horrible acts of violence he commits in *The Dark Knight*, the Joker has fans – and when mass murderers have fans, bad things happen. There's a long list of real people who have either emulated or directly invoked the Joker after 2008. While some of these instances are as benign as donning Joker cosplay while trying to steal movie posters, others are far more sinister, resulting in disfigurement, arson, and murder.

These tragedies have not undercut the Joker's appeal. Quite the contrary, in fact; Todd Phillips' Joker is not only an origin story for a new incarnation of the character (named Arthur Fleck), but one that posits his descent into homicidal madness is at least partially due to society's failings. According to early reviews, Arthur's early killings are seen as an attack on the one-percent[12], inspiring others who are similarly disenfranchised to do the same. That's one of the most sympathetic origins the supervillain has ever had, not least because it feels so timely. *990 words*

Rob Bricken: How Joker became an unlikely icon of anarchy – From fighting Batman, to fighting The Man, Polygon *vom 02. 10. 2019, https://www.polygon.com/comics/2019/10/2/20895027/joker-anarchy-dc-comics-batman-history-movie*

Annotations

3 DC Comics – a comic book publisher
6 cameo – *here:* brief appearance in a movie
7 arch-nemesis – *here:* arch-enemy
9 foil – a character that contrasts with, and therefore emphasizes, the qualities of another character
15 Two-Face – another villain in the Batman comic book series
22 Arkham Asylum – fictional psychiatric hospital and prison for the criminals in the Batman stories
30 reference to *Batman: Detective Comics Vol. 1: Faces of Death*, published in 2011
37 Gotham City – fictional city and home of Batman
49 body count – number of people killed
63 cosplay – *here:* costume to represent a specific movie character
66 Todd Phillips – director of the 2019 movie *Joker*
69 one-percent – reference to the richest one percent of people

Lösungsvorschlag

HÖRVERSTEHEN

Transkript 1 Street Trees

Jason G. Goldman: This is Scientific American, Sixty Seconds Science. I am Jason Goldman. Trees in cities do measurable good for biodiversity and for human health. They scrub pollution from the air. They provide habitat for wildlife. They make streets look nicer. And they even reduce stress and have been linked to reductions in crime.

Back in 2015 a group of Toronto-based researchers discovered that planting just eleven more trees per city block could reduce heart-related conditions by the same amount as if everybody living on that block became a year and a half younger.

But in Detroit between 2011 and 2014 a quarter of eligible homeowners turned down an offer from a local nonprofit for free street trees. Ironic, considering Detroit's nickname was once the City of Trees.

Christine Carmichael: It was actually over 1,800 trees that were rejected out of an eligible 7,425. So it was a big enough issue at that point where it warranted further investigation.

Jason G. Goldman: Forestry researcher Christine Carmichael, who did the research at Michigan State and has since moved to the University of Vermont.

The nonprofit created an education campaign to get more residents to accept the free trees. The assumption being that if people had all the facts, they'd be more likely to take the trees. But when Carmichael talked to residents, she found that they understood the benefits of trees. Their unease was about trust.

Christine Carmichael: Basically what I found was that opposition in Detroit to tree planting among some of these residents resulted primarily from negative past experiences with street trees, particularly in low-income neighborhoods that were grappling with blight from vacant properties, which created an additional burden of care for their neighborhood.

Jason G. Goldman: In the last half-century or so, more than half a million Detroit trees died from disease and neglect. It was primarily low-income African American communities who were forced to deal with the consequences and the hazards, like falling limbs, posed by dead trees.

In speaking with residents, Carmichael found that they would be more willing to accept free trees if they could be more involved in the decision-making process. Locals wanted input on tree size and whether they produced flowers. They also very reasonably wanted to avoid trees that could drop rotting fruits or sap on cars and sidewalks.

TIPP

These text passages will help you find the correct answer:

1 "Trees in cities do measurable good for biodiversity and for human health. They scrub pollution from the air. They provide habitat for wildlife. They make streets look nicer. And they even reduce stress and have been linked to reductions in crime." (ll. 2–5)

2 "Back in 2015 a group of Toronto-based researchers discovered that planting just eleven more trees per city block could reduce heart-related conditions by the same amount as if everybody living on that block became a year and a half younger." (ll. 6–8)

3 "But in Detroit between 2011 and 2014 a quarter of eligible homeowners turned down an offer from a local nonprofit for free street trees. Ironic, considering Detroit's nickname was once the City of Trees." (ll. 9–11)

4 "The nonprofit created an education campaign to get more residents to accept the free trees." (ll. 17/18)

5 "opposition in Detroit to tree planting […] resulted primarily from negative past experiences with street trees, particularly in low-income neighborhoods that were grappling with blight from vacant properties, which created an additional burden of care for their neighborhood." (ll. 21–25); "It was primarily low-income African American communities who were forced to deal with the consequences and the hazards, like falling limbs, posed by dead trees." (ll. 27–29)

6 "In speaking with residents, Carmichael found that they would be more willing to accept free trees if they could be more involved in the decision-making process. […] They also very reasonably wanted to avoid trees that could drop rotting fruits or sap on cars and sidewalks." (ll. 30–34)

1	What are the advantages of street trees according to the presenter? *(Name two.)*	*two of the following:* • good for biodiversity • good for human health • scrub pollution from the air • provide habitat for wildlife • reduce stress • reduce crime • *make streets look nicer*
2	What did a study say about the effect of planting eleven more trees per block?	reduce heart-related conditions (as if people became one-and a half years younger)
3	What was the paradoxical situation in Detroit between 2011 and 2014?	homeowners didn't want free trees although Detroit is called city of trees
4	What was the aim of Christine Carmichael's campaign?	get more residents to accept free trees

5	According to Christine Carmichael, what were some people in disadvantaged neighborhoods worried about?	(that the trees) create (an additional) burden of care / (that the trees) mean extra work
6	What would change these people's attitude towards street trees?	be (more) involved in decision-making process (about which trees are planted) / avoid planting certain trees

Transkript 2 Border

Hinweis: Aus lizenzrechtlichen Gründen ist die ungekürzte Original-Passage der NPR-Sendung abgedruckt. Die in der Abituraufgabe nicht berücksichtigten Passagen sind durch eine kleinere Schriftgröße kenntlich gemacht und für die Bearbeitung der Aufgaben nicht relevant.

Ailsa Chang, *Host:* The conversation on family separation is at a high pitch right now. Youth Radio's team covering the border spoke with young people from El Paso, Texas, and Juarez, Mexico, who grew up never seeing the border as a dividing line. Billy Cruz reports.

Billy Cruz, *Byline:* Along the dry, rocky desert of El Paso, past all the food chains and shopping malls, a brown fence stretches for miles. Is this giant fence that we are looking at right here – is that the border?

Antonio Villasenor-Baca: Yeah. So this freeway right here, like, going, like, in two different directions is I-10. And then you go down, and then there's the actual border. And then you're in Juarez.

Cruz: Antonio Villasenor-Baca is 22. He was born here in El Paso, a huge borderplex that spans the Rio Grande River. But he has an uncle in Juarez. And growing up, Antonio's dad would take him back and forth a lot.

Villasenor-Baca: You know, like, you want to go out and party, you go to Juarez. You have family in Juarez, but you live in El Paso, or vice versa. It really seems like just a huge hassle to, like, go through all of this stuff at the border.

Cruz: For young people like Antonio, life on the border isn't just about the momentous crossings we read about in the news. Commuting between two countries is a part of everyday life. There are even kids with dual citizenship who live in Juarez with their parents and cross the border to go to school.

Villasenor-Baca: It's really weird because growing up as a kid, there's just other kids in your school. And it's not until you get older that you start seeing, well, it's the kids who speak Spanish who are the – doing the daily commute. And it's when the terms like American and Mexican and Mexican-American start coming into place.

Cruz: Many people and goods flow between El Paso and Juarez every day. The culture and economies of both cities rely on each other. Twenty-three-year-old Kenia Guerrero is part of that flow. She grew up in Juarez but just finished college in El Paso. And she crosses the border every day to help out at her parents' cowboy boot shop.

Kenia Guerrero: Yeah, so we are at the Santa Fe Bridge. This is in the central part of El Paso. As you can see, like, cars are coming in from Juarez. It usually takes about half an hour to three hours to cross to El Paso.

Cruz: To make her commute easier, Kenia got something called a SENTRI pass, which cuts down the time it takes to cross. Thousands of people in the El Paso-Juarez region pay the fees and go through the background checks to get one. Kenia says she feels equally at home in Juarez and here in El Paso.

Guerrero: My first 15 years, I didn't know about borders. Like, I live in Juarez, but I would buy my clothes here and would buy certain food items here. It was pretty normal. And now it's not like that anymore because you're sometimes afraid.

Cruz: Now Kenia has to be extra careful whenever she crosses because she says agents have gotten stricter since President Trump took office. If she's caught with a prohibited item like even an apple she packed for lunch and forgot to throw away, Kenia could lose her fastpass. Recently she had a close call.

Guerrero: Had a crushed candy in my cup holder. And the agent asked me, is that cocaine? And I got nervous not because it was cocaine but because it's just a question. Like, how can he think that I'm bringing cocaine? I just told him something along the lines, no, but if you want to try it, you can.

Cruz: The agent passed on the candy and eventually let her cross. As security and media attention at the border increases, Kenia and Antonio are just trying to hold on to their sense of hometown normalcy.

Villasenor-Barca: Yeah, it's a border, and anywhere else in the country will say it as such. But for us, it's just two cities that's divided by a fence.

Cruz: For the time being at least, Antonio and Kenia will keep crossing that fence because for the people who live and work here, these two cities El Paso and Juarez really do feel like one. For NPR News, I'm Billy Cruz in El Paso, Texas.

Chang: That story was produced by Youth Radio.

(SOUNDBITE OF MASSIVE ATTACK'S "MONTAGE")

Billy Cruz: Young People Adapt To A Changing Life At The Texas-Mexico Border, NPR 20. 07. 2018, https://www.npr.org/2018/07/20/630076251/young-people-adapt-to-a-changing-life-at-the-texas-mexico-border

TIPP

These text passages will help you find the correct answer:

1. "Youth Radio's team covering the border spoke with young people from El Paso, Texas, and Juarez, Mexico, who grew up never <u>seeing the border as a dividing line</u>." (ll. 1–3)
2. "It really seems like just a <u>huge hassle</u> to, like, go through all of this stuff at the border." (ll. 14/15)
3. "There are even kids with <u>dual citizenship</u> who live in Juarez with their parents and cross the border to go to school." (ll. 18/19)

4 "Many people and goods flow between El Paso and Juarez every day. The culture and economies of both cities rely on each other." (ll. 24/25)

5 "To make her commute easier, Kenia got something called a SENTRI pass, which cuts down the time it takes to cross." (ll. 31/32)

6 "Now Kenia has to be extra careful whenever she crosses because she says agents have gotten stricter since President Trump took office. If she's caught with a prohibited item […], Kenia could lose her fastpass." (ll. 38–41)

1 According to the female presenter, how do young locals see the border?

c ✓ as having little importance

2 How does Antonio Villasenor-Baca perceive the border?

c ✓ as an annoying measure

3 Why are some children from Juarez able to attend an American school?

d ✓ They have an American and a Mexican passport.

4 What is said about the connection of the two border cities?

b ✓ They are interdependent.

5 Why can Kenia Guerrero cross the border faster?

d ✓ She has bought a special document.

6 What has made crossing the border more difficult for Kenia?

a ✓ a change in politics

Transkript 3 Ship

Alan Johnston, ***Host*****:** It is 1948 in Jamaica and the island is in bad shape. It's still recovering from a hurricane a few years earlier and Sam King remembers the economy being in a desperate state.

Sam King: Things again were very bad because the coconuts were destroyed in '44. It takes five to six years for the coconuts to rebuild. The whole structure of farming was undermined. I didn't see any future. Of course, my father was very glad I was there because I'm the eldest son and like him, eventually I would take over the farm to pick pimento and to plant banana and all that and all that. But I had no intention of planting bananas.

Alan Johnston: Back then, Sam was just 22 years old, but he'd already seen the outside world. He'd volunteered during WWII and served in the Royal Air Force in Britain. With the coming of peace, he'd returned to the hills of Eastern Jamaica. But he knew he wouldn't stay. And within months, he spotted a chance to get away.

Sam King: It was in the daily Jamaican newspaper that this troop ship would call to Jamaica in about two weeks' time. And the passage was 28 pounds 10 shillings.

Let's get that straight: The average man didn't have 28 pounds 10 shillings. It was equivalent to about three cows.

Alan Johnston: So you are sitting, reading the newspaper. And what goes through your mind?

Sam King: I'm going back to England.

Alan Johnston: Eventually nearly 500 passengers boarded the ship, bound for England and a new life. They would turn out to be pioneers. Their journey marked the start of a new wave of migration. In the decade to come, a quarter of a million West Indians would follow in the wake of the Windrush. Sam remembers the mood that evening when she slips slowly out of Kingston harbour.

Sam King: People were waving, things were happening on the docks. Now for about half of us, we had no intention of coming back to our colony. We were looking forward, we were looking towards a new home. But there were some men in their 40s who had wife and children. They were looking back at the yard, they were waving, they – but we, chiefly the young ones, we were not looking back, we were looking forward.

Alan Johnston: Several stowaways had managed to smuggle themselves on board, one was a woman and out of kindness, Sam and some of the other passengers clubbed together and paid to buy her a ticket, enabling her to make the voyage legally. But conditions on the troop ship in those first years after the war were far from luxurious.

Sam King: Sad to say, you have mashed potato in tins from New Zealand two years, they put it on the table, mix it up with water. Now if you didn't eat it then, in the evening they mix it with cabbage and if you didn't eat it then, in the morning they fried it and called it bubble and squeak. I would eat it sometimes before, when I was resident in Britain. Men were playing dominoes and things, but we had the decks, were chiefly blankets and a few bunks. But the women were in cabins. So we just mill around and in the evenings they have boxing competitions and things like that and dance and all things. But the main thing is, it was to mentally get yourself ready to land.

Alan Johnston: And the other young guys who, unlike you, hadn't seen Britain before, were they asking lots of questions?

Sam King: Time and again they would come, "Sam, what, will I have a job?" They were more concerned about jobs. I said, "Settle down." In the evening after supper about 6.30, I would go on the lower deck to you know about ten of them I said, "Look. Food is rationed in England, you can't grasp that, but work is all over the place, so work is not the problem."

From: BBC World Service (20. 06. 2011) Witness History, The Voyage of the Empire Windrush, https://www.bbc.co.uk/programmes/p00h8xkq

TIPP

These text passages will help you find the correct answer:

1 "It is 1948 in Jamaica and the island is in bad shape. It's still recovering from a hurricane a few years earlier" (ll. 1/2); "the coconuts were destroyed in '44. [...] The whole structure of farming was undermined." (ll. 4–6)

2 "my father was very glad I was there because I'm the eldest son and like him, eventually I would take over the farm to pick pimento and to plant banana" (ll. 6–8)

3 "Back then, Sam was just 22 years old, but he'd already seen the outside world. He'd volunteered during WWII and served in the Royal Air Force in Britain." (ll. 10/11)

4 "he'd returned to the hills of Eastern Jamaica. But he knew he wouldn't stay." (ll. 12/13)

5 "the passage was 28 pounds 10 shillings. [...] The average man didn't have 28 pounds 10 shillings. It was equivalent to about three cows." (ll. 15–17)

6 "Their journey marked the start of a new wave of migration. In the decade to come, a quarter of a million West Indians would follow in the wake of the Windrush." (ll. 22–24)

7 "there were some men in their 40s who had wife and children. They were looking back at the yard, they were waving" (ll. 28–30)

8 "Several stowaways had managed to smuggle themselves on board, one was a woman and out of kindness, Sam and some of the other passengers clubbed together and paid to buy her a ticket, enabling her to make the voyage legally." (ll. 32–34)

9 "Sad to say, you have mashed potato in tins from New Zealand two years, they put it on the table, mix it up with water. Now if you didn't eat it then, in the evening they mix it with cabbage and if you didn't eat it then, in the morning they fried it and called it bubble and squeak." (ll. 37–40)

10 "Men were playing dominoes and things [...] we just mill around and in the evenings they have boxing competitions and things like that and dance and all things. But the main thing is, it was to mentally get yourself ready to land." (ll. 41–45)

11 "Time and again they would come, 'Sam, what, will I have a job?' They were more concerned about jobs." (ll. 48/49)

1	Why the economic situation in Jamaica was so serious in 1948	(recovering from a) recent hurricane / a hurricane a few years earlier / coconuts were destroyed (in 1944) / whole structure of farming was undermined
2	What Sam King's father wanted his son to do	(to) take over the farm / (to) pick pimentos / (to) plant bananas

3	Why Sam King had spent time away from Jamaica	volunteered during WW II / served in Royal Air Force in Britain
4	What Sam King realized when back in Jamaica	(he knew) he wouldn't stay
5	What Sam King says about the fare for the passage *(Name **one** aspect.)*	28 pounds, 10 shillings / the average man didn't have 28 pounds, 10 shillings / too expensive for average people / equivalent to about three cows
6	What the journey of the *Windrush* led to	a new wave of migration / a quarter of a million West-Indians emigrating
7	Why some middle-aged passengers found it hard to leave Jamaica	had (to leave their) wives and children / had to leave their families behind
8	What some travellers did when learning a woman was on board illegally	(they) clubbed together and paid to buy her a ticket / (they) bought her a ticket
9	Why Sam considered the food on board bad *(Name **one** reason.)*	old, tinned food / same food served again and again
10	How people spent their time on board *(Name **two** activities.)*	*two of the following:* • playing dominoes • milling around • boxing competitions • dances / dancing • mentally getting (themselves) ready to land
11	What some younger passengers worried about	finding a job

SPRACHMITTLUNG

TIPP

Before you start writing, pay close attention to the assignment. It tells you for whom you have to summarise the information (an American exchange partner) and in what form (a personal email). This will determine the style you should use: write in correct, formal language because your friend needs the information for a presentation at school. However, do not forget to use a more colloquial style when you address your friend and his/her situation. When it comes to content, you should only sum up the pieces of information that are relevant for your friend's presentation: so leave out the concrete personal examples mentioned in the article. Instead, focus on what makes the tradition of travelling journeymen special, where it comes from and why and how it is still practised today.

You should include the following aspects:

- appearance of travelling journeymen:
  - equipment: bindle, hiking pole, logbook
  - traditional clothing: hat, waistcoat, jacket, flared trousers, shirt
  - colour of clothes different depending on craft
  - earring (traditional and current custom of being "nailed down"; original use: payment for funeral costs)
- rules for travelling journeymen:
  - completed apprenticeship, unmarried, no debts, travel for two or three years and one day
  - staying away at least 50 km from hometown
- history of the tradition:
  - dates back to Middle Ages
  - obligatory to become masters until the beginnings of industrialisation
- present situation:
  - 450–550 journeying craftspeople, ten to 20 per cent women
  - custom recognised by UNESCO since 2004
  - many also work abroad
  - normal pay, often free board and lodging
- reasons for travelling:
  - improve skills and learn new techniques
  - gain new experiences, learn about the world and oneself

Hello Cheryl,

Thanks for your email. That's an interesting subject for your presentation. I'd be glad to help you with some information I found in a German newspaper.

introduction

As you might remember from last summer, travelling journeymen can easily be recognised by their traditional clothing, consisting of a hat, a waistcoat, a jacket, flared trousers and a shirt. The colour of these depends on the journeymen's craft. They carry a bindle, a pole and a logbook to record their journey. Another interesting feature is the earring they all wear. Originally, the rings were meant to pay for their funeral in case they died on the trip. They are also reminders of the tradition of nailing the journeymen's earlobes to a post. This custom is still being practised as a symbol of the craftsmen's reliability.

appearance of travelling journeymen

There are more strict rules to observe: the journeymen must have finished their apprenticeship and must be unmarried, free of debt and prepared to travel for two to three years and one day. They must also keep a distance of at least 50 km from their hometown to avoid competing with their masters.

rules for travelling journeymen

The tradition of travelling began in the late Middle Ages. Until the beginning of the Industrial Age, travelling in this way was obligatory for anyone who wanted to become a master of their craft.

history of the tradition

Currently, there are about 450 to 550 journeying craftspeople, ten to 20 per cent of whom are women. They are paid at the standard rate for their trade, with board and lodging often being free. In 2004, the UNESCO recognised the custom's cultural value by giving it world heritage status.

present situation

There are several reasons for its ongoing popularity: the journeymen, who often travel abroad these days, can improve their learned trade by acquiring new techniques. Moreover, they meet many people, gain experiences and learn skills, such as perseverance and pragmatism. All of this can prove helpful when dealing with customers, especially with difficult ones.

reasons for travelling

I hope you'll find this information useful. Please tell me how your presentation went.

ending (fitting to text form)

Love,
Lily

TEXTAUFGABE

Text I **Excerpt from Sophie Mackintosh, *Blue Ticket* (2020)**

1 **TIPP**

The command term "sum up" requires you to state the main points of a text. Thus, you have to write a text which is significantly shorter than the original. Moreover, you mustn't quote from the text but should use your own words. Also remember to use the simple present. Begin your summary by mentioning the title of the story, the author and the year of publication. Then outline what happens in the excerpt. In this case, it is best to proceed chronologically and arrange the events in the same order as they appear in the text.

The following aspects should be included in your solution:
- the narrator arrives at the lottery station with her father
- lines up in front of a ticket machine together with four other girls
- narrator draws a blue ticket, meaning she won't have children → feels relieved
- girl with a white ticket is taken to a different room → returns looking as if she has been crying
- finally, the girls are given refreshments and a compass
- they set out on their own, while their parents stay behind at the lottery station

introduction: title, author, year

The text provided is from the story *Blue Ticket*, which was written by Sophie Mackintosh and published in 2020.

main part: events in chronological order

In the excerpt in hand, the main character Calla arrives at a place called the "lottery station" together with her father. First, she is led into a waiting room, where she carefully observes the other four girls who are also waiting there along with a man in a dark suit. Then they all queue in front of a machine, which eventually produces a ticket for every girl. The protagonist gets a blue ticket and is relieved about this, as this means that she does not have to have children. The same is true for the rest of the girls – except for a girl who gets a white ticket and is ushered into a different room afterwards. When she returns a bit later she looks as if she has been crying. The protagonist first wants to comfort the girl with the white ticket, but then decides against it. In the end, the girls are handed some refreshments and a compass and are free to walk anywhere they want to, but without their parents, who stay behind at the lottery station.

2 **TIPP**

In this task, you have to analyse the atmosphere created in the excerpt. You should write about what the atmosphere is like and how this effect is achieved. The command term "examine" requires you to work closely with the text and back up your findings by means of direct or indirect quotations. The following aspects could be mentioned in your solution:

atmosphere can generally be described as uncanny:

- overall situation of a "lottery" deciding the girls' fates
- rather negative description of the "lottery station":
  - bleak building
  - uncomfortable, loveless furniture
  - floors that have been "varnished aggressively" and worn out by "countless feet" → aseptic ambience, repetition of what happens at the station
  - no decoration except from withering flowers → sense of foreboding
- description of people inside the lottery station:
  - queue up as if "at the butcher's", "plucked chicken" → motif of violence
  - man in suit: superficially friendly, but "terrible benevolence"
  - girls released into the night and the surrounding dark forests → imagery of darkness
  - sombre atmosphere lightened up by the protagonist's determination to find her way in life
- limited point of view of first-person narrator Calla: violence at the core of the story is only hinted at, not told explicitly → unsettling effect

introduction: thesis: uncanny atmosphere

When reading the excerpt from *Blue Ticket*, the reader cannot help but feel uneasy, which is due to the uncanny and threatening atmosphere created. But how is this effect achieved?

main part: situation of lottery deciding girls' fates

Quite often, an "uncanny" (as opposed to straight-out scary) ambience arises, when the setting appears somehow familiar, like something you know from your everyday life – yet at the same time, there are things that seem out-of-place and unsettling. This also applies to the overall situation of the "lottery" in *Blue Ticket*: Expressions such as "lottery" (l. 1) or "full house" (l. 24) are normally used in the context of card games or gambling. Many people enjoy playing games as a leisure time activity and do it for fun. By contrast, what is at stake in the "lottery" in this story is a life-altering question indeed, namely whether or not the girls will have children. Like in a lottery or card game, their fate is determined solely by random luck or bad luck – they do not have any control over their lives.

What further adds to the uncanny atmosphere are the negatively connotated expressions with which the setting of the "lottery station" is described. The building itself is compared to a hospital (cf. l. 1) and described as being made of "pale brick" (l. 1), which from the beginning makes it sound like a bleak place. The furniture inside appears uncomfortable and loveless, consisting of only a hard "wooden bench" (ll. 9/10) and an "orange plastic chair" (l. 7). The floors are described as having been "varnished aggressively" (l. 5), which – together with the glary lights (cf. ll. 6/7, 30) – conveys a rather aseptic ambience. The fact that the floorboards are already worn thin by "[c]ountless feet" (l. 5) suggests that what happens at this place has repeated itself many times before. The only ornamental element in the building which could serve to embellish the place is a "dying flower arrangement at the corner of the sink" (ll. 36/37) in the bathroom. Flowers often serve to symbolise the beauty and abundance of life, yet in this case, all life has been sucked out of them – they are not taken care of and are left to wither.

description of "lottery station":

bleak building

uncomfortable, loveless furniture

worn-out floors and glaring lights

withering flowers

This conveys a sense of foreboding, which can also be observed in the description of people inside the "lottery station". When the girls line up to get their tickets, this is compared to a queue "at the butcher's counter" (l. 14). The example of the "butcher" takes up the theme of dead matter and moreover hints at violence taking place. This becomes even clearer when the narrator later describes herself as a "plucked chicken" (l. 31). The man in the dark suit, or "doctor", as the narrator calls him, appears friendly on the surface, e. g. when he congratulates the narrator on her blue ticket (cf. ll. 21/22). When he later tells the girls with the blue tickets that they have been "spared", it becomes obvious that there is something violent going on beneath the surface and that his seeming benevolence is indeed "terrible" (l. 29).

description of people:

comparison to queue at the butcher's

man in suit: friendliness only superficial

Finally, another aspect that adds to the uncanny atmosphere is the narrative perspective. The story is told from the point of view of the first-person narrator Calla. The reader is limited to her perception of events, such as when the girl with the white ticket is taken away and later returns, looking as if she has been crying. Like the protagonist, the reader can only guess what might have been done to her in-between. The fact that what happens in this core scene is left out and not told explicitly makes the story all the more unsettling.

narrative perspective: limited point of view of Calla; main event omitted

In the end, the girls are released into the "cool night" (l. 58) and the girl with the white ticket walks "directly into the woods" (l. 62). This imagery of darkness again adds to the overall sombre atmosphere. However, the narrator's determination that she "knew [she] could do this" and that her "life was out there, ahead of [her]" (ll. 66/67) makes the story end on a slightly more positive and hopeful note.

ending: sombre atmosphere lightened by narrator's determination

In summary, the atmosphere in the excerpt can be described as uncanny, an effect which is achieved through the overall situation of a "lottery" deciding the girls' fates, the choice of words in the description of the building and the characters, and the limited point of view of the narrator which leaves the reader to imagine the violence taking place at the station. This is only lifted at the very end due to the protagonist's determination to make the best of the situation. **conclusion**

3

TIPP

In this task you have to write an article discussing the question as to whether or not young people can determine their own futures. In the introduction you should refer to the given quotation by the writer Roy T. Bennett and briefly explain it. In your main part, you have to give arguments supporting Bennett's view and arguments opposing it. Moreover, you must refer to the text *Blue Ticket* and to materials studied in class. Finally, you should arrive at a conclusion to what degree you either agree or disagree with Bennett's view. It is probably best to take some notes and sort them before beginning to write to make sure that your text is structured coherently. Don't forget to give your article a proper heading and to use a more formal language register.
The following aspects could be included in your solution:

- introduction:
  Bennett's quotation that "you are not the victim of the world, but rather the master of your own destiny" → young people can determine their own futures
- arguments supporting Bennett's view:
  - declining influence of parents and society → greater freedom of young people to make their own choices
  - "Two Kinds": Jing-Mei manages to emancipate herself from expectations of her mother and culture
  - *Blue Ticket:* Calla determined to make her way in life despite "lottery"
- arguments opposing Bennett's view:
  - *Blue Ticket:* girls' lives determined by mere luck and by society (which invented system of the "lottery")
  - *Never Let Me Go:* fates of clones determined by their status in society
  - marginalised groups in real world: opportunities in life often limited by stereotypes and structural discrimination
- conclusion:
  neither "victims" nor "masters" → chances in life influenced by social structures, but agency to make the best of our situation and change the system from within

Victims of the world or masters of our own destiny?

heading

As young people, we are facing some of life's most important crossroads – the questions of where we want to work, where and with whom we want to live, whether we want to have a family or not, and so on. The writer Roy T. Bennett argues that it is up to us to choose the path for our own future. According to him, "you are not the victim of the world, but rather the master of your own destiny." But is his optimism really justified? And what can works of literature teach us about this question?

introduction: reference to quote by Bennett

At first sight, one is inclined to agree with Bennett. Compared to past centuries or decades, young people nowadays have more possibilities of making their own choices in life. In former times, it was your parents or strict social norms who determined the choice of your partner or profession, for example. Today, most young people decide for themselves how they want to earn their living and who they want to spend their life with. Of course, this varies depending on the cultural context, but the overall tendency seems to prevail.

main part: arguments supporting Bennett's view declining influence of parents and society

Take the protagonist of the short story "Two Kinds", for example. Jing-Mei is an American girl with a Chinese cultural background. Her mother has the best intentions for her and wants her daughter to be a child prodigy. At first, Jing-Mei tries to meet the expectations of her mother and comply with the cultural norm of being the obedient daughter. However, when she realises that she is bound to fail and feels increasingly unhappy, she rebels against her mother's plans. Eventually, Jing-Mei emancipates herself from both the parental and cultural influence and finds her inner peace. This shows that, while it may not always be easy, it is indeed possible to take life into one's own hands and become the masters of our destiny.

reference to "Two Kinds": emancipation from parental and cultural influence

Another case in point is the text *Blue Ticket*. In the story, a lottery decides whether a girl will have children or not, without the girls having any control over it. In spite of this, the protagonist, Calla, is determined to be able to choose her own path in life, which would likewise support Bennett's argument.

reference to *Blue Ticket:* determination to shape own life

However, the same story can be used to counter Bennett's optimism. On closer inspection, it becomes clear that Calla only feels like the "mistress of her destiny", because she didn't want to have children anyway and was lucky enough to get a blue ticket, meaning that she won't have to get pregnant. Thus, she can continue her life as planned and feels free to go where she wants to go and do what she wants to do. For the girl in the story who draws a white ticket and is forced to have a child, the situation looks quite different: her life has been changed in a very far-reaching manner, without her having any say in it. In this story, it is not the characters who determine their future,

arguments opposing Bennett's view reference to *Blue Ticket*

fate decided by luck and society

but mere luck and – in the last instance – society, which designed the cruel system of the "lottery" in the first place.

reference to *Never Let Me Go:* fate determined by society

The strong impact of society on people's lives is also the topic of the novel *Never Let Me Go*. The protagonists are clones who have been created for the sole purpose of donating their organs to "ordinary" humans. Thus, their fate is determined from the start. Two of the protagonists, Tommy and Kathy, fall in love and try to reach a "deferral", which would allow them to spend some more time together. They go to extreme risks to formally request a deferral only to find out in the end that such a thing has never existed in the first place. Thus, their hope of having some agency over their own lives ultimately turns out to be an illusion. They could be described as "victims of the world".

real world: impact of structural discrimination and stereotypes

Of course, the criticism of society in dystopian texts such as *Blue Ticket* and *Never Let Me Go* is somewhat exaggerated. Still, there is a grain of truth to it: In the "real" world, society often severely narrows which paths we can choose. If you are a member of a marginalised group (a person of colour or a member of the LGBTIQ community, for example), your opportunities in life are frequently limited by structural discrimination and unconscious stereotypes. You may work hard for a career and have the best qualification, and still not get the job just because of the colour of your skin or your sexual identity. And it is mere luck which situation you are born into, whether you can start your course in life from a relatively privileged or disadvantaged position. This makes it hard to agree full-heartedly with Bennett's view that we are in complete control of our futures.

conclusion

In summary, Bennett is too optimistic in arguing that we are all the "masters of our destiny", because not everyone is given the same chances in life to do what they want to do. And yet, we do have agency in making the best of our situation, and we can try to change the system from within and create a more just society that grants equal opportunities to everyone. Life can metaphorically deal us bad cards, but it is up to us to play them well and perhaps change the rules of the game.

Text II **Rob Bricken, "How Joker Became an Unlikely Icon of Anarchy" (2019)**

1 **TIPP**

The command term "outline" requires you to state the main points of a text, omitting minor details. Moreover, you are to focus on a particular aspect of the text, namely the question as to what makes the Joker an appealing character. Go through the article again and underline the passages that are relevant to the task. Then paraphrase them in your own words – do not quote from the text. Don't forget to write an introductory sentence in which you name the title and author of the article, the date of publication and the topic.

reasons for Joker's appeal:

- role of misfit who has moved beyond social norms → makes him attractive for people who likewise feel deserted by society and secretly wish to take revenge
- targeting of other villains makes his deeds appear justified
- differs from other villains in his appearance and attitude: flashy colours (instead of dark clothes), mad joy (instead of earnest attitude)

introduction: source and topic

In "How Joker Became an Unlikely Icon of Anarchy" published online in 2019, Rob Bricken explains why the Joker is such an appealing character.

main part: reasons for Joker's appeal

Firstly, Bricken argues, the Joker strikes a chord with the audience because he is a misfit, an underdog in society. The Joker moves completely outside social norms and seeks to create chaos by killing other people. This makes him an attractive figure for people who likewise feel deserted by society and share the secret wish to take revenge. A second aspect that makes him so appealing is that he sometimes targets other villains. In these cases, the viewers might feel that his victims do not deserve any better and consider his deeds to be justified. Thirdly, the Joker differs from other evil characters because of his unique appearance and attitude: While a lot of other villains wear dark clothes, the Joker wears flashy colours and a clown face. He is not as earnest as the other characters but seems to experience a mad joy in what he does.

2 **TIPP**

The command term "compare" asks you to look for similarities and differences between two things. In this case, it is your task to compare the Joker as portrayed in the text with the character of Richard III in Shakespeare's play and in the film version. It is advisable to take some notes before starting to write.

Remember to back up your argument with quotes from Bricken's article and references to *Richard III*.

- similarities:
  - both Richard and the Joker stand out because of their outward appearance
  - both are outsiders who feel they have been failed by society
  - both lack moral scruples and do not even refrain from killing
- differences:
  - Richard uses helpers, while the Joker commits his murders himself
  - Richard kills to achieve a particular goal (to become king), while the Joker merely has a vague desire to create chaos

introduction: reference to task, thesis

At first sight, one could think that a 20th-century comic book character and the protagonist of a Shakespeare play can't have very much in common. And yet, the Joker and Richard III lend themselves perfectly for a comparison. Both can be seen as embodiments of a villain and have quite a few similarities.

similarities: outward appearance

The first thing to mention is that neither the Joker nor Richard III can blend in physically. It stands out that they stand out – Richard with his hunched back and the Joker with his clownish appearance.

role as outsiders

Moreover, both Richard and the Joker are social outsiders. As a man of war, Richard feels unsuited for a society at peace. Although he is a member of the royal family, he appears out of place in elegant society and does not seem to be particularly attractive to women either. This is the reason he himself gives for why he has ultimately turned evil: In the famous opening soliloquy he states that he is determined to "prove a villain" since he "cannot prove a lover". Quite similarly, the Joker is presented as an "anti-establishment figure" (ll. 10/11), someone who does not fit in. At least in Todd Phillips' film version, it is moreover suggested that – as in the case of Richard – his "descent into homicidal madness is at least partially due to society's failings" (ll. 67/68).

lack of moral scruples

Another thing which makes Richard and Joker comparable is their lack of moral scruples, which does not even make them refrain from murder. The Joker shows an "utter disregard for any conventions of society" (l. 35) and will sometimes kill just "for the fun of it" (l. 23). According to the text, "whatever heinous acts he does, he does it all with a laugh" (l. 32). Richard likewise enjoys crossing moral boundaries. For example, he takes a cruel pleasure in winning over Lady Anne, whose husband and father he had killed before. In the film version, he even seems to dance for joy when leaving the morgue after his encounter with Lady Anne. Moreover, he often spreads lies and false accusations, manipulates and deceives other people and chuckles at the thought of his victims being killed.

That being said, there are also a lot of differences beneath the surface. The first, most obvious point is that Richard uses assassins to "do the dirty work". For example, he hires a henchman called Tyrrell to kill his brother Clarence and the princes in the Tower. Only in the very first scenes of the film version, when he is at war, is he seen killing others directly. The Joker, by contrast, is a straight-forward murderer.

differences: using helpers vs. committing murders oneself

What is more, Richard wants to achieve a very particular goal with his murderous scheme, which is to claim the throne. Thus, his victims are primarily people who stand in the way of his ambition. His brother and nephews, for instance, have to die because they are before him in the line of succession. The Joker, by contrast, "will kill for any reason" (l. 21) and without any other aim than to "wreak havoc" (l. 18). Hence, his victims range from police officers (cf. l. 21) to Boy Scouts (cf. l. 23) to other villains (cf. ll. 36–41).

killing to achieve a particular goal vs. to create chaos

Summing up, it can be said that although they have been devised at completely different times, the characters of Richard III and the Joker have many things in common, although they also differ in several aspects.

conclusion

3 **TIPP**

For this task, you have to write an article. This means, your text should have a heading and a well-structured main part. Your target group are readers of a webpage on games and movies – thus, your style should probably not be too formal, but not entirely colloquial either. In your text, you have to comment on the statement that it is the evil characters which fascinate us most, i. e., you have to give your own opinion on it. You can either agree with the statement, disagree or take a stance somewhere in-between. The important thing is to support your opinion by means of arguments and examples. Moreover, the task requires you to refer to the given text about the Joker as well as to the play and the film *Richard III*.
In the following sample solution, it is argued that the given statement is by and large true, although it has to be qualified to a certain extent. The following aspects are mentioned:

- watching villains as a way to give vent to our own anarchic feelings, yet in a harmless way → brief escape from real life, thrill of the forbidden
- identification with "social-outcast-turned-into-powerful-avenger" → appeal to people who similarly feel let down by society
- psychological interest in multi-dimensional characters; fictional villains as a possibility to learn more about the minds of real-life murderers
- fascination with cleverness of the villains' schemes
- conclusion: particular appeal of evil characters, but primarily if they are psychologically complex or their crimes are particularly sophisticated

The thrill of the forbidden – why villains fascinate us

heading

Both in literature and film, villains have always enjoyed great popularity. From Shakespeare's Richard III to DC Marvel's "super-villain" Joker – audiences throughout the centuries have been fascinated by killer figures. In fact, there seems to be quite a bit of truth in the saying that it is the evil characters – rather than the shining heroes – which fascinate us most. But why is this so? And is this true in each and every case? A brief look at the two above-mentioned fictional examples will provide some answers.

introduction: reference to statement, thesis

Although we may or may not admit it, quite a few people somehow feel drawn to evil characters because they allow us a glimpse into the darker sides of our own personality. This is not to argue (as the Joker does) that there is a killer in all of us – that would probably be taking it too far. Yet many of us secretly admire villains for their audacity to do what they want without caring for the consequences or what other people think about them. In this way, they allow us to give vent to our own anarchic feelings – yet in a socially acceptable manner and without causing any harm in real life.

main part: arguments supporting the statement giving vent to own anarchic impulses

The Joker, for example, does whatever he wants, just for the fun of it. He kills and settles scores at whim – and gets away with it. By watching the Joker, we can imagine just for two hours what it would be like to completely ignore all social conventions. A lot of people enjoy such a brief escape from their everyday lives and experience a secret thrill. And perhaps, for a few people, cheering for the Joker may not even feel like a "forbidden" pleasure. As the Joker sometimes kills other villains, they consider his deeds to be somehow justified, and root for him without a guilty conscience.

escapism / thrill of the forbidden

The examples of the Joker and of Richard III also point at another possible reason why we are often spellbound by evil characters. In both cases, it is hinted that the protagonists become evil because they feel rejected by society. This feeling of being an outsider is something a lot of people can relate to or even sympathise with to a certain extent. The Joker's development into a powerful avenger moreover makes him attractive for those viewers who similarly feel like failures and dream of getting back at society. By identifying with the Joker, they can play out their secret fantasies. Disturbingly, in some cases, this identification has gone so far as to reach a point where viewers have imitated the Joker's deeds in real life.

identification with outsider figure

Yet villains don't just speak to our emotions and subconscious drives. Sometimes we may also be fascinated on a more intellectual level.

A lot of us take a general psychological interest in complex characters that have more than one dimension to them. Often, we watch fictional villains in the hope of learning more about the minds of real-life murderers and understanding their motivations. For example, in the film version of *Richard III*, the whole setting reminds us of the Nazi era in Germany. This makes us reflect on the question as to whether there are parallels between Richard III and other dictators in history, and what might be the reasons for their evilness and complete lack of empathy.

psychological interest in complex characters / learning about real-life murderers

On an intellectual level, we may also marvel at the cleverness and sophistication of a villain's intrigues. For example, in his soliloquies, Richard III gives us an insight into his murderous plans, such as when he talks about how he wants to get rid of his two brothers Clarence and King Edward to claim the throne. In consequence, we are curious to see whether his schemes will actually work out. In the film version he often speaks directly to the camera, thereby putting the viewers into the role of "partners in crime".

fascination with artistry of crime

In brief, evil characters seem to exert a particular appeal because they take us to a dark place, yet leave us in the comfort zone of our sofas at the same time. Often, they engage both our more primitive impulses as well as our brains. However, most people would probably feel repulsed or become bored merely watching a "bad guy" set out on a killing spree. As the examples of Richard and the Joker have shown, there has to be a certain psychological depth to the characters or their crimes have to be particularly artful in order for them to truly captivate the audience.

conclusion

Niedersachsen Englisch ▪ Abiturprüfung 2022
Erhöhtes Anforderungsniveau

Um Ihnen die Prüfung 2022 schnellstmöglich zur Verfügung stellen zu können, bringen wir sie in digitaler Form heraus.
Sobald die Original-Prüfungsaufgaben 2022 freigegeben sind, können sie als PDF auf der Plattform **MyStark** heruntergeladen werden. Ihren persönlichen Zugangscode finden Sie auf den Farbseiten vorne im Buch.

Prüfung 2022

www.stark-verlag.de/mystark